THE CAMBRIDGE COMPANION TO
SHAKESPEARE'S LAST PLAYS

Which plays are included under the heading 'Shakespeare's last plays', and when does Shakespeare's 'last' period begin? What is meant by a 'late play', and what are the benefits in defining plays in this way? Reflecting the recent growth of interest in late studies, and recognising the gaps in accessible scholarship in this area, leading international Shakespeare scholars address these and many other questions. The essays locate Shakespeare's last plays – single and co-authored – in the period of their composition, consider the significant characteristics of their Jacobean context, and explore the rich afterlives, on stage, in print and other media of *The Winter's Tale*, *Cymbeline*, *The Tempest*, *Pericles*, *The Two Noble Kinsmen* and *Henry VIII*. The volume opens with a historical timeline that places the plays in the contexts of contemporary political events, theatrical events, other cultural milestones, Shakespeare's life and that of his playing company, the King's Men.

CATHERINE M. S. ALEXANDER is a Fellow of the Shakespeare Institute, University of Birmingham.

A complete list of books in the series is at the back of this book

THE CAMBRIDGE
COMPANION TO

SHAKESPEARE'S
LAST PLAYS

EDITED BY
CATHERINE M. S. ALEXANDER

CAMBRIDGE
UNIVERSITY PRESS

CAMBRIDGE UNIVERSITY PRESS
Cambridge, New York, Melbourne, Madrid, Cape Town, Singapore, São Paulo, Delhi

Cambridge University Press
The Edinburgh Building, Cambridge CB2 8RU, UK

Published in the United States of America by Cambridge University Press, New York

www.cambridge.org
Information on this title: www.cambridge.org/9780521708197

First published 2009

Printed in the United Kingdom at the University Press, Cambridge

A catalogue record for this publication is available from the British Library

ISBN 978-0-521-88178-4 hardback
ISBN 978-0-521-70819-7 paperback

CONTENTS

Notes on contributors   *page* vii

Illustrations   x

Historical timeline: Clare Smout   xi

Introduction

CATHERINE M. S. ALEXANDER   1

1   What is a 'late play'?

GORDON McMULLAN   5

2   Blackfriars, music and masque: theatrical contexts of the last plays

DAVID LINDLEY   29

3   The literary and dramatic contexts of the last plays

CHARLES MOSELEY   47

4   Politics, religion, geography and travel: historical contexts of the last plays

KAREN BRITLAND   71

5   'You speak a language that I understand not': listening to the last plays

RUSS McDONALD   91

6   *The Winter's Tale*: shifts in staging and status

PATRICIA TATSPAUGH   113

7   *Cymbeline*: the afterlife

CATHERINE M. S. ALEXANDER   135

8   Literary invocations of *The Tempest*

VIRGINIA MASON VAUGHAN   155

9   *Pericles*: the afterlife
    EUGENE GIDDENS   173

10 *The Two Noble Kinsmen* and *King Henry VIII*: the last last plays
    SUZANNE GOSSETT   185

    Further reading: Clare Smout   203
    Index   213

NOTES ON CONTRIBUTORS

CATHERINE M. S. ALEXANDER is a Fellow of the Shakespeare Institute, University of Birmingham, and researches and writes on eighteenth-century Shakespeare. For CUP she has edited *Shakespeare and Politics* and *Shakespeare and Language* and, with Stanley Wells, *Shakespeare and Race* and *Shakespeare and Sexuality*. She has recently completed *Henry VIII* for Penguin and the illustrated and documented *Shakespeare: The Life, The Works, The Treasures* for Andre Deutsch and the RSC.

KAREN BRITLAND was a Senior Lecturer at the University of Keel before leaving in 2008 to take up a position as Associate Professor in the English Department of the University of Wisconsin-Madison. Her first book, *Drama at the Courts of Queen Henrietta Maria*, considered the political and cultural activities of Charles I's French queen. She is currently working on a study of women, theatre and early modern tragedy as well as an edition of Elizabeth Carey's *Mariam*.

EUGENE GIDDENS is Skinner-Young reader in Shakespeare and Renaissance Drama at Anglia Ruskin University. He edited *Pericles* for the Penguin Shakespeare series and is a general editor of the forthcoming Oxford *Complete Works of James Shirley* and an associate editor of *The Cambridge Edition of the Works of Ben Jonson*.

SUZANNE GOSSETT is Professor of English at Loyola University Chicago. She is General Editor of Arden Early Modern Drama, for whom she is completing an edition of Beaumont and Fletcher's *Philaster*. She writes on issues of editing, feminism, and collaboration, and is the editor of many early modern plays, including Shakespeare's *Pericles* for Arden Three (2004), Middleton and Rowley's *A Fair Quarrel* (*Collected Middleton*, 2007), and Chapman, Jonson and Marston's *Eastward Ho!* for the *Cambridge Edition of the Works of Ben Jonson* (forthcoming).

DAVID LINDLEY is Professor of Renaissance Literature at the University of Leeds, where he has worked since 1978. He has published widely on the court masque, on music and poetry, and has edited *The Tempest* for the Cambridge Shakespeare. His edition of eleven Jonson masques is forthcoming as part of the *Cambridge Edition of the Works of Ben Jonson*.

RUSS McDONALD is the author of *Shakespeare's Late Style* (Cambridge 2006) and a variety of books and articles on Shakespeare and Renaissance Culture. Having taught in several American universities, including the University of North Carolina at Greensboro, where he was North Carolina Professor of the Year in 2003, he is currently Professor of English Literature at Goldsmiths, University of London.

GORDON MCMULLAN is Professor of English at King's College London and a general editor of Arden Early Modern Drama. His most recent books are a monograph, *Shakespeare and the Idea of Late Writing: Authorship in the Proximity of Death*, and a collection of essays, *Reading the Medieval in Early Modern England*, co-edited with David Matthews (both Cambridge, 2007). He has edited *Henry VIII* for Arden Shakespeare (2000) and *1 Henry IV* for Norton Critical Editions (2003).

CHARLES MOSELEY was for many years Programme Director of the University of Cambridge International Shakespeare Summer School. He is Fellow and Tutor of Hughes Hall, Cambridge, and Affiliated Lecturer in the Faculty of English. Recent publications include an edition of *The Travels of Sir John Mandeville* (2005), *English Renaissance Drama: A Very Brief Introduction* (Humanities E-books, 2007) and studies of *King Henry IV* (2007), *Richard III* (2007) and *The Tempest* (2007). He is a Fellow of the English Association and of The Society of Antiquaries.

CLARE SMOUT spent many years as a director and dramaturg. She is currently studying for a D. Phil. at Magdalen College, Oxford, and teaches for the universities of Birmingham, Oxford and Cambridge. Forthcoming publications include a chapter on Mariah Gale for Routledge's *Actors' Shakespeare* plus RSC performance histories for Jonathan Bate's editions of *The Winter's Tale*, *The Merry Wives of Windsor* and *Timon of Athens*. She reviews regularly for *Cahiers Elisabéthains* and *Shakespeare*.

PATRICIA TATSPAUGH who has held academic and administrative posts in the USA and directed a study-abroad programme and lectured in the UK, has published *The Winter's Tale* in the series Shakespeare at Stratford (general editor Robert Smallwood, Arden Shakespeare, 2002) and contributed a performance history of *The Winter's Tale* for the New Variorum edition (eds. Robert Kean Turner and Virginia Westling Haas, Modern Language Association, 2005), essays on Shakespeare in performance and on film, and reviews of performances in *Shakespeare Bulletin* and *Shakespeare Quarterly*.

VIRGINIA MASON VAUGHAN is Chair of the English Department at Clark University in Worcester, Massachusetts, where she teaches courses in Shakespeare and early modern English drama. She is the author of two monographs, *Othello: A Contextual History* (1994) and *Performing Blackness on English Stages, 1500–1800* (2005). She also authored *Caliban: A Cultural History* and edited *The Tempest* for the Third Arden Series, both with historian Alden T. Vaughan. She is currently working on *'The Tempest': Shakespeare in Performance* for Manchester University Press.

ILLUSTRATIONS

1. Inigo Jones's design for Jupiter descending on an eagle, in Aurelian Townshend's masque *Tempe Restored* (1632). From the Devonshire Collection, Chatsworth, reproduced by permission of the Duke of Devonshire and the Chatsworth Settlement Trustees; photograph from the Photographic Survey, Courtauld Institute of Art.   *page* 54

2. Monochordum mundi: an illustration from Robert Fludd's *Utriusque cosmi maioris scilicet et minoris metaphysica, physica atque technica historia* (Oppenheim: Johann Theodore de Bry, 1617–18).   58

3. Hermione's trial, from William Creswick's promptbook, Shakespeare Centre Library.   117

4. *The Winter's Tale* (National Theatre, 1988): Leontes (Tim Pigott-Smith), Polixenes (Peter Woodward), and Hermione (Sally Dexter). Photograph by John Haynes.   123

5. *The Winter's Tale* (RSC, 1992): Hermione (Samantha Bond), Leontes (John Nettles), Polixenes (Paul Jesson), Perdita (Phyllida Hancock) and Paulina (Gemma Jones). Photograph by Richard Mildenhall.   124

6. *The Winter's Tale* (RSC, 1999): Leontes (Antony Sher), Hermione (Alexandra Gilbreath), and Paulina (Estelle Kohler). Photograph by Malcolm Davies.   126

7. *Cymbeline* at the Lyceum Theatre, 1896, with Henry Irving as Iachimo and Ellen Terry as Innogen. Drawing by H. M. Paget in *The Graphic*.   142

8. *Cymbeline* (RSC, 1962): Innogen (Vanessa Redgrave) with Cloten's corpse in William Gaskill's production at Stratford-upon-Avon. Photograph by Gordon Goode (Shakespeare Centre Library, Stratford-upon-Avon).   151

Early print and performance history

Pericles written 1607–8; seen by the Venetian and French Ambassadors at the Globe in 1607/8; performed by touring actors in a Catholic context in Yorkshire in 1609–10; presented at court in 1619; printed in quarto in 1609 (twice), 1611 and 1619, but excluded from the 1623 Folio, and finally included in Shakespeare's complete works in a supplement to the second issue of the Third Folio, 1664.

The Winter's Tale written 1609–10; seen by Simon Forman at the Globe in 1611; performed at court in 1611, 1618, possibly 1619, and 1624, as well as during the 1612–13 betrothal celebrations for Princess Elizabeth; first printed in the 1623 Folio.

Cymbeline written 1610–11; seen by Simon Forman at an unspecified venue in 1611; first printed in the 1623 Folio.

The Tempest written 1610–11; recorded performances at court in 1611 and again during the 1612–13 betrothal celebrations for Princess Elizabeth; first printed in the 1623 Folio.

Cardenio written 1612–13; two recorded performances at court in 1613; entered in the Stationers' Register in 1653 but apparently not published at that point; no copy survives.

Henry VIII written 1613; recorded performance at the Globe in 1613; first printed in the 1623 Folio.

The Two Noble Kinsmen   written 1613–14; recorded performance at court in 1619; first published in 1634, in quarto, attributed to Fletcher and Shakespeare; not included in Shakespeare's collected works until the mid-nineteenth century.

Date	Political events	Shakespeare and the King's Men	Other theatrical events	Cultural context
1603	Death of Elizabeth I Accession of James I Surrender of Hugh O'Neill, Earl of Tyrone and leader of the Irish Plague closes London theatres from May until April 1604	Chamberlain's Men become the King's Men Jonson: *Sejanus* Shakespeare: *Measure for Measure* Shakespeare: *A Lover's Complaint* Shakespeare: additions to Munday's *Sir Thomas More*	Heywood: *A Woman Killed with Kindness* Middleton: *The Phoenix*	Gibbons becomes a musician of the Chapel Royal
1604	Peace concluded with Spain Hampton Court Conference between Anglican clergy and Puritan leaders Tax on tobacco introduced	King's Men march in livery in King James's coronation procession Shakespeare: *Othello* King's Men acquire Marston's *Malcontent*	Daniel: *Philotas* Marston: *The Fawn* Middleton: *Michaelmas Term*	Dowland: *Lachrimae*
1605	Gunpowder Plot	Munday: *The Triumphs of Reunited Britannia* Shakespeare: *King Lear*	First collaboration between Jonson and Jones: *Masque of Blackness*	Bacon: *The Advancement of Learning* Byrd: *Gradualia*, Book One

	Shakespeare and Middleton: *Timon of Athens*	Playwrights of *Eastward Ho!* imprisoned for anti-Scottish portrayals Red Bull Theatre opens Rose Theatre closes	Cervantes: *Don Quixote* Caravaggio: *Ecce Homo*
1606	London and Plymouth Companies given charters to colonise Virginia The first Union Flag introduced Theatres closed due to plague, June to December	Fletcher: *The Noble Gentleman* Jonson: *Volpone* Middleton: *The Revenger's Tragedy* Shakespeare: *Macbeth* Shakespeare: *Antony and Cleopatra* Wilkins: *The Miseries of Enforced Marriage*	Parliament passes *Act to Restrain Abuses of Players* prohibiting blasphemy onstage Boy actors from Children of the Queen's Revels imprisoned for involvement in *The Isle of Gulls* Death of Lyly Birth of Davenant	Birth of Rembrandt
1607	The 'Midlands Rising' against the practice of enclosures Jamestown founded, the first successful British colony in North America Theatres closed all year due to plague, except for one week in April	Shakespeare: *All's Well That Ends Well* Shakespeare and Wilkins: *Pericles* Amateur performances of *Hamlet* and *Richard II* aboard an East India Company ship off Africa Marriage of Shakespeare's daughter	Beaumont: *The Knight of the Burning Pestle*	Halley's Comet observed by Keppler Jones: *First Set of Madrigals* Monteverdi: *L'Orfeo*

		Susanna to John Hall Death of Shakespeare's actor brother Edmund and his son		
1608	Theatres reopen in April, close again due to plague in late July.	King's Men start performing at the Blackfriars, though also continuing to use the Globe in summer Shakespeare: *Coriolanus* Birth of Shakespeare's granddaughter Elizabeth Death of Shakespeare's mother	Whitefriars Theatre opened Fletcher: *The Faithful Shepherdess*	Birth of Milton Wilkins: *The Painful Adventures of Pericles, Prince of Tyre* (prose narrative)
1609	*The Sea Venture* wrecked in the Bermudas (source for *The Tempest*) The Moors expelled from Spain Theatres remain closed due to plague	Beaumont and Fletcher: *Philaster* Shakespeare: *The Winter's Tale* Shakespeare's *Sonnets* printed, probably without permission	Jonson: *Epicene* Jonson: *The Masque of Queens*	Galileo demonstrates the telescope Death of Dr Dee
1610	Theatres reopen in January Prince Henry created Prince of Wales Henri IV of France murdered; Louis XIII succeeds	Shakespeare: *Cymbeline* Shakespeare: *King Lear* reworked	Daniel and Jones: *Tethys' Festival* Buc replaces Tilney as Master of the Revels	Death of Caravaggio Galileo discovers Jupiter's four largest moons Herriot is first to observe sunspots

	Guy leads expedition to colonise Newfoundland			
1611	Plantation of Ulster begins Roe explores 300 miles up the Amazon River	Fletcher: *The Tamer Tamed* Jonson: *The Alchemist* Shakespeare: *The Tempest* Tourneur: *The Atheist's Tragedy*	Heywood: *The Brazen Age* Heywood: *The Silver Age* Middleton: *The Roaring Girl*	King James Bible published Byrd: *Psalmes, Songs, and Sonnets*
1612	Death of Prince Henry (aged eighteen) Execution of the Lancashire Witches	Shakespeare and Fletcher: *Cardenio* Death of Shakespeare's brother Gilbert	Webster: *The White Devil* Heywood: *An Apology for Actors*	Cervantes's *Don Quixote* published in English (source of *Cardenio*) Drayton: *Poly-Olbion* Gibbons: *The First Set Of Madrigals and Motetts* Dowland appointed lutenist to James I Death of Gabrieli
1613	Marriage of Princess Elizabeth to the Elector Palatine	Shakespeare and Fletcher: *Henry VIII* Globe Theatre burns down during a performance of *Henry VIII*	Beaumont: *Masque of the Inner Temple and Gray's Inn* (source of the morris dance in *The Two Noble Kinsmen*) Middleton: *A Chaste Maid in Cheapside*	

1614	'Addled Parliament' summoned but dissolved having passed no legislation Native American Pocohontas marries Englishman Rolfe in Virginia	Shakespeare and Fletcher: *The Two Noble Kinsmen* Webster: *The Duchess of Malfi* Rebuilt Globe Theatre opens	Jonson: *Bartholomew Fair* Hope Theatre opens	Death of El Greco
1615		Death of Armin	Representatives of four leading theatre companies including King's Men summoned before Privy Council for performing in Lent	Rubens: *The Death of Seneca* Donne ordained
1616	Prince Charles created Prince of Wales Rolfe and Pocohontas visit London	Marriage of Shakespeare's daughter Judith to Thomas Quiney Death of Shakespeare Jonson: *The Devil is an Ass* Middleton: *The Witch*	Jonson's *Workes* printed in folio Cockpit Theatre opens Death of Henslowe Death of Beaumont	Chapman: *Whole Works of Homer* Rubens: *Hippopotamus and Crocodile Hunt* Hals: *Banquet of the Officers of the St George Militia Company* Galileo argues in support of Copernicus's theory of the solar system Copernicus's *De Revolutionibus* banned by the

				Catholic Church Death of Cervantes
1617			Jonson becomes Poet Laureate Cockpit Theatre destroyed in apprentice riots and rebuilt as the Phoenix	Death of Breugel
1618	Bacon appointed Lord Chancellor Raleigh executed Start of the Thirty Years War			Harvey lectures on the circulation of blood
1619	Death of Queen Anne	Death of Burbage King's Men block an attempt by Pavier and Jaggard to print a collection of ten of Shakespeare's plays (including *Pericles*)	Alleyn founds Dulwich College	Whitehall Banqueting House designed by Inigo Jones Schütz: *Psalms of David*
1620	The *Mayflower* takes settlers from Plymouth to Cape Cod	Middleton: *Hengist, King of Kent*	Middleton appointed Chronologer of the City of London	Bacon: *Novum Organum* Artemisia Gentileschi: *Judith Decapitating Holofernes*
1621		Dekker, Ford, Rowley: *The Witch of Edmonton* Fletcher: *The Island Princess* Middleton: *Women Beware Women*	Fortune Theatre burnt down	Burton: *Anatomy of Melancholy* Wroth: *Countess of Montgomery's Urania*

1622	Ignatius Loyola canonised		Middleton and Rowley: *The Changeling*	Birth of Molière
1623		Shakespeare: First Folio printed Fletcher: *The Sea Voyage* Death of Shakespeare's wife, Anne	Herbert appointed Master of the Revels	Velázquez: *The Investiture Of St Ildefonso With The Chasuble* Death of Byrd
1624	Pope orders Luther's German translation of the Bible to be burned Cardinal Richelieu appointed adviser to Louis XIII	Massinger: *The Parliament of Love* Middleton: *A Game at Chess* has continuous nine day run before being banned		
1625	Death of James I; Accession of Charles I Dutch settlement in Manhattan	Death of Fletcher Massinger becomes principal playwright for the King's Men		Death of Gibbons

Dates of composition of Shakespeare's plays have been taken from *William Shakespeare: The Complete Works*, ed. Stanley Wells *et al.*, 2nd edn (Oxford: Oxford University Press, 2005); dates of Middleton's plays taken from *Thomas Middleton: The Complete Works*, ed. Gary Taylor and John Lavagnino (Oxford: Clarendon Press, 2007); all other play dates taken from *Annals of English Drama, 975–1700*, ed. Alfred Harbage, revised by S. Schoenbaum and Sylvia Stoler Wagonheim, 3rd edn (London and New York: Routledge, 1989).

CATHERINE M. S. ALEXANDER

Introduction

Ordering works by the date of their composition is a common taxonomic principle, evident in the numerical classification of many art forms. The Shakespearean canon is frequently considered chronologically (that is to say, in the order in which it is assumed the plays were written although revision theories can thwart the ostensible simplicity of such an organising principle) and editions of the Complete Works sometimes arrange the plays in such a way. But writing about six plays from a large canon of work, gathered according to the probable date of their composition, would be an odd, indulgent and even pointless activity if the only reason for grouping them was the concluding place they occupied in the chronological output of their author. When does a last period begin? Why not the last eight (which in this case would accommodate *Coriolanus* and *Lear*) or the middle six? Grouping 'last' works together is usually predicated on two assumptions: that there is discernible difference from what has gone before, and in that difference is an identifiable progression or change – in style, subject matter and ideas, the use of language or the constituents of the work and, in the case of a dramatic piece, of stagecraft. It has been the fate of the Shakespeare's last plays to have their dates attached to specific biographical readings that identify 'meaning' or account for subject matter in ways that plays from other periods of the author's life have escaped. The persona that has been extrapolated from the art, covering the period between 1608 and 1612, has been characterised variously as religious and mystical, perhaps mentally unstable, probably cynical and disillusioned and with, at its emotional heart, an intense attachment to a daughter (it is never specified which one). It is such reading that is responsible for the erroneous belief that *The Tempest* is Shakespeare's final play and is a work of autobiography in which, disguised as Prospero, he bids farewell to the stage and his craft. The elision is evident as early as 1669 in the Prologue to Davenant's and Dryden's adaptation *The Tempest, or the Enchanted Island*, where Prospero's power becomes 'Shakespear's Magick' and the 'Enchanted Isle' a synonym for the playwright's work.

It was in response to late nineteenth- and early twentieth-century biographical readings that Lytton Strachey made his notorious comment on the author of the last plays (alluded to by Russ McDonald on p. 91), 'It is difficult to resist the conclusion that he was getting bored himself. Bored with people, bored with real life, bored with drama, bored, in fact, with everything except poetry and poetical dreams.'[1] Strachey had already pointed out the fallacy of suggesting that a character in a play can be 'a true index to the state of mind of the dramatist composing it' (p. 41) but played with the idea, and reached his different and not wholly serious conclusion after quoting from Dowden (whose arguments are considered by McMullan on pp. 6–7) and from Furnivall's description of Shakespeare's later years:

> the gloom which weighed on Shakespeare (as on many men) in later life, when, though outwardly successful, the world seemed all against him, and his mind dwelt with sympathy on scenes of faithlessness of friends, treachery of relations and subjects, ingratitude of children, scorn of his kind; till at last, in his Stratford home again, peace came to him, Miranda and Perdita in their lovely freshness and charm greeted him, and he was laid by his quiet Avon side. (p. 42)

Biographical readings cast a long shadow: they were implicit in Daniel Mesguich's *La Tempête* for the Comédie-Française in 1998, where Prospero was indistinguishable in dress and manner from Shakespeare and the visions presented to Ferdinand and Miranda during the masque were characters and scenes from other Shakespeare plays. Biography is the starting point, too, for the opening essay in this volume, 'What is a "late play"', in which Gordon McMullan begins his provocative exploration of Shakespearian classification with Edward Said's work on lateness.

Part of the difficulty in resisting biographical readings lies in the adult nature of the last plays, not in the x-rated sense but in their insistent focus on the problems of maturity: parenting (particularly the relationship between fathers and daughters), succession, inheritance, ageing and loss. They are pervaded by a sense of experience (of life and playwriting) that, for many, seems beyond the capacity of a youthful dramatist, however gifted. So while this volume is not driven by biography it remains a useful starting point because of its implicit recognition of difference. While Strachey's assessment, 'bored', might seem seriously outmoded, risible even, it is clearly a response to the question that might follow McMullan's – 'why are the plays as they are?' – that serves to point to perceptions of dissimilarity. Identifying and explicating distinguishing features is part of the function of this present volume. The last plays are relocated in the period of their composition; in Jacobean performance culture (David Lindley); in the literary and dramatic conventions of the period (Charles Moseley) and in the contexts of politics, religion and travel

(Karen Britland). Russ McDonald explores the distinctive features of the plays' language.

The use of 'last' rather than 'late' in the title of this *Companion* is determined, in part, by the connotations in the word of survival and endurance – Shakespeare's *lasting* plays – and one of the characteristics shared by these works, prompted perhaps by their difference and the experimental nature of their stagecraft, is their rich afterlives evident not only in criticism, textual and authorship studies but in the imaginative responses that they have generated on the stage and in new media. The presence in the plays of unexpected sounds and visual elements (deities, personifications, animals, statues, banquets, dance)[2] has inspired or licensed new work. From the Dryden/Davenant adaptation of *The Tempest* onwards the plays have attracted musical treatments: Carlo Barbieri's *Perdita* (1865), Max Bruch's *Hermione* (1872), Arthur Sullivan's incidental music for *Henry VIII* (1878), Arne Eggen's *Cymbeline* (1951), Michael Tippett's *Tempest*-derived *Knot Garden* (1970) and the rock musical *Marina Blue* (2002) up to Thomas Adès' *The Tempest* that premièred at Covent Garden in February 2004. The second half of this volume is devoted to the life of the plays in the 400 years after their composition. Undoubtedly it is *The Tempest* that has the highest reputation and most varied legacy (might this be because of biographical readings again?) and not only in music: its afterlife in art from Hogarth and Hayman onwards is probably the richest in the canon and it has spawned countless adaptations in new media. Its legacy is even evident in science: triggered perhaps by the sci-fi film derivative *Forbidden Planet* (1956) 'Prospero' was the name of the satellite launched into orbit in 1971 as Britain entered the space-race. Critically *The Tempest* is the play that has received the most attention of the group, particularly following the disintegration of the liberal humanist consensus, with theoretical readings that draw on analyses of race, gender and class/power leading to significant revisions in the reading of character and context. Prospero has been subject to the greatest reassessment with a shift of interpretation from a benign duke, god or magician to a malign manipulator, a change of emphasis that has created more sympathetic readings of Caliban – a victim of colonialism rather than a rapacious ingrate. It is Prospero's art, central to any reading of the play, that is the impetus for Virginia Mason Vaughan's essay on the afterlife of *The Tempest* as she focuses on the literary appropriations that are responses to those elements of the play that explore the role of art in human consciousness. The other essays are obliged, in part, to write about an afterlife that is less consistent and sustained: reception is patchy and responses have sometimes been hostile and all the authors are required to acknowledge the poor or problematic reception of their plays at some point. Patricia Tatspaugh focuses on the performance of *The Winter's Tale* and the reclamation of the play – on stage and page – over the last fifty years; Catherine Alexander considers the enduring effect of Johnsonian criticism and the strategies employed to make *Cymbeline* playable; Eugene Giddens writes of the checkered stage and critical history of *Pericles*; Suzanne Gossett explores the problems of co-authorship, tone and genre before considering the recent reclamation of *The Two Noble Kinsmen* and *Henry VIII*.

This volume reflects the recent growth of interest in the last plays, singly and as a group, but is not simply a reaction to trends in criticism, textual studies and performance. It recognises that there are gaps in accessible scholarship, that the Jacobean age is less well known than the Elizabethan period, that co-authored plays are as worthy of study as single-authored works, and that the 'afterlife' of these extraordinary creations – on page, stage or beyond – is an important area of scholarship. In the last scene of *Cymbeline* the king, ignorant of the identities of Belarius, Guiderius and Arviragus, rewards their valiant efforts in the battle against the Romans:

> Arise my knights o'th'battle. I create you
> Companions to our person, and will fit you
> With dignities becoming your estate. (5.4.20–22)

The Cambridge Companion to Shakespeare's Last Plays makes no claim for dignity (which is hardly a quality of the eclectic plays themselves) but it does aim to 'fit' the reader with an enjoyable, challenging and high quality encounter with these extraordinary creations.

NOTES

1. Lytton Strachey, *Books and Characters: French and English* (London: Chatto and Windus, 1928), p. 52.
2. For the visual culture of the plays see Frederick Kiefer's *Shakespeare's Visual Theatre: Staging the Personified Characters* (Cambridge: Cambridge University Press, 2003).

I

GORDON McMULLAN

What is a 'late play'?

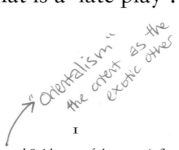

I

At the end of his life, Edward Said, one of the most influential cultural critics of the later twentieth century, wrote, appropriately enough, about last works. *On Late Style*, which was published posthumously, rejects the presumption that old age equals creative decline, endorsing instead the critical counter-argument that, for certain major writers, artists and composers, the last few years of life, far from tracing a gradual and irreversible process of decay, in fact mark a period of renascent creativity, a coherent, if brief, burst of artistic energy embodying a return to the engagements of the artist's youth which functions at the same time as a prophecy of subsequent developments in his chosen form.[1] In the late stylists Said admired – Strauss, Lampedusa, Beethoven – lateness manifests itself as a raging against the dying of the light, a resistance or obtuseness quite different from the resigned, serene abstraction more usually associated with the art of old age. For Said, the 'prerogative of late style' is to 'render disenchantment and pleasure without resolving the contradiction between them', and he argues that

> [w]hat holds them in tension, as equal forces straining in opposite directions, is the artist's mature subjectivity, stripped of hubris and pomposity, unashamed either of its fallibility or of the modest assurance it has gained as a result of age and exile'.[2]

'[L]ate-style Beethoven', Said argues, citing his single most admired late stylist, is music in 'a somewhat unattractive, not to say repellent, idiom'; it 'is not, as one might expect, all about reconciliation and a kind of restful summing-up of a long, productive career' – which is at best a second-tier kind of lateness, one that can be found, according to Said, 'in Shakespeare's late romances like *The Tempest, The Winter's Tale* and *Cymbeline*, or in Sophocles' *Oedipus at Colonus*, where, to borrow from another context, ripeness is all'.[3] Shakespeare, for Said, is thus a key instance of the version of late style he disliked – work manifesting a sense of calm resignation or resolution in old age and lacking the edge, the jaggedness, the difficulty that, for him, marks true lateness.

In making Shakespeare his primary exemplar of the serene form of late style, Said (consciously or not) invokes the work of the late nineteenth-century critic Edward Dowden, who, while not precisely the first to ascribe a late phase to Shakespeare, was certainly the most influential.[4] Dowden divided the life into four sections, mapped as apprenticeship ('In the work-shop'), young manhood ('In the world'), mature crisis ('Out of the depths') and resolution in old age ('On the heights'). This final phase, for Dowden, writing in 1875, is characterised by

> a certain abandonment of the common joy of the world, a certain remoteness from the usual pleasures and sadnesses of life, and at the same time, all the more, a tender bending over those who are like children still absorbed in their individual joys and sorrows.[5]

Thus, '[t]he spirit of these last plays is that of serenity which results from fortitude, and the recognition of human frailty; all of them express a deep sense of the need of repentance and the duty of forgiveness' (Dowden, p. 415). In the wake of the crisis which yielded unremittingly grim mid-period trage-dies such as *King Lear* and *Timon of Athens*, it seems, Shakespeare discovered a new lightness of heart which 'demanded not a tragic issue' but rather 'an issue into joy and peace': the 'dissonance' characteristic of the tragedies could now 'be resolved into a harmony, clear and rapturous, or solemn and profound, a reconciliation' (Dowden, p. 406). This steadily became the con-trolling understanding of Shakespeare's late work: a small subset of plays that post-date the major tragedies, forming a chronologically, generically and stylistically distinct group characterised by the sensibility of an old man reaching the end of an extraordinary career and ready to drown his art. 'The transition from these plays [i.e. the later tragedies] to Shakspere's last plays', wrote Dowden, 'is most remarkable. From the tragic passion which reached its climax in *Timon of Athens*, we suddenly pass to beauty and serenity'.[6] Dowden's influence was sustained well into the twentieth century: Robert Sharpe, for instance, writing in 1959, argued that the romances are Shakespeare's 'fourth period, of a serenity and tolerance allowing little in the way of bitter intensity, but much in that of a cosmic, almost godlike irony such as Prospero's', adding that 'Shakespeare has now made his peace with God and man'.[7] And it is clear also in recent criticism that still defines the plays as 'romances' and assumes their 'serenity': Joe Nutt, for example, writing in 2002, suggests that '[i]f the late plays are united in a romantic concern to evoke pleasure, that pleasure appears yet again to be inescapably rooted in what are perceived as the superior joys of family life, forgiveness and harmony' (and, of course, the same assumptions govern Said's reading of late Shakespeare).[8] Dowden's is, in other words, an understanding of the late plays that held sway for an astonishingly long time and that continues, to a perhaps surprising degree, to exercise a low-key influence on Shakespearean scholarship.[9]

But what are the plays in question? Which plays constitute 'late Shakespeare'? The plays that Said lists are those that Dowden groups as 'romances', the final serene, reconciliatory group:

> Cymbeline, The Winter's Tale, The Tempest.

Critics in Dowden's wake – and especially in the 1930s and 1940s, the heyday of late-play criticism – typically addressed these three plays in this exact order, seeing Cymbeline as an experiment in a new style, if perhaps a not very successful one; thinking of The Winter's Tale as more of a success, if still a little flawed; and treating The Tempest as the finished product, the retirement gesture par excellence, after which the ageing playwright could return to the town of his birth to live the remainder of his days in peace.[10] All three plays were written at roughly the same time and they all share generic similarities which are strong even as they are hard to pin down precisely: 'romance' or 'tragicomedy' or the hybrid 'romantic tragicomedy', plays in which time goes by, voyages are undertaken, storms and human sinfulness separate friends, lovers and families, yet eventually, at the last, usually over a period of a decade-and-a-half (time, that is, for daughters to grow to marriageable age), reconciliations are effected, families reconstructed and the generational future assured. Equally, they share certain stylistic features – ellipsis, asyndeton, convoluted syntax, heavy dependence on parenthesis and repetition – that Russ McDonald has recently delineated in impressive detail in Shakespeare's Late Style.[11] In all of this, it seems clear that the understanding offered in the 1930s and later by the German philosopher and critic Theodor W. Adorno of the late work of great artists as a form of catastrophe – that is, as discontinuity, as an ending that results from sudden change, from a distinct and marked caesura or division in the creative life – applies well to late Shakespeare. After the tragedies, in or around 1608, it seems, he shifted gear, producing three plays that share certain key characteristics and are thus unified chronologically, generically and stylistically.

Many critics, however, have chosen to add a fourth play to the mix (Dowden did so himself in his later Shakespeare 'Primer'), one which pre-dates the originary trio, producing a slightly modified group:

> Pericles, Cymbeline, The Winter's Tale, The Tempest.[12]

Pericles is so similar generically to the other three plays, they argue – it is a play about a father and his daughter, involving chivalric motifs, storms and shipwrecks, wide geographical wanderings and powerful emotional wrenches, and it concludes with recognition and reconciliation – that it must be included as the first experiment in the late-play form, even though its oddly archaic language and the sheer messiness of the text – we know *Pericles* not from the First Folio, but from a quarto of 1609 (two quartos of the play were published in 1609, as it happens, plus one in 1611 and another in 1619) which is fragmentary and error-strewn – mean that critics find it relatively hard to warm to, despite the evidence of its apparent popularity when first performed (as attested by those multiple early editions) and of some magnificent and deeply moving productions in recent years.[13] Still, for these critics, generic similarities outweigh textual uncertainties, making *Pericles* inescapably a 'late play': 'The last four plays of William Shakespeare,' announces Robert M. Adams, 'form a distinct group, similar to one another in several respects, different from the other plays in several respects' (Adams, p. 3).

Certain issues arise, however, with the incorporation of *Pericles* into the late-play group, one of which is that the play spoils a possible material explanation for the change in style apparent in the late work. Critics, beginning to resist the dominance of Dowden's purely (and fictionally) biographical reading of these plays, suggested that it is not so much a change of mood in the playwright that should be held responsible for the late-play caesura but the occupation by the King's Men of a second playhouse, the Blackfriars, out of use for several years due to the objections of local residents but brought back into service in the second half of 1608 (with financing from a group of investors that included Shakespeare).[14] This indoor theatre offered new possibilities for staging – including mechanisms in the roof for flying scenes (Ariel, say, in *The Tempest* or Jupiter descending on his eagle in *Cymbeline*) and the potential for lighting effects offered by an indoor playhouse illuminated not by daylight, as at the Globe, but with candles, and these factors, along with its smaller size and the different nature of the music required for such a space, perhaps account for the shift in tone. The problem created by the incorporation of *Pericles* into the late-play group, however, is that it cannot but pre-date the occupation of the Blackfriars by the company by at least several months and it thereby spoils the story of a clear-cut stop-and-begin-again for Shakespeare the playwright. Moreover, it introduces a further problem, because *Pericles* is a collaboration, a joint venture by Shakespeare and an obscure writer called George Wilkins, and so, critics sense, it can only be viewed partially or fragmentarily at best as late writing. After all, if the key definition of late work is that it is the product of an artist in old age, what can be done with work which is created by more than one artist, only one of whom is in the last phase of his life?

These awkwardnesses aside, critics could still argue that they had established a coherent group of four plays with a clear dynamic building up to the climax of the life's work in *The Tempest*. This is an argument still made in print: Nutt, for instance, baldly states that

> [a] glance at any list of Shakespeare's plays covering the end of his theatrical career from 1589 to 1612 will show the four plays ... *Pericles, Cymbeline, The Winter's Tale* and *The Tempest*, huddled together at the end, perhaps with *Henry VIII* added on as the very last play. (Nutt, p. 1)

The problem with this is that, as the 'perhaps' grudgingly acknowledges, *The Tempest* is not the last play that Shakespeare wrote. There are no fewer than three plays – *Cardenio, Henry VIII* and *The Two Noble Kinsmen* – which unavoidably post-date *The Tempest* and which therefore need to be added in some way to the late-play grouping, which would begin to look like this:

Pericles, Cymbeline, The Winter's Tale, The Tempest, Cardenio,
  Henry VIII, The Two Noble Kinsmen

This extended list of course presents serious problems for the maintenance of the neatly delimited group with which we began, not least because, like *Pericles*, the additional plays are collaborative, not with the obscure Wilkins this time but with John Fletcher, newly famous at the time for his collaborations with Francis Beaumont – histrionic, almost operatic plays which toy wilfully with convention in order to establish a new English form of tragicomedy – and destined before long to inherit from Shakespeare the role of principal playwright for the King's Men. *Cardenio* we know of only because of mentions in the records and its possible partial survival in the form of *Double Falsehood*, a play claimed by its eighteenth-century 'reviser', Lewis Theobald, to be an adaptation of Shakespeare's original.[15] But *Henry VIII* is present in the First Folio, the last in the group of plays depicting the lives of English kings, and although *The Two Noble Kinsmen*, like *Pericles*, does not feature in the Folio, there is a 1634 quarto of the play with a clear title-page ascription to Shakespeare and Fletcher.

Critics remain, as Suzanne Gossett points out, highly chary of these plays, since they spoil the serene-late-play story so very thoroughly – especially the *Kinsmen*, a dark, tense reworking of Chaucer's *Knight's Tale* by way of *A Midsummer Night's Dream* that, in any subjectivist reading (any reading, that is, which presumes that a given work of art reflects that artist's state of mind at the time of composition), offers us an ageing Shakespeare quite different from the image of the contented retiree amid the green fields of

Stratford. Moreover, these plays form what appears, in effect, to be a further stylistic caesura, disrupting the clear division between the late work and what went before. For Russ McDonald, Shakespeare's style in these post-*Tempest* plays is still, like it is in the earlier 'late plays', 'elliptical, roundabout, crowded, and extravagant, but the sense of *possibility* no longer seems to obtain' (McDonald, p. 254). In other words, there is a noticeable further shift of tone after *The Tempest*, a move away from reconciliation to something distinctly bleaker, offering a group of 'late late' or (as Gossett calls them) 'last last' plays and thereby undermining the 'final' status of the group of three (or four) with which we began. Shakespeare 'seems', McDonald suggests, 'to be changing his mind again' (McDonald, p. 254). And in any case, of course, as with *Pericles*, more than one 'mind' is in play here: the plays' status as collaborations between Shakespeare and Fletcher again presents the problem of the co-written play which is late for one of its authors and early for the other.

And this is by no means all. The most current Shakespearean chronology in circulation at the time of writing is that to be found in the second edition of the Oxford *Complete Works*, published in 2005.[16] It looks like this (I have included the editors' proposed dates):

> *All's Well That Ends Well* (1606–7), *Pericles* (1607–8), *Coriolanus* (1608),
>   *The Winter's Tale* (1609–10), *The Tragedy of King Lear* (1610),
> *Cymbeline* (1610–11), *The Tempest* (1610–11), *(Cardenio)* (1612–13),
>   *Henry VIII (All Is True)* (1613), *The Two Noble Kinsmen* (1613)

The editors move *All's Well That Ends Well*, traditionally lumped a little earlier with the other inappropriately named 'problem plays', *Measure for Measure* and *Troilus and Cressida*, into close and generically telling proximity to *Pericles* (with this simple, if undefended, chronological change, the romance elements in the *All's Well* plot take on entirely new significance), suggesting an easing-into the late-play genre, not the abrupt caesura of critical tradition ('Suddenly in 1608 there was a change,' announced Kenneth Muir, but it doesn't seem to be true).[17] The Oxford editors had, in fact, already, in their first edition, made the quietly bold move of reversing the order of *The Winter's Tale* and *Cymbeline*, thereby in part undermining the 'experimental' thesis which finds a convenient 'natural' order for the four 'romances'; and they had also already disrupted the late-play sequence by locating two tragedies – *Coriolanus*, a play in which it is effectively impossible to find traces of romance, and folio *King Lear* – both firmly inside the chronological bounds of the last work. We have come a long way, in other words, from Said's group of three clear-cut, singly-authored, generically distinct, serene late romances. Genre becomes a far less obvious way than it at first seemed to differentiate the 'late' work from the 'mature' period, the 'last plays' from the 'tragedies'; the caesura becomes far harder to locate than it is when certain convenient exclusions are made.

Moreover, the presence in this chronology of a version of *King Lear* as a 1610 play throws a particularly fat cat among the late-play pigeons. *Lear* is, after all, considered one of the two greatest tragedies in the Shakespeare canon (critics regularly put it into the ring with *Hamlet*, but there has yet to be a knockout – though a citation index would no doubt give *Hamlet* the victory on points).[18] So what is *King Lear* doing in the midst of the late work, of the so-called 'romances'? The answer (at least, the answer that became canonical in the last decades of the twentieth century) is *revision*, the argument that Shakespeare reworked his own material, thereby foregrounding the permeable boundaries of the creative process within the individual career. Shakespeare, it seems, wrote more than one version of several of his plays – not just of *King Lear* but also, notably, of *Hamlet* and *Othello* – and editors and critics have begun to explore what this might mean for the way we interpret these plays now. Gary Taylor, taking the lead, insists on the differences between quarto and folio *Lear*, rejecting the usual solution of conflation (that is, merging of the two texts to form a composite, so as to keep the individual features of both, a process which produces a text that is significantly longer than either of the originals), and he points out the distinct identity of each of the two texts, arguing that the later one is Shakespeare's own revision of his earlier play, a revision made in light both of the experience of four or five years' performance and of the ways in which he himself had developed as a playwright in that time. And he proceeds to point out a series of verbal parallels between folio *Lear* and the plays of 1610 or 1611, *The Winter's Tale* and *Cymbeline* especially, suggesting that the Folio version dates from the time of the late plays.[19] John Jones, in turn, both endorses and reverses Taylor's argument by demonstrating that it is the *earlier* version, not the one apparently written around the time of the late plays, that displays more traces of romance (in, for instance, the description of Cordelia's discovery of her crazed father in scene 17 which is excised from the later version) and arguing that, in revising the play, Shakespeare was wilfully de-romanticising, cutting lines and short scenes that, he now in hindsight realised, made his tragedy look a little too much like a late play *avant la lettre*.[20] *King Lear*, then, in its revised form, disrupts the late-play sequence, drawing on and resisting the mode that we have learned to call Shakespearean lateness.

Taylor's insertion of folio *King Lear* into the late-play group raises a further major problem for the incorporation into the canon of late work of Shakespeare's last plays, and that is the problem of old age. For H. B. Charlton, writing in 1938, the late plays are, famously, 'an old man's compensation for the inescapable harshness of man's portion'; for Marco Mincoff, in 1987, *The Tempest* is 'very much an old man's play'.[21] Yet this, like the belief that *The Tempest* is Shakespeare's last word, is simply untrue. Shakespeare was forty-three when he wrote *Pericles* and forty-five at the time of *The Tempest*, a man, then, in distinctly *middle* age. Critics, at this point, usually make one of two turns: arguing either that forty-five *was* old in Shakespeare's day, that people aged much faster back then – but this is to misunderstand actuarial statistics: average age at death was low because so many died in childhood, and if you survived till you were, say, thirty, you had a decent chance of making it also to sixty, the age at which you were relieved of civic obligations and thus officially considered old – or that a genius who dies young, through the sheer intensity of his genius, has lived the equivalent of a full life into old age – which is a fine romantic fantasy, but still only a fantasy.[22] Even *The Tempest* fails to be an old man's play: Prospero is typically represented on stage as (in one critic's words) a 'mixture of Father Christmas, a Colonial Bishop, and the President of the Magician's Union', but early illustrations of the role show a man in his late thirties or early forties at most, and his claim that the fifteen-year-old Miranda is 'a third of [his] own life' may simply mean that he is, like the playwright who created him, forty-five as the play opens.[23] Shakespeare was not old, in other words, when he wrote his 'late plays' and while these plays may perhaps be seen as examples of what German scholarship traditionally refers to as *Spätstil* ('late style'), they cannot be referred to by the supposedly synonymous term *Altersstil* ('old-age style').

So critics turn elsewhere, to *King Lear*, in their search for the ageing Shakespeare. Said, as we have seen, quoted the phrase 'Ripeness is all' to summarise the characteristic mood of late Shakespeare, words drawn not, as you might expect, from *Pericles* or *Cymbeline* but, tellingly, from *King Lear* (it is one of Edgar's several unconvincing aphorisms, spoken to try to comfort his comfortless father). For mid-century late-play critics, seeking a way both to mark the late-style caesura and yet also to insist on a fundamental redemptive continuity between the tragedies and the romances, *Lear* was the pivot, the play that provided the connection between mid- and late Shakespeare. For Cyrus Hoy, 'Shakespeare's tragedies are the necessary prelude to the romances; the romances are inconceivable without the tragedies; and among the tragedies, *King Lear* stands out' as the interconnecting link; for Robert Speaight, working with a pre-Taylor chronology but keen to make the connection with the late plays, '*Lear* is not Shakespeare's last word, but it is the overture to his last act'.[24] In their search for a late play which emphasises old age and which might therefore have a kind of metonymic effect upon Shakespeare the author, making him old before his time, critics have, then, repeatedly settled on *King Lear*, the play of old age, and the Oxford editors are the latest in that line. I'm not, I should add, suggesting that this is deliberate – it is a side-effect of Gary Taylor's search for evidence for a late date for folio *Lear* in order to make a convincing case for Shakespeare as reviser of his own work – but the dating of Folio *Lear* to 1610 (to, that is, the same date, roughly, as *The Winter's Tale* and *Cymbeline*) allows the play to bring the imprimatur of old age within the borders of the late phase and thereby serves to alleviate the underlying problem that Shakespeare's late plays were not in fact the work of an old man.

The requirements of chronology, of the stylistic caesura, of genre and of old age, then, all cause problems for the excavation of a classic 'late period' from the Shakespeare canon. And in any case, as I have argued elsewhere, the conditions for theatrical production in Shakespeare's day were wholly inim-ical to the subjectivist understanding of art required for an attribution of late style. Shakespeare, contrary to the image familiar to us from *Shakespeare in Love* and other popular representations of the playwright's creative process, was not a lone genius, awaiting inspiration in an attic: he was a professional early modern playwright, working – sometimes overtly in collaboration with other playwrights, always tacitly in collaboration with his fellow actors in the King's Men – for his audiences, adjusting to new genres and new styles as they had success in rival theatres and with rival companies (I will come back to this in the final section). He was not (as C. J. Sisson pointed out as early as 1934) writing his own life story in his plays, consciously or otherwise.[25] The Romantic conception of authorship – the belief that the work directly repre-sents the development of the mind that produced it and that it should there-fore be understood principally in its relation to that mind – post-dates him by a couple of centuries. It is critics such as Dowden, intent on establishing a coherent life-span for a demonstrable genius, who invented 'late Shakespeare' in the sense in which we have come to understand it, privileging coherence and teleology over fragmentation and impersonality. And contemporary Shakespeareans – sentimentally (though deniably) attached to the image of Shakespeare-as-Prospero, the all-powerful writerly mage finding a new and profound lease of creative life late in the day – continue to be complicit in the process through which we have come to think of the late plays as we do.

2

Where, then, does this leave us? Is there no such thing as a Shakespearean 'late play'? I have tried in the previous section to set out the problems involved in establishing the shape and nature of the Shakespearean late phase not in order to reject out of hand the idea that there is something different about the plays of Shakespeare's last writing years but to do two things: to demonstrate the exclusions required to produce the mainstream understanding of the late plays and to clear the air of some of the presumptions and myths that seem to me to stand in the way of an adequate view of these plays. 'Late play', like 'problem play', is, after all, a term created a couple of hundred years after Shakespeare in order to negotiate a perceived grouping of plays felt by nineteenth- and twentieth-century critics to be inadequately served by the categories available in the early seventeenth century. The First Folio offers 'comedies', 'histories' and 'tragedies' (it doesn't have a 'tragicomedies' section, though it might have done; 'romance', on the other hand, was not a term applied to drama at the time), but most definitely not 'problem plays' or 'late plays': in the folio, the plays we think of as the 'late plays' are divided between the 'comedies' (*The Tempest*, *The Winter's Tale*), 'histories' (*Henry VIII*) and 'tragedies' (*Cymbeline*), and three of them do not, as we have already seen, appear in the First Folio at all (*Pericles*, *Cardenio*, *The Two Noble Kinsmen*). 'Late play' is, then, a subsequent invention, one which, though often (and understandably) treated by critics as a 'neutral term' in comparison with the heavily laden options of 'tragicomedy' or 'romance', is in fact burdened with meanings imposed a very long time after these plays were first performed.[26]

If, then, as a kind of simple thought-experiment, we take as our material for critical analysis not Shakespeare's *late* plays – that is, a group consisting of some, though not all, of the plays in the Shakespeare canon written between 1607 or 1608 and 1613, with the choices for inclusion made on the basis of style and/or genre and defined in relation to what I have elsewhere called the 'discourse of lateness' – but rather Shakespeare's *last* plays – that is, the entire group of plays within those chronological bounds – and insist that any account of these plays has to exclude none of them, then the situation is to a significant degree altered. What we would be working with, in this scenario, is simply a set of plays viewed within certain chronological bounds and without prior thematic, generic or stylistic selection (though care would be needed not to treat the group as a monolith with no internal dynamic or development). The plays in question, then, if we accept provisionally the dating work undertaken by the editors of the Oxford *Complete Works*, would, as we have seen, be these: *All's Well That Ends Well*, *Pericles*, *Coriolanus*, *The Winter's Tale*, *The Tragedy of King Lear*, *Cymbeline*, *The Tempest*, *Cardenio*, *Henry VIII* and *The Two Noble Kinsmen* – a list given its working logic, it would seem, solely by chronology. Clearly this group is not adequately defined on the basis of the kinds of description we have seen of the privileged four 'romances'. Yet if we were to compare this set of ten plays with another set of ten from a little earlier in Shakespeare's career – let us say the plays written (according again to the Oxford chronology) between 1599 to 1604, that is, *Much Ado About Nothing*, *Henry V*, *Julius Caesar*, *As You Like It*, *Hamlet*, *Twelfth Night*, *Troilus and Cressida*, *Sir Thomas More* (only one scene, perhaps, but it is important nonetheless not to forget this collaborative play), *Measure for Measure* and *Othello* – then we can see that the ten last plays, though they certainly don't all fit readily into the mould outlined for them by the Dowden tradition, do nonetheless offer a good deal more overall coherence than the earlier group. There is, in other words, some shared difference about them. I do not wish to claim that this exercise would automatically involve seeing Shakespeare's last work 'whole', because that implies a governing, authorising unity that would be inappropriate as a basis for interpretation of these plays, not least because it might resist the necessary incorporation of the collaborations into the group. The group is, in any case, stable neither generically nor stylistically. Yet there do appear to be certain cross-currents and interconnections amongst the plays in question that have the potential to be critically productive.

If, then, we include in our group plays such as *Coriolanus* and *The Two Noble Kinsmen*, the usual generalisations – ones which work perfectly well for the exclusive group-of-four of *Pericles*, *The Winter's Tale*, *Cymbeline*, *Tempest* – are severely disabled: we are unable to make very many of the standard statements about the late plays. Take this, for instance, from Raphael Lyne's recent introduction to the late plays, *Shakespeare's Late Work*: '[T]here are tortuous voyages towards self-discovery, and the endings of the plays see marvellous discoveries and recoveries of lost things'.[27] This is a perfectly accurate assertion about the group-of-four, but it would not work for a group that includes *Coriolanus* or *The Two Noble Kinsmen*. Yes, in these plays too, there is something that could fairly be described as a 'tortuous voyage towards self-discovery', but the discoveries are neither integrated nor redemptive and the endings of both plays are crushingly bleak. So, in discovering that the identity that was constructed for him by his mother is hollow (in what in post-Althusserian discourse we might call an ideological effect), Coriolanus will inevitably be destroyed. Again, Palamon may end up married to Emilia, as he wished to be, but since that situation has only come about through the death of Arcite, his more-than-cousin, he is encompassed by the debilitating logic of the play's closing paradox: 'That we should things desire which do cost us / The loss of our desire'.[28] Yet to exclude either play from a discussion of Shakespeare's late or last plays would be chronologically arbitrary – and especially so in the case of *The Two Noble Kinsmen*, which is, after all, the 'latest' or 'very last' play, a position of privilege that critics remain reluctant to wrench away from *The Tempest*.

In any case – and this is where, in my thought-experiment, I would suggest that critical energy might be focused – some generalisations about late Shakespeare still hold true, arguably, for the entire group. The traditional centrality of the *father/daughter* binary to late Shakespeare, for instance – the focus in so much work on the late plays on the reconciliation of Pericles and Marina or of Leontes and Perdita, as well as the subtle changes of dynamic in the relationship between Prospero and Miranda across the length of *The Tempest* – works also, if in a stilted, forced manner, both for *Henry VIII* as the infant Elizabeth appears in the final scene in order silently but effectively to upstage her father and, arguably, for *The Two Noble Kinsmen* in the dysfunctional relationship of the Jailer and his daughter and the discomfort of the daughter's 'cure' at the end of the play (that she remains the 'Jailer's Daughter' throughout and is never named serves to emphasise the relationship with her father over any individual identity that might be claimed for her). This said, the binary would need to be modified in a whole-group analysis to the gender-unspecific *parent/child* in order to incorporate the *mother/son* focus of *Coriolanus*, and indeed there is a deal to be gained by doing so: the generational dynamic would remain clear, but the sentimentalism of the 'romances' would be put under severe pressure, and the shift of gender-focus would permit, for instance, a fuller incorporation into the overall discussion of relationships such as that of *Cymbeline's* Queen and Cloten, *The Winter's Tale's* Hermione and Mamillius and (more contentiously) *All's Well's* Countess of Roussillon and Bertram. Moreover, Janet Adelman's psychoanalytic reading of *King Lear* suggests that, even in a play with such an overt father/daughter focus, the repressed mother is present just beneath the surface, ready to return to appalling effect.[29]

This serves as a reminder that perhaps the most prominent thematic concern insistently to remain when all the plays written between 1607 and 1613 are taken into account is the issue of *return*. If there is one thing that connects these last plays, it is their habit of looking back in order to look forward, of rehearsing, reshaping and reinventing past concerns in new contexts. This is a truism, of course, both as an observation about Shakespeare's late plays and also as a claim about late work in general – and in any case, as Ruth Nevo has pointed out in her surprisingly overlooked book *Shakespeare's Other Language*,

> Shakespeare is *throughout* the most reiterative of poets – his returns and recurrences are as incessant as they are exfoliating and diversified; his imagination kindles afresh to each redevelopment of familiar components or, perhaps it would be truer to say, every work leaves in its wake a detritus of un- or not yet resolved or integrated components which leads on to the next. (Nevo, p. 2)

That this is true right across the Shakespeare canon, however, does not detract from the particular foregrounding of the return/rehearse/revise process enacted repeatedly in the last plays – one which happens to work, on its own terms, even for the very *final* play, since if Shakespeare did not subsequently negotiate the 'detritus' of the *Kinsmen*, then Fletcher unquestionably did, as Suzanne Gossett notes in her essay in this volume.[30] On the contrary, it provides one way, at least (and I hope this essay might provoke others into finding more such ways), of making sense of the *full* set of plays within the chronological bounds specified, not just of those that confirm a prescribed generic grouping, and of course it encompasses the characteristic language – renunciation, reconciliation, revelation, redemption, release – that will appear prominently in any randomly chosen critical work on the late plays. Moreover, *return* also encompasses both the revision process that is apparent in Folio *Lear* – Shakespeare turning back to an earlier play and rewriting it – and that apparent in a play such as *Pericles* in its relationship with the much earlier *Comedy of Errors* or such as *The Two Noble Kinsmen* with the earlier *Midsummer Night's Dream* or, as Suzanne Gossett notes in her essay, with the even earlier *Two Gentlemen of Verona* (or, for that matter, in its restaging of a tournament of anonymous knights, with the only-just-earlier *Pericles*) – Shakespeare turning back to an earlier play and rewriting it in a new form. And it incorporates not only the kinds of return that critics find in the group-of-four – for Nevo, for instance, *Pericles* 'obsessively reiterates, is, indeed, the rhythm of vicissitude in human life, the rhythm of maturation: separation, dispossession, return, under the cross of guilt, where three roads meet' (Nevo, p. 47), something that can be said just as effectively of the plays she doesn't address, such as *The Two Noble Kinsmen*, which, in its most quotable couplet, ensures that we are aware of the centrality of death to this process of separation and return: 'This world's a city full of straying streets, / And death's the market-place where each one meets' (1.5.15–16) – but also, in a very different generic setting, Coriolanus's return to Rome and to his mother in all of that moment's profound destructive power. The idea of return, then, offers a means of addressing the whole chronological group without determining or limiting generic affiliation, suggesting at least one way in which the decision to include all the last plays, not just a selected few, might offer the potential for new readings.

I hope in these brief sketches to have given a sense of what is to be gained in resisting prior exclusions when addressing Shakespeare's last plays. Yet there is, at the same time, no doubt that redefining late Shakespeare in this way as the last work on purely chronological grounds necessarily excises a great deal which critics will be reluctant to lose: that is, the very stylistic and generic features which have been the primary focus of late-play criticism. And we cannot, in any case, pretend (even if we wished to) that Shakespeare criticism, and literary criticism in general, is a rigorous, scientific mode; it is, of course, no such thing. Critics have emotions, and one of those emotions is nostalgia, the continued calling-to-mind of what has gone even in the process of moving on, preferring to retain both a belief in *The Tempest*'s finality, despite the unavoidable evidence that it is not the last play (a preference that encourages a reluctance to acknowledge the collaborations) and the sense of wonder, of resolution, of forgiveness that can be found – arguably, though so much late-play criticism over the last thirty years, not least the powerful array of postcolonial readings of *The Tempest*, suggests otherwise – in the 'romances'. Nonetheless, the comprehensive view that is available to those prepared to look at *all* the last plays and to dwell on the reasons made by others for leaving some of them out and foregrounding others seems to me to be worth the effort required to achieve it. Shakespeare's last plays – all of them, not just selected highlights – provide critics and students alike with a glorious array of interpretative currents and counter-currents to provoke exploration of genre, style, history, context, culture, gender, psychology, ideology and per-formance (to name just some of the available avenues) and offer a deal of potential for new readings – which is a cherishable thing in respect of such an overdetermined and relentlessly consumed canon as Shakespeare's. To define these plays according to the limitations implicit in the term 'late play', it seems to me, is unnecessarily to reduce their impact and to limit their potential as objects of critical analysis. To think of them instead as Shakespeare's *last plays*, in the very arbitrariness of that term, is to enhance, not deny, the possibility of genuinely new accounts of these marvellous plays.

3

There are, nonetheless, critical issues which a solely chronological principle cannot embrace with any great comfort, because attempts to isolate these plays chronologically tend to make apparent the *diachronic* nature of the creation of meaning – in other words, that meaning is made across time, not just made once, at a single time, and then developed, eroded or corrupted in ways that can always be detached and subordinated. Let us take, for instance, the textual nature of the late plays. As we have seen, *Pericles* is a particularly complex case, a text sufficiently fragmented and incomplete that editors, even editing as lightly and conservatively as possible, have little choice but to reconstruct from Wilkins's prose version of the story certain scenes, so that the text of the play read by students in any of the current editions (especially the Oxford *Complete Works* and its derivatives) is to a considerable degree one which cannot be said to date strictly from 1607–8. Again, the stage-directions for which the late plays are renowned can form a further barrier to clarity: those in *Henry VIII*, for instance, are at times near-verbatim Holinshed (Shakespeare's principal source for his historical plays) and appear to be more literary than theatrical – that is, they seem to be words doing more work than, or work other than, that required to assist a group of actors to stage the scene in question – which makes it that little bit more difficult to work out the relationship of the First Folio text to the first performances. In other words, the late plays we read and see performed are not necessarily texts that provide us with a direct line back to the date of first performance but are, rather, the products of a series of inputs and negotiations across time. Out of this material history, a clear-cut chronology does not necessarily carve a cohering interpretation, because the process through which the plays have reached us is part of what they have become for us and that process has taken far longer than the seven years we ascribe to 'late Shakespeare'.

Nonetheless, even without expanding the interpretative timeframe beyond the period during which Shakespeare acted as playwright for the company, there is one further thought-experiment that might be made, one which grows out of an approach to early modern drama that has emerged in the last decade or so and which puts into serious doubt the entire line of thinking that prompts the questions I have so far been trying to answer, at least as far as Shakespeare and his professional contemporaries are concerned. In a sense, it requires me to relocate the emphasis in the sentence with which I finished the previous section, so that it would read as follows: 'To think of them instead as *Shakespeare*'s last plays, in the very arbitrariness of that term, is to enhance, not deny, the possibility of genuinely new accounts of these marvellous plays'. I have already briefly argued, at the close of the opening section, that we misrepresent the Shakespeare canon if we imagine that Shakespeare can be treated as if he were a laureate-style poet consciously carving out a career – by which I mean either in the early modern sense of shaping a poetic selfhood, as for instance did Spenser, on the basis of the inherited classical models of Ovid or (especially) Virgil, or in the later, Romantic sense of the inspired figure in the garret working in isolation to pour out onto the page the record of his current emotions – rather than a professional playwright working within the conditions, physical and institutional, of the early modern theatre, and I wish now to return to this in slightly more detail.

We have already seen the extent to which collaboration threatens a clear-cut understanding of Shakespeare's late plays. Early modern playwrights collaborated a great deal – G. E. Bentley conservatively estimated that 'as many as half of the plays by professional dramatists in the period incorporated the writing at some date of more than one man' and noted that '[i]n the case of the 282 plays mentioned in Henslowe's diary (far and away the most detailed record of authorship that has come down to us) nearly two-thirds are the work of more than one man' – and this calls for an appropriate critical response.[31] The simple fact that a playwright worked with another playwright requires the critic to examine the extent of the role of each in the play they wrote together and authorship analysts, using linguistic and other methods, work hard to differentiate between collaborating playwrights in a given play so as to be clear which sections should be attributed to whom. Yet audiences rarely find themselves noticing the joins – the moments at which the other playwright takes over the writing – and, even if the authorship analysis performed is close to foolproof (and techniques have advanced rapidly over the last couple of decades), it is arguable that the hermeneutics of collaboration – that is, the interpretative framework within which they need to be addressed – is such that simple differentiation between the collaborating writers' sections is not sufficient to deal with the impact of collaboration on our reading of the play. For one thing, as Jeffrey Masten argues, dramatic collaboration militates against the assumption that an individual style will be detectable for a given playwright. A playwright, he points out,

> im/personates another (many others) in the process of writing a play-text and thus refracts the supposed singularity of the individual in language. At the same time, he often stages in language the *sense* of distinctive personae, putting 'characteristic' words in another's mouth.[32]

For Masten, there is always a negotiation of the playwright's voice with those of the characters he creates as well as between the two or more collaborating playwrights, so that in the process identity appears far more fluid than attributional analysts care to admit: 'In attribution study's terms', he argues, 'textual "habits" are taken ... to convey or express individual identities', but analyses of this kind 'fail to register the ways in which "habits", however seemingly concrete in a given text, can be broken, emulated, adopted, adapted, thrown off, unintentionally lost, and contextual'.[33] And there is, in any case, a more fundamental problem with treating a piece of theatrical writing – at least of the kind that Shakespeare produced – as the writing of an individual with complete creative autonomy, because Shakespeare the professional playwright did not write plays at random, as the mood took him; on the contrary, he wrote plays *for his company*, for the King's Men, the single most successful acting troupe of the age and one which had its own distinctive style – a style which had of course substantially been created by Shakespeare himself in collaboration with his company peers (Heminges, Condell, and the rest) but which nonetheless came into being through more agencies than just that of Shakespeare himself. It is, then, to the concept of repertory and the repertory company to which I wish to turn for my second and final thought-experiment.

Suppose we ordered things differently. Suppose we had never chosen the *author* as the arbiter of meaning in a text. Suppose instead that libraries located books on shelves not according to the name of the author but on a different basis: the name of the patron or of the publisher, say, or the place of publication – even the colour of the spine, perhaps. Or rather, in the case of early modern plays – because system would naturally be preferred to the arbitrariness and instability of something like jacket design – according to the acting company for which the play was written, so that we would include the plays in the Shakespeare canon not under 'S' for 'Shakespeare' but under 'K' for 'King's Company'. This is, in a way, the work that the field known as 'repertory studies' has begun to do in the last fifteen or so years. The landmark texts are Rosalyn Lander Knutson's *The Repertory of Shakespeare's Company*, Scott McMillin and Sally-Beth MacLean's *The Queen's Men and Their Plays*, Andrew Gurr's *The Shakespeare Company* and Lucy Munro's *Children of the Queen's Revels*.[34] Each of these books begins from the same basic premise – that, as Munro phrases it, '[t]he author is a useful organising principle, but it is not the only one available' (Munro, p. 4) and that the plays of a given company 'were created not only by the dramatists, but also through the ideas and desires of the company's shareholders, licenser, patrons, actors and audience' (Munro, p. 165).

Were we to see the logic of this through in relation to the late plays, we would seek to make sense of the plays not only in relation to the earlier work in the Shakespeare canon but also in relation to the other plays in the King's Men's repertory and in the rival repertories with which that company competed. 'Companies', Munro points out, 'reacted to the plays performed alongside their own, with influences and sources bouncing back and forth between adult and children's companies alike' (Munro, p. 165). In this context, the biography of the playwright becomes a less significant factor in our understanding of the shifts in genre and style that we find in a given play at a given time than does the place of the play in the commercial structures of the theatre, and we would look to the interactions of repertories for the logic of some, perhaps many, of those changes. So, for instance, we might assess the writing of *Cymbeline* and *The Winter's Tale* not, as some have done, in relation to the awareness of last things provoked in Shakespeare by the deaths of his son and his brother but rather to the impact of the revival of the Elizabethan pastoral romance play *Mucedorus* just prior to, and in the middle of, the 'late phase' – as Knutson suggests of *Mucedorus*,

> [k]nowing as do that it was on stage both around 1605–06 and 1610–11, we see that it was in a position to influence the romances and tragicomedies throughout 1607–1613, a period which includes the composition and production of the early pastoral tragicomedies of Beaumont and Fletcher as well as those of Shakespeare. (Knutson, pp. 142–3)

From this perspective, the similarities between certain scenes in *The Winter's Tale*, for instance, and in *Mucedorus* are not so much a record of Shakespeare's memory of seeing the play several years earlier but rather the effect of a company seeking to perform new work which capitalises on a revival success. Similarly, we might look at *Henry VIII* in relation to the publication in 1613 of a new edition of Samuel Rowley's *When You See Me You Know Me*, a Prince's Men play about the reign of Henry VIII first performed in 1604–5, so that we would become aware of the possible significance, in a year in which the King's son died catastrophically at the age of only eighteen, of the otherwise curious omission from the King's Men play of any mention of Queen Elizabeth's brother Edward VI, who also died young (and who features prominently in *When You See Me*).

Moreover, were we to adopt the perspective of Ashley Thorndike in *The Influence of Beaumont and Fletcher on Shakespeare* (a book that was anathema to Bardolaters at the beginning of the twentieth century, who wished to see Shakespeare precisely as free from the influence of 'lesser' writers) in order to understand the emergence of the new hybrid genre of 'romantic tragicomedy' at this time in the contrasting, competing and complementary work of Daniel, Marston, Beaumont, Fletcher and Shakespeare in adaptating and negotiating the theory and practice of Giambattista Guarini, the most influential source of information about tragicomedy available to Jacobean playwrights, we would begin, perhaps, to see one basis for the productive cross-currents in motion in 1608/9/10. Nobody has yet produced proof of which of *Philaster* and *Cymbeline* was written first, so that Knutson's observation that '[a]mong the offerings new (or relatively new) to London playgoers [in spring 1610] were *Cymbeline*, *Philaster*, and *The Alchemist*' (Knutson, 137) – the latter in part parodying romance excess – gives a helpful sense of the audience's perspective on the interrelations of plays in the repertory. And we might look, as Knutson has so valuably done, at the triple pattern of continuations, new work and revivals within a single repertory in order to see a possible institutional basis for the process of renew-and-return that we have mapped thematically within late Shakespeare. So, in 1610–11, 'when *The Winter's Tale* was new', she notes,

> *Cymbeline* and *Othello* were continued from 1609–10 and his *Macbeth* was being revived. In 1611–12, he supplied *The Tempest* to the new offerings and *The Winter's Tale* to the continuations. In 1612–13, he supplied *Cardenio* for the new offerings in the winter and *Henry VIII* in early summer. In addition, he supplied *The Tempest* and *The Winter's Tale* to the continuations; and *Othello*, *Much Ado About Nothing*, and *Julius Caesar* to the revivals, as well as (apparently) *1 Henry IV* and *The Merry Wives of Windsor*.   (Knutson, p. 166)

In other words, it begins to be clear that we need to look as closely as we can at the relative chronologies both of the plays within the King's Company repertory itself and of those in the repertories of other key companies in order to establish a kind of flow-diagram of the movement of generic and other influences within and across company lines. In this way, Lucy Munro, assessing the relationship between the King's Men repertory and that of the Children of the Queen's Revels, maps the unfolding of events from the differing fates of two tragicomedies in the children's repertory, Beaumont's successful *Cupid's Revenge* and Fletcher's flop *The Faithful Shepherdess*, plotting a trajectory that would remain hidden were authors' intentions the sole basis for critical analysis:

> The attempt [by Fletcher in *The Faithful Shepherdess*] to naturalise Italian pastoral tragicomedy failed, but the Queen's Revels' other attempts to develop English tragicomedy succeeded. Hired by the King's Men around 1609, after that company had regained the Blackfriars theatre, Beaumont and Fletcher set to work in an attempt to combine the popularity of *Cupid's Revenge* with the lessons learnt from *The Faithful Shepherdess*. The pair also had an impact on their new colleagues. The repertory of the King's Men when the theatres reopened included the tragicomic *Philaster* and *Cymbeline* – both of which rework the stabbing of Amoret [a female character in *The Faithful Shepherdess*] – together with revivals of *Pericles* and *Mucedorus*. The new tragicomedies reinterpreted many of the preoccupations of the Queen's Revels' version of the form, such as the concern with the relationships between sexuality and political structures, and used many of the same sources. The place of English tragicomedy, together with the future of the King's Men after the uncertainties of the plague years, looked to have been assured, but it was the interplay between satyr and shepherd in the Queen's Revels tragicomedies that fuelled the emergence of the genre.　　(Munro, pp. 132–3)

Munro's is an exemplary account of the impact of company rivalry and emulation and of the transfer of playwrights from company to company: the agency of certain playwrights figures in this reconstruction, too, of course, but it is one of several reasons, not the only reason, for the kind of play that emerged in 1609 or thereabouts – and there is, crucially for our purposes, nothing in the story that might encourage the use of the words 'late' or 'last'.

In this way, then, we might begin to establish an understanding of the creative process in the early modern theatre that sees authorship not as the sole creative source for the shape and nature of a given play but rather as one (a principal one, it goes without saying) in a series of intersecting influences, impetuses and inputs. This is a little inelegant as a formula, admittedly, but it allows us to think again, I hope, about the process through which early modern professional plays came into being, and it offers us a perspective on dramatic authorship which allows us to step back a little from the Romantic inheritance that continues, anachronistically, to dominate critical thinking about early modern drama. The point, of course, is that the terms 'late' or 'last' apply only if we persist in treating Shakespeare as the interpretative hub of the plays in question. Treated as Shakespeare's creations, these plays are, indeed, 'late' or 'last', but we have seen the obstacles that exist to make such a decision problematic. Treated as plays in the repertory of the King's Company, however, they are neither early nor late; they mark, rather, a major transition for the company, from the period in which Shakespeare was the principal house playwright to the period of Fletcher's dominance (which in turn would become the period of Massinger and then of Shirley, in a natural process of creative turnover, while the institution these playwrights served went from strength to strength, determining the nature of London theatre in the 1620s and 30s and far beyond the Civil War). The Shakespeare/Fletcher collaborations, from this perspective, suddenly become pivotal, not supplementary or fragmentary but the locus of institutional transition, as the Elizabethan theatrical dispensation is reshaped by way of the intrreraction of company repertories a decade into the reign of James VI and I.

Perhaps, then, in the end, to think and write of 'Shakespeare's late plays' is to miss a certain amount (or even a great deal) of the point, to take a view which is at best partial. Agencies other than, or in addition to, that of the playwright determined the shape and nature of the plays in the Shakespeare canon; Shakespeare's own agency was a significant, no doubt a major, factor in the conjunction of creative forces that produced the 'late plays', but it was not necessarily the exclusive one that critical history has demanded. The terms 'late' or 'last' play emerge from an understanding of the creative process that foregrounds the author at the expense of other significant determining elements in the construction of a play, arguably denying us as much perspective as it provides. It will not, of course, go away in any foreseeable future to be replaced by some sort of alternative, non-authorial hermeneutic, and nor should it: those, such as Munro, who argue now for the value of repertory studies would strongly resist any over-reaction which negated or underplayed the role of the playwright in the collaborative process that is the production of a play. There is, however, little danger of that in any imaginable future. And, in any case, as I have tried to suggest in the course of this essay, there is a great deal to gain from thinking of the late plays *as* 'late' or 'last' plays, as long as the critic bears in mind the extent to which the category so delineated is *constructed* rather than *given*. The 'late' or 'last' plays are richly rewarding works of art for the student of early modern theatre – we have, happily, come a long way from where we were a century ago, when these plays were viewed, more often than not, with a combination of suspicion and disappointment – and they deserve (and will reward) our continued, attention. It is important, then, to be aware of the implications of thinking of them as 'late' or as 'last' and to dwell on those implications, if only because in the history of Shakespeare criticism shifts of perspective of this kind have tended to produced the most exciting new readings, helping make anew these wonderfully endless plays.

NOTES

1. My choice of the masculine possessive pronoun is deliberate. One of the markers of the timeboundedness and contingency of the supposedly 'transhistorical' idea of late style is its general exclusion of women. Very few women have had a late style attributed to them: like 'genius', 'lateness' has been treated by critics, implicitly rather than explicitly, as a male prerogative.

2. Edward Said, *On Late Style* (London: Bloomsbury, 2006), p. 148; reworked from Said, 'Thoughts on Late Style', *London Review of Books* 26 (5 August, 2004), pp. 3–7.

3. Edward Said, 'Untimely Meditations,' *The Nation* 277 (September 2003), pp. 38–42, at p. 40, reprinted in Said, *Music at the Limits*, with a foreword by Daniel Barenboim (New York: Columbia University Press, 2008), p. 302.

4. The shape of the late period is arguably already apparent in Hermann Ulrici's *Shakespeare's Dramatic Art: And his Relation to Calderon and Goethe* (London: Chapman, 1846), and Dowden's own work was to a certain extent intertwined with that of F. J. Furnivall, the founder of the New Shakspere Society. See Gordon McMullan, *Shakespeare and the Idea of Late Writing: Authorship in the Proximity of Death* (Cambridge: Cambridge University Press, 2007), Chapter 3.

5. Edward Dowden, *Shakspere: A Critical Study of His Mind and Art* (London: Henry S. King, 1875), p. 415.

6. Edward Dowden, *Shakspere* (London: Macmillan, 1879), pp. 54–5. Dowden's spelling of the playwright's name, odd to our eyes, was fashionable amongst Shakespeareans in the later nineteenth century.

7. Robert Boies Sharpe, *Irony in the Drama: An Essay on Impersonation, Shock, and Catharsis* (Chapel Hill: University of North Carolina Press, 1989), p. 53.

8. Joe Nutt, *An Introduction to Shakespeare's Late Plays* (Houndmills: Palgrave, 2002), p. 127.

9. For a fuller account of this and other issues summarised in this essay, see McMullan, *Shakespeare and the Idea of Late Writing*, esp. Chapters 2–5.

10. Critics addressing the strict three-play group include, across the twentieth century, E. M. W. Tillyard, *Shakespeare's Last Plays* (London: Chatto and Windus, 1938); Robert Ornstein, *Shakespeare's Comedies: From Roman Farce to Romantic Mystery* (Cranbury, NJ: Associated University Presses, 1986); Robert Henke, *Pastoral Transformations: Italian Tragicomedy and Shakespeare's Late Plays* (Newark: University of Delaware Press, 1997).

11. Russ McDonald, *Shakespeare's Late Style* (Cambridge: Cambridge University Press, 2006); see also his essay in this volume.

12. The group-of-four critics include Derek Traversi, *Shakespeare: The Last Phase* (London: Hollis and Carter, 1954); Frank Kermode, *William Shakespeare: The Final Plays* (London: Longman, 1963); Douglas L. Peterson, *Time, Tide,*

and Tempest: A Study of Shakespeare's Romances (San Marino, CA: Huntington Library, 1973); Ruth Nevo, *Shakespeare's Other Language* (New York: Methuen, 1987); Marco Mincoff, *Things Supernatural and Causeless: Shakespearean Romance* (Newark: University of Delaware Press, 1992; first published Sofia, 1987); Robert M. Adams, *Shakespeare: The Four Romances* (New York: W. W. Norton, 1989); Maurice Hunt, *Shakespeare's Romance of the Word* (Lewisburg, PA: Bucknell University Press, 1990); Cynthia Marshall, *Shakespearean Eschatology: Last Things and Last Plays* (Carbondale and Edwardsville: Southern Illinois University Press, 1991); and Simon Palfrey, *Late Shakespeare: A New World of Words* (Oxford: Clarendon Press, 1997).

13. On the textual history of *Pericles*, see Suzanne Gossett's Arden edition (London: Thomson Learning, 2004), pp. 10–38. A good recent instance of the impact the play can have in the theatre was the spectacular and emotionally powerful Japanese production by Yukio Ninagawa, performed at the National Theatre, London, in 2003 – 'this superlative production', in Michael Billington's words (review in the *Guardian*, 31 March 2003).

14. The prompt for this work was G. E. Bentley's essay, 'Shakespeare and the Blackfriars Theatre', *Shakespeare Survey* 1 (1948), pp. 38–50.

15. *Double Falshood, or, The Distrest Lovers … Written Originally by W. Shakespeare; And now Revised and Adapted to the Stage By Mr. Theobald* (London, 1728). This might not bear traces of Shakespeare's hand (authorship analysts tend to suspect the presence of Fletcher rather more than of his more significant collaborator), but it continues to exercise a fascination for scholars: an edition of the play is in preparation for the Arden Shakespeare series; Gary Taylor has written a recreation of *Cardenio* as a development of his creative 'reconstruction' of *Pericles* in the Oxford *Complete Works*; and Stephen Greenblatt's play, *Cardenio*, co-written with the playwright Charles L. Mee, was performed by the American Repertory Theatre company at the Loeb Drama Center in Cambridge, MA, in early summer 2008 (the publicity claimed, provocatively, that 'Shakespeare's fingerprints are all over this sparkling new version' of a play 'that was lost soon after its first performance').

16. William Shakespeare, *The Complete Works*, ed. Stanley Wells, Gary Taylor, John Jowett and William Montgomery, 2nd edn (Oxford: Clarendon Press, 2005).

17. Kenneth Muir, *Shakespeare's Comic Sequence* (Liverpool: Liverpool University Press, 1979), p. 148.

18. For an account of the debate, see R. A. Foakes, *'Hamlet' versus 'Lear': Cultural Politics and Shakespeare's Art* (Cambridge: Cambridge University Press, 1993).

19. Gary Taylor, '*King Lear*: The Date and Authorship of the Folio Version,' in Gary Taylor and Michael Warren (eds.), *The Division of the Kingdoms: Shakespeare's Two Versions of* King Lear (Oxford: Clarendon Press, 1983), pp. 351–468.

20. John Jones, *Shakespeare at Work* (Oxford: Clarendon Press, 1995), p. 208.

21. H. B. Charlton, *Shakespearian Comedy* (London: Methuen, 1938), p. 267; Mincoff, *Things Supernatural and Causeless*, p. 118.

22. On old age in early modern England, see, e.g., Ralph Houlbrooke, *Death, Religion, and the Family in England, 1480–1750* (Oxford: Clarendon Press, 1998), p. 7; and E. A. Wrigley and R. S. Schofield, with contributions from Ronald Lee and Jim Oeppen, *The Population History of England, 1541–1871: A Reconstruction*

(Cambridge: Cambridge University Press, 1989; first published by Arnold, 1981), pp. 528–9.

23. Ivor Brown, review of 1940 Old Vic *Tempest*, cited in John Gielgud, with John Miller, *Shakespeare: Hit or Miss?* (London: Sidgwick and Jackson, 1991), p. 17.

24. Cyrus Hoy, 'Fathers and Daughters in Shakespeare's Romances', in Carol McGinnis Kay and Henry E. Jacobs (eds.), *Shakespeare's Romances Reconsidered* (Lincoln: University of Nebraska Press, 1978), pp. 77–90, at p. 77; Robert Speaight, *Nature in Shakespearian Tragedy* (London: Hollis and Carter, 1955), p. 89.

25. See C. J. Sisson, *The Mythical Sorrows of Shakespeare*, Annual Shakespeare Lecture of the British Academy, From the Proceedings of the British Academy, vol. xx (London: Milford, 1934).

26. On 'late play' as the 'neutral term', see Henke, *Pastoral Transformations*, p. 31.

27. Raphael Lyne, *Shakespeare's Late Work* (Oxford: Oxford University Press, 2007), p. 3.

28. John Fletcher and William Shakespeare, *The Two Noble Kinsmen*, 5.6.110–111, in Wells, Taylor, Jowett and Montgomery, (eds.), *Complete Works*, pp. 1, 279–81, 310.

29. See Janet Adelman, *Suffocating Mothers: Fantasies of Maternal Origin in Shakespeare's Late Plays, 'Hamlet' to 'The Tempest'* (London: Routledge, 1992), pp. 103–29.

30. See Gossett in this volume, pp. 85–202.

31. G. E. Bentley, *The Profession of Dramatist in Shakespeare's Time 1590–1642* (Princeton: Princeton University Press, 1971), 199.

32. Jeffrey Masten, 'Beaumont and/or Fletcher: Collaboration and the Interpretation of Renaissance Drama', *ELH* 59 (1992), pp. 337–56, at p. 342.

33. Jeffrey Masten, '*More* or Less: Editing the Collaborative', *Shakespeare Studies* 29 (2001), pp. 109–31, at p. 115.

34. Roslyn Lander Knutson, *The Repertory of Shakespeare's Company 1594–1613* (Fayetteville: The University of Arkansas Press, 1991); Scott McMillin and Sally-Beth MacLean, *The Queen's Men and Their Plays* (Cambridge: Cambridge University Press, 1998); Andrew Gurr, *The Shakespeare Company 1594–1642* (Cambridge: Cambridge University Press, 2004); Lucy Munro, *Children of the Queen's Revels: A Jacobean Repertory* (Cambridge: Cambridge University Press, 2005). See also, *inter aliis*, Mary Bly, *Queer Virgins and Virgin Queans on the Early Modern Stage* (Oxford: Oxford University Press, 2000), and Knutson, *Playing Companies and Commerce in Shakespeare's Time* (Cambridge: Cambridge University Press, 2001).

2

DAVID LINDLEY

Blackfriars, music and masque: theatrical contexts of the last plays

In 1948 Gerald Eades Bentley was confident that one of the most important events in the affairs of the King's Men, and one that 'influenced decidedly the dramatic compositions of Shakespeare',[1] was the acquisition of the Blackfriars playhouse in 1608. He was certain that all Shakespeare's plays from *Cymbeline* onwards were composed specifically with the indoor theatre in mind, and aimed at 'the sophisticated audience attracted to that house'.[2] It would, at first sight, seem entirely likely that the adoption of a new performance space might have exercised an important influence on the way Shakespeare wrote, but exactly how and to what extent is far from self-evident.

James Burbage originally took over two properties in the former Blackfriars priory in 1596 to provide winter accommodation for his theatre company, the Chamberlain's Men. He constructed a galleried playhouse of some 66 by 46 feet, and if his plans had gone ahead, Andrew Gurr conjectures, 'the Globe might never have been built, and London playing would have moved indoors far earlier than it did'.[3] In the event, protests by the inhabitants of the area against the noise and inconvenience of the presence of actors and audiences persuaded the Privy Council to prevent him from performing in his new theatre. Instead it was leased to one of the children's companies which performed much less frequently than the adult companies, and so, presumably, were tolerable to the easily antagonised neighbours. In their brief existence the children's companies at Blackfriars and at St Paul's were able to call on the services of distinguished playwrights – Marston, Chapman, Jonson, and later Beaumont and Fletcher among them – who provided a varied repertory that included topical satire, for which they were not infrequently in trouble with the authorities, and which, in the end, contributed to their collapse, as offence given to the French ambassador by Chapman's *Byron* plays led King James to dissolve the company.[4] With that collapse came the opportunity for Richard Burbage to reclaim his property and finally to put into practice his father's plans. By now protected by royal patronage as the King's Men, the company had, it seems, no further problems with the other residents of Blackfriars.

Though the theatre was acquired in 1608, the incidence of the plague kept theatres closed until 1610. Nonetheless it would seem at least likely that, while composing *Cymbeline* and *The Winter's Tale*, Shakespeare would have been aware of the planned future winter home for the company and might, as Bentley suggests, have written in some way specifically for it.

Quite what this might have meant has been the subject of controversy, and there is no real critical consensus on the implications of the creation of the two playing places at the Globe and Blackfriars for the nature of the performances at each, at least at this early stage. Physically the environments were very different. The Blackfriars stage was much smaller than that of the Globe, and even this relatively cramped area was occupied by fashionable self-regarding members of the audience. This almost certainly meant that large-scale history plays with battles could not be performed indoors unadapted, and, as Gurr observes, 'the much less free floorspace of the Blackfriars must have inhibited Hamlet when he fought Laertes'.[5] Tiffany Stern argues that the proximity of the audience encouraged writers to 'exploit miniature devices and tiny props', and suggests that 'the fact that the audience was crammed into the same world as the actors and equally visible will also have shaped production ... the story of stage and audience frequently meld together, and Blackfriars plays often have internal events – masques, songs, dances – that call for a "staged" audience of actors'.[6] It might be objected that such devices are not exactly absent from plays written for the Globe theatre, and furthermore that the actors were already used to indoor performance, in town halls or inns on tour and in the much more prestigious, but no less cramped confines of the various venues in which they played at court.

One difference, however, that may have affected authors rather more obviously was the need in the indoor theatres for breaks in the action to allow for attention to the candles. Whereas at the Globe plays were probably performed straight through with no interval, and any 'five-act structure' in the writing was only implicit to an audience, in the Blackfriars breaks were necessary and expected, and could therefore be designed for.[7] So, for example, in *The Tempest* (the Shakespeare play that seems most evidently written with Blackfriars in mind), not only does Prospero have an exit at the end of Act 4 and immediate re-entrance at the beginning of Act 5, clearly signalling the need for an act break, but each act builds towards a climactic moment or situation that might help to preserve momentum across the periods of audience inattention. How long these breaks were is not clear, though as time went on they might have become more like the modern interval. What is evident, however, is that music was performed during this time – and to the implications of that we will return shortly.

How far the physical environment affected playwrights and actors is one consideration; far more often the object of critical speculation is the effect of the different audience on the nature of the King's Men's repertoire after 1608. Attendance at the new theatre was significantly more expensive than the Globe, since 'a lord's room at the Globe [was] worth only the price of the cheapest place in an upper gallery at Blackfriars'.[8] Whereas at the Globe the bottom price was paid by those standing nearest to the stage with the more expensive seats in the galleries, protected from the weather, at the Blackfriars, as in the modern theatre, proximity to the action came at a higher price. If the audience was by definition wealthier, it has been argued that its gender balance was also significantly different. Andrew Gurr suggests that :

> The acquisition of the Blackfriars altered company practices quite drastically. One reason was the prevalence of women in Blackfriars audiences compared with the Globe. Commentators began to write more and more about the women in the audiences, and the plays written for the new repertory started providing a woman-centred perspective.[9]

It has often more generally been assumed that the audience at the Blackfriars was more sophisticated than that at the Globe (though one might doubt whether there was any more necessary a connection between wealth and taste then than there is now), and that this influenced the direction of the evolution of the King's Men's repertoire, especially its turn towards tragicomedy. Martin Wiggins, however, comments that:

> This argument, that the Blackfriars theatre itself begat the genre, style and tone of the plays performed there, needs to be treated with caution. It may contain an element of truth, not least because the fashion for romantic tragicomedy seems initially to have been associated with the King's Men alone, continuing with plays like Beaumont and Fletcher's *A King and No King* (1611) and Fletcher and Shakespeare's *The Two Noble Kinsmen* (1613–14) ... But it is difficult to sustain the case that this was a symptom of a progressive gentrification of drama.[10]

As many writers have pointed out, the argument for two distinct repertoires indoors and out founders on the simple fact that the King's Men seem to have played the greater part of their repertoire indifferently at both playhouses. Simon Forman saw both *The Winter's Tale* and *Cymbeline* at the Globe in 1611, and it was, famously, the discharge of a cannon in *Henry VIII* which caused the fire which burned down the Globe theatre in 1613. Testimony to the fact that the company saw both of its venues as necessary to its work is the fact that the Globe was rebuilt after this disaster, when it might have seemed altogether simpler and more profitable to use the more exclusive environment of Blackfriars throughout the year.

Russ MacDonald has attempted to salvage something of once-axiomatic assumptions:

> it is worth considering that the conventional, simplified accounts of the tastes of these two groups might be accurate, that the Blackfriars audience, particularly those members of the literary and social elites, preferred a more sophisticated and aggressively "modern" style of drama, whereas the Globe patrons enjoyed a simpler, perhaps old-fashioned, more generally "popular" kind of play. Since most of the plays discussed herein were performed at both the Globe and Blackfriars, it is possible that the divergent tastes of this double audience are partly responsible for their unusual mixture of elements, the modish and the outmoded, and particularly the complex tone, with its combination of artlessness and sophistication[11]

Though this argument might sound rather like the frequent student invocation of 'the groundlings' in order to explain away uncomfortable vulgarity, it does valuably draw attention to the way in which the emergence of tragicomedy as a fashionable genre involves both a forward-looking attempt to import contemporary Italian theory into English drama and at the same time more than a gesture towards dramatic and narrative modes of the past. The turn to romance or tragicomedy, of course, preceded the return to Blackfriars in the composition of *Pericles* in 1606, which Andrew Gurr called 'Shakespeare's biggest innovation'.[12] In turning to this 'mouldy tale' as Jonson was to call it, as in his adaptation of Greene's *Pandosto* into *The Winter's Tale*, Shakespeare seems very self-consciously to be looking backwards, and towards a popular rather than a learned tradition. Barbara Mowat, speaking of 'these creakily old-fashioned, deeply resonant, Shakespearean tragicomic romances' argues that we should see the late plays 'as deliberate transformations of very old forms that appear in new guises as part of the King's Men repertory, in competition with the more Italianate, courtly forms produced by Shakespeare's fellow playwrights'.[13] Helen Cooper, too, sees these plays as an ending rather than a beginning when she writes:

> Romance itself remained important for a few more decades after Shakespeare's death, but in forms that had largely lost touch with the roots of the genre, not least its roots in England. His own last plays are almost the final works to profit from the power of those endlessly transforming traditions.[14]

From this perspective Shakespeare is Fletcher's competitor, as well as collaborator, alert to the new directions the younger man is taking, but resistantly finding his own distinctive line in a process of generic recuperation and revision. In the end, of course, Fletcher won the contest – in the later Caroline period it was his plays, much more than those of Shakespeare, which were revived as a mainstay of the repertory of the King's Men. Nonetheless it is clear that there can be no simple appeal to the assumed 'sophisticated' tastes of a Blackfriars audience to explain (or explain away) the nature of Shakespeare's last single-authored plays.

Gordon McMullan valuably suggests that one should consider the repertory of a company as a whole as one of the factors influencing the development of styles. But a brief moment in Ben Jonson's *Bartholomew Fair* suggests how problematic it is to balance the various different elements that might contribute to the character of Shakespeare's last plays. In the Induction the Scrivener, speaking on behalf of the author, comments:

> If there be never a servant-monster i' the Fair, who can help it, he says, nor a nest of antics? He is loath to make nature afraid in his plays, like those that beget *Tales*, *Tempests*, and such-like drolleries, to mix his head with other men's heels, let the concupiscence of jigs and dances reign as strong as it will amongst you.[15]

This dig at Shakespeare is not easy to interpret. Jonson, who had set the action of his previous play *The Alchemist* in the Blackfriars, where it was played in 1610, and in a time of plague such as that which had delayed the theatre's opening, is here writing for the Hope, a venue at the other end of the scale from the exclusive indoor theatre, designed to host both plays and animal-baiting. In the Induction Jonson pokes fun at the tastes of the 'understanding gentlemen o' the ground here' (49–50), and their fondness for old plays like *The Spanish Tragedy*. Yet he also assumes that this audience will be familiar enough with the offerings of the King's Men to understand and appreciate the contrast he is making between his own London-based satire and the extravagances of Shakespearean romance. Interestingly, he is also, by associating the taste for such plays with the 'concupiscence of jigs and dances', by this time distinctly old-fashioned and confined to the most popular end of the market, making the same kind of judgement that he was later to do in his apologia for the failure of *The New Inn* in castigating the taste for the 'mouldy tale of *Pericles*'. The Shakespearean romances do not merely offend his neo-classical generic criteria, they also seem to him a throwback to out-of-date modes. Exactly the tone of Jonson's implied jibe at Shakespeare's last two single-authored plays is difficult to determine – Jonson had a history of falling out and in with the King's Men, and this might be no more than an affectionate joke – but it is a potent indicator of the fluidity of the theatrical world at this period, when authors might write for different companies, audiences attend the offerings at different theatres, and the old co-exist with the new. Over the ensuing decades the demarcation of theatrical practices at different venues and by different companies became clearer and stronger, but in the immediate aftermath of the Blackfriars acquisition boundaries were perhaps more permeable than it is sometimes convenient to acknowledge.[16]

If it is too simple to see the acquisition of the Blackfriars as sufficient explanation for the turn in Shakespeare's writing, there is one unmistakeably important consequence of the King's Men's move into new accommodation: the access it gave them to the famed consort of musicians who had accompanied the children's company in the theatre.

The boy's companies, initially choristers of St Paul's and the Chapel Royal, had made music of central importance to many of their performances in both phases of their existence, in the 1580s and again at the beginning of the seventeenth century. Not only did there tend to be more songs inserted into the action of the plays, but a consort of musicians entertained audiences before the performance began, and then covered the gaps between the act-breaks. The most famous testimony to their practice is that of Frederic Gerschow, a visitor to London accompanying the Duke of Stettin-Pomerania. He went to the Blackfriars on 18 September, 1602 and left this account of his experience:

> The origin of this boy company is this: the Queen keeps a group of young boys who work hard at the art of singing and learn a wide variety of musical instruments while pursuing their studies. They have special teachers in all the arts, and in particular some outstanding musicians. To help them learn good manners, they are required to act a play once a week, for which the Queen has erected a special theatre and given them many expensive costumes ... They do all their plays by artificial light, which makes an impressive effect. For a whole hour before the play begins there is a delightful performance with musical instruments, organs, lutes, bandores, mandolins, violins and flutes, and a boy sings *tremolo* in a double bass so tunefully that we have not heard anything like it in our entire journey, except perhaps for the nuns in Milan.[17]

Quite what is implied about the boy's singing style is unclear (does *tremolo* indicate rapid ornamentation rather than a vocal vibrato? What on earth is meant by the 'double bass'?), but Gerschow's admiration of the performer's skill is evident. This must have been one of the few places in London where it was possible at this time to listen to a public concert (though the London Waits gave regular performances on Sundays before the Royal Exchange from 1571 onwards.[18]). The range of instruments being used is also worth noting, adding organs to a range of plucked and bowed strings and the flute. The boy's companies also used the cornetto, or cornett – a curved woodwind instrument with finger-holes like a recorder but a trumpet-style mouthpiece (nothing to do with the modern brass band cornet) – that substituted in the indoor theatre for the trumpets which provided a good deal of the instrumental music in the amphitheatres. It was a flexible instrument, able to scale down to accompany voices, or to rise to the fanfares which characteristically welcomed those of high status onstage. It is not an easy instrument to play, and was the preserve of professional musicians. These resources, both in personnel and equipment, were significantly greater than those which had been available to the King's Men at the Globe. Probably most, if not all, the music that was used before 1608 was provided by members of the acting company themselves and their apprentices. Henslowe bought brass and other instruments for his company, and Augustine Phillips, a sharer in the King's Men, bequeathed a cittern, bandora, lute and bass viol to his apprentices. This suggests a certain instrumental versatility amongst the actors, but, nonetheless, it was almost certainly the case that fewer performers, and probably less expert musicians, were available at any one time than was the norm in the indoor playhouses.

Gerschow's testimony is the only record of pre-performance concerts; presumably they continued after 1610, though there is no evidence either way. What certainly did continue, and what may have been of much more importance to the theatrical experience of theatre-goers at the Blackfriars, was the provision of inter-act music. This had not been the practice in the outdoor theatres. In Webster's Induction, added to Marston's *The Malcontent* when the play was stolen by the King's Men, Burbage answers Sly's question 'what are your additions':

> Sooth, not greatly needful; only as your salad to your great feast, to entertain a little more time, and to abridge the not-received custom of music in our theatre.[19]

The 'custom' here is, precisely, the provision of musical interludes between the acts. As Linda Austern observes, 'inter-act music appears to have been a normal feature of performances in all three children's theaters, but few specific details about it have survived'. It is evident, however, that it could take many forms:

> The tantalizing tidbits relating to inter-act music that remain scattered throughout the repertoire imply extreme variety and many degrees of relationship to the main drama. Inter-act music seems to have sometimes been instrumental, sometimes vocal, and sometimes a mixture of both. Inter-act music occasionally accompanied dance, occasionally mimed action, and occasionally neither … Sometimes inter-act music set the stage for the action to follow, sometimes it reinforced previous action, sometimes it followed the antics of minor characters that had little bearing on the main plot, and sometimes it was not at all related to the play.[20]

In the event, mention of act music is only made at the beginning of Act 2 (though the play opens with 'the vilest out-of-tune music', emanating symbolically from the Malcontent's chamber). It is a great pity that no act music survives which can clearly be identified as provided for this or any other play, for the care with which Marston specifies the instrumentation of the various interludes in his *Sophonisba* suggests that it was a matter to which some thought was given, and that instruments were chosen with care. So, for example, at the end of Act 3 the stage is cleared 'with a full flourish of Cornetts', but 'Organs, Viols and Voices play for this Act' as a prelude to the entrance of Sophonisba and Zanthia 'as out of a cave's mouth', whereas between Acts 4 and 5, as Syphax hastens, as he thinks, to Sophonisba's bed, 'A bass lute and a treble viol play for the act', perhaps ironically hinting at the erotic activity taking place within the curtains before Syphax realises he has been tricked by the witch Erictho.

The relative infrequency of choirboy company performances (they played only once a week) must have allowed time for the choice and preparation of appropriate music, and even have permitted new compositions to be supplied for specific plays. It is true that, like the adult companies, the boy players appropriated a good number of tunes from the popular repertory of unaccompanied ballad, giving them new or modified words,[21] but they also took pre-existing material from published song-books and madrigal collections, and some few songs survive which seem to have been composed specifically for performance in particular plays.[22] As is the case with the adult companies, there is a significant number of 'blank' songs, where the words are not printed in the text – presumably any generally appropriate song from repertoire might be performed in such cases. In general, then, the musical fare at Blackfriars and St Paul's while the children's companies performed was rather more varied, and certainly more extensive, than anything the adult companies could aspire to.

All this changed in 1610. By then, during the plague closure, it seems probable that a curtained music room was created out of a reconstruction of the stage balcony. Before that, as Richard Hosley demonstrated, music at the Globe and other amphitheatre playhouses heard from offstage was performed 'within', or behind the *frons scaenae*.[23] When Ferdinand, in *The Tempest*, claims of the music 'I hear it now above me' (1.2.406) he reflects what had always been the positioning of musicians in the Blackfriars, but what was only just now possible at the Globe. This is perhaps the clearest example of Shakespeare writing for, and taking advantage of, new arrangements of theatrical space. There is other scattered evidence that specifically musical arrangements changed after 1608. In the Folio text of *A Midsummer Night's Dream*, for example, the stage direction '*They sleepe all the Act*' appears at the end of Act 3, as the weary lovers slumber. The direction is not present in the quarto text of 1600 and its derivative quarto of 1619. Though editors have expended a good deal of effort over this direction, it seems certain that the folio text reflects the fact that an act tune was inserted into the play for a post-1610 revival at this point, and the lovers continued to sleep while it played. The specification of 'cornets' in folio *Merchant of Venice* to introduce the Prince of Morocco (3.1.0 SD), where the quartos mention no instruments at all, reflects the availability of the softer instruments in the indoor theatres; and the softening of 'trumpets' to 'hoboyes' between quarto and folio *Titus* (5.3.25 SD) might imply the same amelioration of the louder sound in the more confined space. In *Coriolanus* the fact that directions both for trumpets and for cornets are found might suggest that instrumentation changed according to where the play was performed. Though there is no unambiguous evidence, Taylor's researches seem to indicate that gradually the five-act structure and therefore, in all probability, the provision of inter-act music spread to all of the playhouses during the second decade of the seventeenth century.[24]

If 'the new music consort brought the largest single alteration to the King's Men's practices when they took over the Blackfriars playhouse', and if 'in the next few years stage-music and song was what differentiated the King's Men at the Globe from the other amphitheatre companies',[25] then that transformation is nowhere more clearly marked than in *The Tempest*. It is not only Shakespeare's most musical play in terms of the number of instrumental and sung items called for during its performance, it is the work above all others which explores the dramatic and thematic potential of music to its fullest extent. In many of the earlier choirboy plays (and indeed in much of the King's Men's later repertoire) musical items not infrequently seem to be bolted on, and scarcely integrated into the action. They are often detachable 'turns' to show off a good voice or provide an interlude in the action. Shakespeare had always been careful to give good occasion for his music cues, but in *The Tempest* he takes this further, in that music is not merely integrated with the action, but is its cause and engine as the means by which Prospero exercises his power and control. It brings Ferdinand on stage in 1.2, it charms the lords to sleep in 2.1. and clears their addled brains in 5.1. It accompanies the most rare vision of the masque, but also leads Caliban and his co-conspirators into the stinking pond. Music's power and Prospero's magic are intimately linked, and both contribute to the exploration of ideas of command and control with which the play is deeply concerned. The published text makes no mention of any act tunes, but if, as is entirely likely, they were performed, then they would have contributed further to the atmosphere of the island, its 'noises, sounds and sweet airs' to which Caliban refers (3.2.127–8).[26]

The other noteworthy feature of the music of these late plays is that for a number of songs – 'Hark, hark the lark' in *Cymbeline*, 'Get you hence' in *The Winter's Tale*, 'Full fathom five' and 'Where the bee sucks' in *The Tempest* – settings survive which are likely to have been used in the first performances, or for early revivals. All of them have been attributed to Robert Johnson (*c*.1583–1633). He was originally a servant of George Carey, Lord Chamberlain and patron of Shakespeare's company in the last years of Elizabeth's reign, before becoming one of the lutenists to the King in 1604. His association with the King's Men seems to have begun with these settings, and continued for some years afterwards. The significance of his settings is not simply their musical merit – though the Shakespeare settings are graceful airs, and one or two of Johnson's later dramatic compositions (including 'Oh let us howl' from Webster's *Duchess of Malfi*) explore a more advanced, declamatory musical style. It is the very fact that these settings survive as 'art-song' compositions which to all appearances were designed for the plays themselves which betokens the important change in musical provision which the company had undergone. Though the lack of any surviving settings of songs from earlier Shakespeare plays does not necessarily indicate with absolute certainty that no such settings were made (then, as indeed now, the survival of musical manuscripts in theatrical company archives must have been a chancy business), there is a high probability that it was only with the new musical regime made possible after the acquisition of Blackfriars that the adult company was able to commission settings for individual songs.[27] All in all, these settings, and the increased variety of musical resources that could be deployed, must have contributed a very different and rather more sophisticated atmosphere to the King's Men's performances after 1610.

Robert Johnson not only composed music for plays, he also wrote songs and dances for the court masque. It has often been suggested that another influence on the theatrical practice of Shakespeare's last plays is this distinctive courtly genre. In two of them, *The Winter's Tale* and *Two Noble Kinsmen*, there seems to be actual borrowing of dances from court entertainments. The satyrs' dance in *Winter's Tale* is introduced by a servant who claims of the dancers that 'One three of them, by their own report, sir, hath danced before the King' (4.4.332–3), and just such a dance was performed in Jonson's *Oberon* before the King in January, 1611. In *Two Noble Kinsmen*, 3.5.101, a Schoolmaster introduces his 'country pastime', and the participants he names for the morris dance (124–32) are identical with those specified in Beaumont's *Masque of the Inner Temple and Gray's Inn*, performed as part of the celebrations for the marriage of the King's daughter, Princess Elizabeth, in 1613.[28] Since the King's Men were likely to have provided the speaking parts and the antimasquers for these court events, it is entirely possible that there would be some degree of cross-fertilisation between this most courtly of genres and the dramas enacted at Blackfriars and the Globe – and much has often been claimed for the influence of one upon the other.

Such claims, however, need to be scrutinised carefully. Shakespeare, after all, unlike Beaumont, Chapman, or Jonson, never – as far as we know – provided the text for an entertainment at court. Indeed, what precisely is meant by critical invocation of the generic label 'masque' itself is worth consideration. The arrival of masked revellers at court, or at private houses, was part of seasonal entertainment throughout the sixteenth century. In an oft-quoted account, Edward Hall in 1512 described Henry VIII and eleven of his court who 'wer disguised, after the maner of Italie, called a maske, a thyng not seen afore in Englande'. He continued:

> thei … came in, with sixe gentlemen disguised in silke bearyng staffe torches, and desired the ladies to daunce, some were content, and some that knew the fashion of it refused, because it was not a thyng commonly seen. And after thei daunced and commoned together, as the fashion of the Maskes is, thei toke their leave and departed, and so did the Quene, and all the ladies.[29]

It is precisely this form of simple disguising that Shakespeare deployed in *Love's Labours Lost*, where the attempts of the lords to 'common' (converse) with the ladies are defeated by their adoption of masks and swapping of the tokens by which they might be identified. In *Henry VIII* Fletcher incorporates just such another masked dance at Wolsey's palace (following Holinshed's historical account fairly closely). Here, however, the ladies are not disguised, only the visitors, who represent themselves as strangers dressed as shepherds. They take out the ladies to dance, and the King (unhistorically) chooses Anne Bullen as his partner. In a brief dialogue Wolsey suggests that 'Your grace / I fear, with dancing is a little heated', to which the King replies 'I fear too much' (1.4.99–101). The association of dancing, masquing and heated, even illicit desire was to be repeatedly asserted by critics of the court throughout the history of the genre, and is not unimportant, as we will see, to Shakespeare's most extended imitation of the form.

Though the entry of masked courtiers to participate in dancing remained the core of the court masque, in the reign of James, at the instigation of his wife, Queen Anne, and through the determination, ambition and abilities largely of two men – Ben Jonson and Inigo Jones – the genre was significantly developed.[30] Jonson's aim, above all, was to bestow a seriousness on the device of the masque that would enable it to outlive the transitory day of its presentation and the particular occasion for which it was designed. He aspired to 'lay hold on more removed mysteries' in his ' high and hearty inventions', drawing heavily upon his own classical knowledge, and on the many Renaissance handbooks and treatises, which together validated the masques by their grounding 'upon antiquity and solid learnings'.[31] In the quarto publications of his early masques Jonson ensured that this intellectual ambition was emphatically signalled to his readers by the plethora of footnotes which presented the masques visually as if they were the heavily annotated texts of the classics. By 1609 he had also established a template for the masque whereby the entry of the courtly masquers was preceded by a 'foil or false masque' as he called it in the preface to *The Masque of Queens*.[32] The relationship between the 'false' and the 'true' masque might be of different kinds – as is indicated by its variant spellings 'antimasque', 'antemasque' and 'antic masque' – but in general it presented some sort of moral imperfection or vice which the virtues symbolised by the courtly masquers themselves either dispelled or else revised and reformed.

Inigo Jones's contribution was to bring the theatre design of continental Europe to the English court. Perspectival settings of increasing elaboration provided the backdrop for gorgeous costumes; carefully deployed lighting glittered on jewellery; as time went on rapid transformations from one scene to the next became possible, and complex machinery enabled spectacular effects of many kinds. Poet and designer called upon the collaboration of dancing masters and the rich resources of the royal music, both vocal and instrumental, to fashion their multi-media events. The devices were organised to compliment the King, to celebrate the magnificence of monarch, court and courtiers, and to manifest that opulence to foreign as well as domestic observers.

For all the intellectual effort that both Jonson and Jones expended upon their inventions, the central focus of the masque in the eyes of the select audiences who watched was primarily upon the participants, both on the masquers who exhibited their prowess in the dances, and on the response of the most important members of the audience. King James could, and not infrequently did, intervene in the unfolding masque – he, for example, asked for the antimasques of Beaumont's *Inner Temple* to be repeated, as the printed text reports: 'It pleased his Majesty to call for it again at the end, as he did likewise for the first anti-masque, but one of the Statues by that time was undressed'.[33] The masque, then, was tied firmly to its occasion, and was embedded in the social exchange of which its dramatic representation was only a part. The bulk of the evening was taken up, not with the performance of Jonson's learned script, but in the dances of the revels in which masquers first took out carefully selected distinguished guests before gradually widening the circle of those involved in these dances.

No play could possibly reproduce accurately the complex, composite effect of a Stuart court masque; whenever such a masque is staged in a play it is always, as it were, in quotation marks. The question is, what are the essential basic qualities that must be represented for it to be seen as commenting on or derived from the masque? The essentials remain some form of disguise, and dancing. Though masques frequently deployed mythological figures in their fictions, the simple appearance of such figures in a play does not constitute a citation of the court masque. So, for example, the appearance of Jupiter in *Cymbeline*, or of Diana in *Pericles*, draws on the long-established practice of divine descents in amphitheatre plays at least as much as it does on the appearance of as such figures in the court masque. Indeed, as Martin Butler observes, 'such effects were uncommon at the indoor Blackfriars playhouse and more in vogue at the open-air theatres', and he cites Heywood's Red Bull plays, *The Golden Age* (1609–11), as the closest parallel to *Cymbeline*, and points out that at this time descents were actually rare in court masques.[34] These theophanies have less to do with the masque even than the appearance of Hymen in *As You Like It* – where there is at least dancing to celebrate the ceremonious marriages.

In the drama of the earlier Stuart period, many of the citations of the masque actually gesture towards the Tudor, rather than the Jacobean, form – it is a good deal easier to stage. But, especially in tragedy, staged masque comes frequently to stand as an emblem of, or a metonymy for, the court world and its corruption. In *The Maid's Tragedy*, *The Revengers' Tragedy* and *Women Beware Women*, to name but three plays, the courtier disguised is emblematic of courtly hypocrisy and deceit, the gorgeous outside of the masque concealing immorality, and murderous desire. A dialogue at the beginning of Beaumont's and Fletcher's *The Maid's Tragedy* represents the cynical attitude such dramas take towards the form:

LYSIPPUS.   Strato, thou hast some skill in poetry,
             What thinkst thou of a masque, will it be well?
STRATO.   As well as masques can be.
LYSIPPUS.   As masques can be?
STRATO.   Yes, they must commend their king, and speak in praise of the
             assembly, bless the bride and bridegroom in person of some god:
             they're tied to rules of flattery.[35]

Shakespeare does not seem to have shared this impulse to bitter satire of the masque. But in *The Tempest* he does conduct a subtle negotiation with the genre in his most extended imitation of the Stuart form, the betrothal masque for Ferdinand and Miranda in Act 4. In the first place, this entertainment deploys its mythological figures precisely and appropriately, as a well-behaved court masque should. Venus, the goddess of love, is absent because this is a celebration of a betrothal, not (as is frequently implied by those who carelessly call it a 'marriage masque') a wedding. The physical consummation of the marriage is to be postponed until after the return to Milan, and so here the masque is presided over by Juno, and offers a fertile future with the presence of Ceres, the goddess of harvest. The dance of water nymphs, or naiads, and fiery sicklemen dramatises the standard image of marriage as a uniting of female coldness and male heat. If Ferdinand and Miranda join in the dance (though no stage direction indicates that they should, they have done so to good effect in a number of productions) then the formal gesture towards courtly performance is further emphasised. But, of course, this masque then collapses into a *'strange, hollow and confused noise'* (4.1.132 SD) as Prospero recalls the conspiracy of Caliban. Prospero then delivers perhaps the most famous speech in the play, 'our revels now are ended ...' in which the ending of the masque becomes an image of the ending of the individual life, and an apocalyptic prefiguring of the end of time when all shall dissolve.

Stephen Orgel registered the significance of this masque episode in the play, calling it 'the most important Renaissance commentary on the subject ... Shakespeare's essay on the power and art of the royal imagination'.[36] The immediate context of the masque in the play is the rumbling debate between Samuel Daniel and Ben Jonson about the claims that could be made for the genre. Daniel in 1610 was commissioned to write a masque for the investiture of Prince Henry as Prince of Wales. In the published version of *Tethys' Festival* he pointedly distanced himself from Jonson's parade of learning, claiming that he did not print the work 'out of a desire to be seen in pamphlets, or of forwardness to show my inventions therein; for I thank God, I labour not with that disease of ostentation'. He argued against Jonson's ambition to give the masque permanence through its laying hold on 'removed mysteries', saying that masque-writers were 'poor engineers for shadows' who 'frame images of no result'.[37] *The Tempest* takes Daniel's side; Prospero sees the masque as a 'vanity of mine art', and attempts to persuade Ferdinand to be 'cheerful' precisely *because* he recognises the masque's evanescence. One of the things *The Tempest* is concerned with is the limits of art, and of magic, to bring everyone within the charmed circle of forgiveness. Its interrupted masque images both the appeal and the limitations of theatrical spectacle. (As an aside – one wonders whether Jonson's public irritation with *The Tempest* in *Bartholomew Fair* derives in part from the line Shakespeare takes on the masque, whether, indeed, in the irascible masque-maker Prospero Jonson saw some barb aimed at himself.)

Ernest Gilman argued that the play as a whole reversed the normal masque pattern of antimasque followed by masque in presenting this vision evaporating before the threat of the 'antimasque' figures of Caliban and his cronies.[38]

To argue that the masque penetrates the deep structure of the play, however, seems to me very debatable. Yes, Caliban is a monstrous figure who has some parallels in the grotesques of the court masque, as do the 'shapes' who carry in the banquet in 3.3 (though the clearest parallels in court masques post-date the play). The parody 'court' of Stephano can be coerced into the mould of an antimasque distortion of the 'true' courtly prince. But Caliban is far more than a grotesque; Prospero is far more ambiguous than the monarch who is the centre of the court masque. The court masque aims at an absolute clarity of moral distinction, and its reliance on allegory which, however rich and learned, is aimed at pinning down and confining the interpretation of attributes and qualities in the figures it depicts. In very important and fundamental ways it therefore operates at the other end of the spectrum from the moral complexity and ambivalences of Shakespearean drama. The vocabulary of the court masque was important to the drama, and became increasingly so, as Inga-Stina Ewbank long ago demonstrated.[39] For Shakespeare, however, it was a genre to be challenged even as it was exploited in this most allusive and elusive of plays.

The changes in the theatrical conditions under which the King's Men operated after they took over the Blackfriars theatre in 1608 were undoubtedly important. The opportunities for additional and more elaborate musical arrangements were seized by Shakespeare and his successors. Audiences gradually became more differentiated as time passed, and as a consequence the repertoires of different companies became more distinct. But it remained true that the King's Men played both indoors and out throughout the period and that new plays jostled old in the repertory. Visiting ambassadors went to bear-pits as well as theatres. If the audience at the Blackfriars was more 'sophisticated', as is so often claimed, the behaviour of gallants sitting on the stage was frequently satirised as ignorant and boorish. Changing theatrical conditions, then, must have influenced dramatists. They are not, of course, sufficient explanations of the exploratory and experimental nature of Shakespeare's late plays.

NOTES

1. G. E. Bentley, 'Shakespeare and the Blackfriars Theatre', *Shakespeare Survey* 1 (1948), p. 38.
2. Ibid., p. 48.
3. Andrew Gurr, *The Shakespeare Company, 1594–1642* (Cambridge: Cambridge University Press, 2004), p. 5.
4. See Michael Shapiro, *Children of the Revels: The Boy Companies of Shakespeare's Time and Their Plays* (New York: Columbia University Press, 1977); Reavley Gair, *The Children of Paul': The Story of a Theatre Company, 1553–1608* (Cambridge: Cambridge University Press, 1982); Lucy Munro, *Children of the Queen's Revels: A Jacobean theatre repertory* (Cambridge : Cambridge University Press, 2005).

5. Gurr, *Company*, p. 37.

6. Tiffany Stern, 'Taking Part: Actors and Audience on the Stage at Blackfriars', in Paul Menzer (ed.), *Inside Shakespeare: Essays on the Blackfriars Stage* (Selinsgrove: Susquehanna University Press, 2006), pp. 35–53, at pp. 46, 47.

7. For an exhaustively detailed account of the coming of the act intervals see Gary Taylor and John Jowett, *Shakespeare Reshaped 1606–1623* (Oxford: Clarendon Press, 1993), pp. 1–50.

8. Gurr, *Company*, p. 11

9. Ibid.

10. Martin Wiggins, *Shakespeare and the Drama of His Time* (Oxford: Oxford University Press, 2000), pp. 113–14.

11. Russ McDonald, 'Fashion: Shakespeare and Beaumont and Fletcher', in Richard Dutton and Jean E. Howard (eds.), *A Companion to Shakespeare's Works* (Oxford: Blackwell, 2003), vol. IV, pp. 150–74, at p. 170.

12. Gurr, *Company*, p. 137.

13. Barbara Mowat, '"What's in a Name?" Tragicomedy, Romance, or Late Comedy', in Dutton and Howard (eds.), *Companion*, pp. 129–49, at p. 143

14. Helen Cooper, *The English Romance in Time: Transforming Motifs from Geoffrey of Monmouth to the Death of Shakespeare* (Oxford: Oxford University Press, 2004), p. 23.

15. Ben Jonson, *Bartholomew Fair*, ed. Suzanne Gossett (Manchester: Manchester University Press, 2000), Induction, pp. 130–5. Jonson had earlier made a similar complaint about the tastes of audiences in the address to the reader prefaced to the quarto of *The Alchemist* (1612).

16. See Andrew Gurr, *Playgoing in Shakespeare's London* (Cambridge: Cambridge University Press, 1987), pp. 164–9, for an account of the evolution of distinct audiences.

17. The diary is transcribed in *Transactions of the Royal Historical Society*, n.s. 6 (1892), pp. 1–35. This is Andrew Gurr's translation, in *Company*, p. 80. He draws attention to the oddity of the 'double bass', which must surely be an error of some kind.

18. See Walter L. Woodfill, *Musicians in English Society from Elizabeth to Charles I* (Princeton: Princeton University Press, 1953), Chapter 2.

19. John Marston, *The Malcontent*, ed. George K. Hunter (Manchester: Manchester University Press, 1975), Induction, pp. 81–4.

20. Linda Phyllis Austern, *Music in English Children's Drama of the Later Renaissance* (Philadelphia: Gordon and Breach, 1992), p. 83. This extremely useful survey of the field has been rather overlooked by scholars.

21. For the suggestion that most of the songs in Shakespeare's plays were written to fit existing ballad tunes see Ross Duffin, *Shakespeare's Songbook* (New York: Norton, 2004), pp. 31–2. His collection suggests tunes for all the songs in the canon, taken from the popular repertoire.

22. See Austern, *Music*, pp. 203–32 for a full account of the sources of the music.

23. Richard Hosley, 'Was there a Music-Room in Shakespeare's Globe?', *Shakespeare Survey*, 13 (1960), pp. 113–23.

24. Taylor and Jowett, *Shakespeare Reshaped*, pp. 32–4.

25. Gurr, *Company*, pp. 36–7.

26. For full discussions of the functions of music in the play, see David Lindley, *Shakespeare and Music* (London: Thomson Learning, 2005), pp. 218–33; Robin Headlam Wells, *Elizabethan Mythologies: Studies in Poetry, Drama and Music* (Cambridge: Cambridge University Press, 1994), pp. 63–80.

27. It is (just) possible that Thomas Morley composed his setting of 'It was a lover and his lass' specifically for *As You Like It*; much more likely that the pre-existing song was taken over into the play. There are one or two song lyrics, such as 'Love, love, nothing but love' in *Troilus*, which seem too complex to fit to ballad tunes, and perhaps might have been specially set. It is an area where discoveries remain to be made.

28. Lois Potter in her Arden edition of *The Two Noble Kinsmen* (Walton-on-Thames: Nelson, 1997) prints the complete text of Beaumont's *Masque of the Inner Temple and Gray's Inn* and speculates on the possibility of the knights taking over costumes from the masque, and even of some elements of scenery (pp. 340–55).

29. Quoted in Enid Welsford, *The Court Masque* (Cambridge: Cambridge University Press, 1927), p. 130.

30. The literature on the court masque is large. Among the most important studies are Stephen Orgel, *The Jonsonian Masque* (Cambridge, MA: Harvard University Press, 1965), David Bevington and Peter Holbrook (eds.), *The Politics of the Stuart Court Masque* (Cambridge: Cambridge University Press, 1998), Martin Butler, *The Stuart Masque and Political Culture* (Cambridge: Cambridge University Press, 2008). On Inigo Jones, see Stephen Orgel and Roy Strong, *Inigo Jones: The Theatre of the Stuart Court* (London: Sotheby Parke Bernet; Berkeley: University of California Press, 1973), and John Peacock, *The Stage Designs of Inigo Jones* (Cambridge: Cambridge University Press, 1995).

31. Ben Jonson, *Hymenaei* (1606), in Stephen Orgel (ed.), *Ben Jonson: The Complete Masques* (New Haven and London: Yale University Press, 1969), pp. 74–5.

32. Orgel (ed.), *Ben Jonson*, p. 122.

33. Potter (ed.), *The Two Noble Kinsmen*, p. 346.

34. Martin Butler (ed.), *Cymbeline* (Cambridge: Cambridge University Press, 2005), p. 15.

35. Beaumont and Fletcher, *The Maid's Tragedy*, ed. T. W. Craik (Manchester: Manchester University Press, 1988), 1.1.5–10.

36. Stephen Orgel, *The Illusion of Power* (Berkeley: University of California Press, 1975), p. 45.

37. David Lindley (ed.), *Court Masques* (Oxford: Oxford University Press, 1995), p. 55.

38. Ernest B. Gilman, '"All Eyes": Prospero's Inverted Masque', *Renaissance Quarterly* 33 (1980), pp. 214–30.

39. Inga-Stina Ewbank , '"These Pretty Devices": A Study of Masques in Plays', in T. J. B. Spencer, Stanley Wells and G. E. Bentley (eds.), *A Book of Masques in Honour of Allardyce Nicoll* (Cambridge: Cambridge University Press, 1967), pp. 405–48.

3

CHARLES MOSELEY

The literary and dramatic contexts of the last plays

Elizabethan and Jacobean drama is an untidy thing, growing from classical roots and also, more importantly, from the allegorical moralities and interludes and the old mystery drama, cycles dramatising the history of the world from Creation to Last Judgement. The experience of those plays, whatever the polite dressing on top, provided the theatrical language of Shakespeare's generation. The mysteries were played in some parts until well into the 1570s, despite Privy Council prohibition. Their mix of highly ritualised performance, grotesque and horrifying suffering and broad vulgar comedy is all held within a frame where the tragedy of Calvary is not the end but the necessary preparation for the moment of Resurrection and the challenge of forgiveness.

At the same time a growing body of critical theory, based on Aristotle and his Italian interpreters, was beginning to define tragedy more severely than simply the turning of Fortune's wheel – a concept Shakespeare never, in fact, quite abandons. Comedy recognisably divided into 'City' comedy, using elements of the Roman comedy of Plautus and Terence and based on a money nexus, and romantic comedy, based on 'love will find a way'. But, though he could keep minutely, as in *The Tempest*, to the three unities if he wished, Shakespeare throughout his career showed scant concern for purist classical generic prescriptions enunciated by critics like Sidney in his *Apologie for Poesie*, and cheerfully mingles classical dramatic forms with the modes of vernacular drama.

It was once fashionable to call the late plays 'romances',[1] a label more helpful than modern sneers might suggest. For the frequent editions suggest that popular taste for the now neglected narrative chivalric romances, like *Amadis de Gaule*, *Bevis of Hampton*, *Guy of Warwick* or the works of Malory, eventually deriving from medieval romance Arthurian or not, was consistent and influential, and affected dramatic writing. The Queen's godson, Sir John Harington, translated Ariosto's *Orlando Furioso*. Philip Sidney's influential *Arcadia*[2] Shakespeare knew well. The normal trajectory of romance narrative is comedic: the hero is separated from apparent stability, put through moral and physical trials, often in a wilderness, which we know (and he does not) he will survive, before finally being reintegrated into a society more stable because of those trials. There is always the *potential* for tragedy, but we know it will not happen. Furthermore, not only chivalric romance but also Hellenistic romance was popular: for example, *A Midsummer Night's Dream* echoes Apuleius' *The Golden Asse* (translated by William Adlington in 1566). Heliodorus' *Ethiopica* was translated from Latin by Thomas Underdowne in 1569. Angel Day translated Longus' *Daphnis and Chloe* from Amyot's French version, and the story was used by Honoré d'Urfé, by Montemayor, and in *Aminta* by Tasso. These Greek romances are full of children lost in infancy, of travel (often by sea), and usually climax in a series of recognitions (sometimes by tokens). Obviously *Pericles*, *Cymbeline*, *The Tempest* and the second half of *The Winter's Tale* borrow these structures, which would be familiar, and which are used by playwrights other than Shakespeare. Reading such romances must affect, perhaps unconsciously, the strategies of response used when *reading texts* of plays when these begin to appear, and will qualify how the reader fills the imaginative space round printed dialogue. That then will affect how the plays are watched, will alter what people want from drama, and indeed how plays are written – indeed, it may affect the conception of dramatic character.

'Tragicomedy', beginning to become respectable as a genre in polite circles, plays to this taste for 'romance'. Sidney's *Apologie* inveighed against the 'mungrell tragicomedies' of the 1580s, castigating the type of English romantic play that, ignoring the unities of time, place and action which purists were coming to admire, mixed high and low characters in improbable actions. But Italian theory and practice claimed tragicomedy as a regular genre, with discernible rules. Giovanni Battista Cinthio (1504–73) claimed, indeed, that what he called *tragedia de lieto fin* ('tragedy-with-happy-ending') was the appropriate modern form. Giambattista Guarini's *Il Pastor Fido* (1590) provoked much critical debate, which provoked Guarini to defend generic innovation.[3] Guarini's play, adapted as *The Faithful Shepherdess* by John Fletcher in 1608, led its mannered characters along a careful line between comedy and tragedy. In 'To the Reader', Fletcher, drawing on Guarini's *Compendio*, defines 'tragicomedy': 'A tragi-comedie is not so called in respect of mirth and killing, but in respect it wants [lacks] deaths, which is enough to make it no tragedy, yet brings some neere it, which is inough to make it no comedie.' Guarini and Torquato Tasso, moreover, saw tragicomedy as a specifically Christian form. It might be well to remember this when we consider its use on the Jacobean stage.[4]

The romantic comedy *Mucedorus*, (probably *c.* 1590) was the most frequently reprinted play of its age, with seventeen quartos before 1700: Q3's title page (1610) claims it was played at the Globe. An expanded version was performed at Shrovetide at Whitehall early in James's reign. It may draw on Sidney's *Arcadia*, as generically it certainly draws on pastoral and on the *commedia dell'arte*. This 'very delectable' comedy is stuffed with romantic adventure as well as the clowning of Mouse. Mucedorus disguises himself first as a shepherd and then as a hermit; there is a wild man of the woods (with cannibal propensities) who has a taste for romance; a clownish rustic; and a bear which teaches Princess Amadine how to distinguish between the coward and her hero lover Mucedorus. The Induction and Epilogue present Envy and Comedy, allegorical figures straight from a morality. (The bear was frequently a real one and perhaps suggested the bears in Jonson's masque *Oberon* (1611) and in *Winter's Tale*.) It is difficult to see a commercially alert company like the King's Men not noticing this play's success, and wanting new work that appealed to those who had enjoyed it.

Shakespeare was an eclectic and voracious reader. He knew his Bible well and had been well grounded in Latin literature at school. He knew his Roman and English history. He was thoroughly *au fait* with the developing canon of English literature – Chaucer, Gower, Lydgate – as well as with the fashionable writing of the moment. His response is never simple, and it is sometimes teasing – especially with contemporaries. He was soaked in Virgil – the *Aeneid* is a sort of ghost constantly glimpsed in *The Tempest* – and Ovid, especially the *Metamorphoses*, which led him to that interest in metamorphosis, change and the creative as well as destructive effects of time and nature which seem to lie at the heart of these late plays. Five of them look explicitly to the relation between past suffering and crime and future reconciliation and regeneration. In these plays, too, he seems to be reconsidering books he had read much earlier – Chaucer, Gower, Virgil, Greene – as well as some of his own earlier work, for he was a great borrower from himself. He is more prepared to alert audiences to his sources and invite those with ears to hear to enjoy a delicate intertextuality. These plays are openly 'literary'.

Furthermore, as David Lindley explains above, they all draw on the discourse of masque and pageant, possess features which may respond to the resources and audience profile of Blackfriars and, in *Pericles*, *The Winter's Tale* and *The Tempest*, use music not just as decoration but structurally, symbolic of a supernature interacting with nature: Hermione's and Thaisa's awakenings, for example, or the large body of music in *The Tempest*. All reflect a more optimistic ideology: noticeable especially in *Winter's Tale* and *Tempest* is an interest in the 'post-tragic', in 'what happens next?' What happens when the tragic trajectory has run its course *if* there were to be a second chance? Acts 1–3 of *The Winter's Tale* have a verbal texture and a plotting economy that we would expect of a tragedy, and indeed the rhetoric of the deluded Leontes is reminiscent of Othello. But after that fulchral storm, the key changes, and we move into pastoral comedy, with young lovers, parental opposition, flight and eventual marriage. The integration of the two worlds is achieved by the *coup de théâtre* of Hermione's resurrection, where the painted funeral monument, the work of art to be appreciated by connoisseurs, takes life like Pygmalion's Galatea in Ovid and becomes Truth, the Daughter of Time:[5] and 'great creating nature', as Perdita calls it, makes reconciliation possible. The sins of the fathers seem to be the necessary prelude to the happiness of the young and the marriage of kingdoms.

In *The Tempest* the action is even leaner: the tragic movement has happened in the past, recalled only in Prospero's long exposition after the catalytic and emblematic storm. His past could well have been Lear's present; but through Gonzalo and the winds of Providence he gets a second chance. So the trajectory of the play is now firmly *past* revenge and punishment to reconciliation and forgiveness – and a recognition of Providential purpose: 'Was Milan thrust from Milan, that Milan's heirs should be kings of Naples?' *Pericles, The Winter's Tale, The Tempest, Cymbeline* all point through the tragic to the reconciliation, healing, calm after storm, but never without recognition that the suffering was genuine. Mamillius remains dead. Indeed, the late plays seem to develop a theme Shakespeare would have noticed in Virgil's *Georgics*, where the farmer ploughing his peaceful fields on the plain of Philippi uncovers the bones and rusty swords of those who fell in that battle in which the old Rome died: is past suffering the condition for present peace to grow from – and will it last? Further, that post-tragic trajectory to restoration and reconciliation receives support from another quarter. In *Metamorphoses* 1, 145–50 the virgin Astraea, goddess of justice, last of the immortals to leave the earth after the golden age, will return in the Last Days to usher in an era of peace and justice. That imagery was systematically appropriated by Elizabeth,[6] and there were indeed many of considerable calibre, like Bishop Aylmer of London, or John Foxe, in her and in James's reign who thought that they were living at the end of time.[7] The stress Shakespeare gives to young women as resolvers of ancient grudge and male confusion, from Portia through Marina and Innogen to Perdita, Miranda and the infant Elizabeth, picks up the Astraea theme, and several of these plays turn on the crucial conceit of Truth the Daughter of Time. Their post-tragic structure takes them beyond the *catastrophe* that is the last of the four movements of classical tragedy recognised by ancient and early modern critics (*protasis, epitasis, katastasis* and *catastrophe*) but that leaves Shakespeare with the problem of representing Time. For the reconciliation comes only after *prolonged* suffering.

If an action should be single and complete, as Aristotle recommended, and ideally within one day, a dramatist has problems in representing growth and development over time. In several of the late plays development over time is of the essence of the fable, and they require a vastly extended time and space. Time as destroyer and as restorer is an important feature of Ovid's concept of time in *Metamorphoses*, and several of these plays strain to find ways of representing metamorphosis through time. *Pericles*, *The Winter's Tale* (based on Greene's *Pandosto; or, The Triumph of Time*, after all) and *The Tempest* all require the daughter to grow up sixteen years.[8] The plays adopt different strategies to cover the problem. *Henry VIII* gets over it by presenting the baby Elizabeth and the prediction of her future reconciliatory glory – and her death – by Cranmer – the future taken back into the present, so to speak. But the methods of the others are equally inventive. Narrators extraneous to the action like the emblematic Time, or Gower, cleverly frame it and suggest ways in which it may be considered. In *Cymbeline*, the 'long time' needed by the plot – a journey to Rome and back, or a walk to Wales, doesn't happen in forty minutes – is finessed by the rapidity of narration and its tension. In *The Tempest* the problem is elegantly overcome by integrating the dark backward and abysm of the pre-plot into the instant of the play in Prospero's narrative in 1.2. *The Tempest*, indeed, is *bravura* in explicitly matching the time of the events represented to the time of the representation. Shakespeare may be playing a pleasant teasing game, for a few months earlier the company had performed Jonson's *Alchemist*, set in Blackfriars itself, a wee bit into the future, and also played with the same self-referential timing. It is entertaining to consider how an audience that saw both plays would enjoy the extra-dramatic ironic opposition between Burbage as the fake magus Subtle and as the serious magus Prospero, and there are other points of direct contrast in mechanisms and themes between the two plays. It would be a fun to have the same boy play Dol Common and Miranda …

Pericles

Pericles and *The Tempest* can be seen as examples of the sub-genre of 'travel plays'. Such plays engage with Europe's increasing interest in, and response to, the previously unknown, and can test easy European certainties.[9] Certainly *The Tempest* capitalises on the interest in accounts of far places and voyages demonstrable from the amount of 'travel writing' published. *Pericles*, written before the Blackfriars became available, anticipates in many of its concerns and techniques the plays that exploit that theatre's resources. Its tournament requires elaborate staging, and the *imprese* must be properly painted for their significance to be interpreted. At this very time, *impresa* painting, a complex visual language related to the sophisticated emblem form, was highly fashionable, and the annual Accession Day Tilts in Whitehall – for 6d the public could come and watch – had reached a level of elaborateness that would make audiences critical judges of attempts to represent anything similar on stage. The awakening of Thaisa in 3.2, to music, anticipates the spectacular awakening of Hermione: the moment must be slow, and the props elaborate and beautiful. At 5.1.232 machinery must be used to lower Diana for her theophany – the same technique used in *Cymbeline* for Jupiter's theophany and in *The Tempest* in Prospero's Masque of 'goddesses'. In Cerimon we perhaps anticipate the *magus* figures of Paulina and Prospero, and they require a convention of stage credibility for them to work. The magical and super-natural paraphernalia of the Court masque provided just such a language. Finally, *Pericles* anticipates the elaborate sonic and perhaps visual effects of the storms of *The Winter's Tale* and *The Tempest*.

Born during the symbolic, pivotal storm that features also in *The Winter's Tale* and *The Tempest*, Marina requires time to grow into the woman who heals her father and converts Lysimachus. The scenes are widely scattered: Tyre, Tarsus, a ship at sea, Pentapolis, Antioch. This could hardly be more removed from Aristotelian economy. The main source, Gower's story of Apollonius, sums up the themes of the preceding (well over 100) tales in the *Confessio Amantis*, which in essence relate to the proper rule of the self and, by extension, of the kingdom. Medieval writers often use incest as a metaphor for the ultimate test of tyranny, what St Augustine called *amor sui*, 'love of oneself, or one's own', as against pursuing 'common profit'. The tale is thus structured on the oppositions between Antiochus and his daughter, Pericles/Apollonius and the daughter Shakespeare calls symbolically Marina – reminding us of the 'sea change' – and Cleon and the Good Steward Helicanus. Lysimachus adds a counterpoint which directly anticipates the more innocent Florizel and Ferdinand, each of whom must master the 'fire i'th blood'. But what might cohere in a narrative poem could easily fall into incoherence in a play, which must to some degree show not tell. Shakespeare's solution is the device of Gower, who intervenes no less than seven times to frame, summarise and move the action forward through time and space.

But the wit of this device is not simply structural. Gower's current neglect makes us overlook the respect accorded him in the Renaissance, when he is often cited in the same breath as Chaucer. Chaucer and Gower appearing in *Greenes Vision* (1590? printed 1592), for example, reflect a tradition of paired citation of them to represent rival literary values and styles. Chaucer, to whom Shakespeare and Spenser went many times, is being appropriated to 'Englishness',[10] but with time, his conceptual language proves increasingly intractable and difficult for imitators, and so the short comic tales become his 'typical' work. This raises problems for humanist writers, with their ideas about the moral authority of poetry. Chaucer never, in fact, claims any authority for himself. Gower, by contrast, does make such claims, and clearly offers morality as distinct from mere mirth – in his own words, 'lore' as well as 'lust' (pleasure) (Prologue, *Confessio Amantis*, 19): a model for the humanist agenda. Further, the style, verse and vocabulary, with occasional archaisms (e.g. 3.0.1, 3.0.5, 3.0.11, 3.0.13), Shakespeare gives 'Gower' allude to his elegant octosyllabics (though his later speeches move into heptasyllabics, decasyllabics, and cross rhyme). Using 'Gower' solves the issue of time and the structural coherence of the story, and also self-referentially raises the issue of what that story may be made to mean – how in fact 'lust' becomes 'lore'. A further effect is to make the events themselves demonstrative, with an accompanying distancing of the audience from immediate engagement to a point where thoughtful awareness of the total force of the story qualifies emotional response. After all, as in any romance, medieval or Renaissance, the audience know, as Pericles or any hero cannot, that all shall be well, all manner of thing shall be well, in the end. The how and why is of the essence.

Cymbeline

One of the several remarkable things about *Cymbeline* is its generic indeterminacy, its unprecedented holding-together of a farrago of different elements: histories of Britain; Italian novella (perhaps); echoes of *Titus Andronicus* and *Rape of Lucrece*; 'folk-tale' motifs of hidden noble children; tests of chastity; pastoral; romance restoration. Even more than *The Winter's Tale*, there are generous doses of potentially tragic material – echoes of *Othello*, of *Lear*, are obvious. It almost collapses into chaos in the first four acts, and needs divine intervention to pull it right, but ... in the end the Dry (family?) Tree fruits, and the fruit may hang there till the tree die, and the reborn Phoenix, the 'sole Arabian bird', perch in its branches. And it uses a *deus ex* (a fashionable) *machina* as a visually spectacular catalyst of the uncovenanted resolution into harmony. If the comedies disturbingly indicate how strong a role accident, not necessity, has in their resolution, this play makes explicit the mechanism of that accident – and hints it might not be accident at all.

Earlier I noted the taste for Hellenistic romance, and for romance in dramatic form, like *Mucedorus*. This play exploits that taste, besides looking back to plays fashionable thirty years earlier. Indeed, the parallels and similarities in names between *Cymbeline* and the anonymous *The Rare Triumphs of Love and Fortune* (c.1582) led J. M. Nosworthy to suggest in his 1955 Arden edition (p. xxv) that the old play had been where Shakespeare started. Possibly: but the general debt may be more important than any specific one. Wagers on

1. Inigo Jones's design for Jupiter descending on an eagle, in Aurelian Townshend's masque *Tempe Restored* (1632).

or tests of a wife's chastity have many analogues in folk tale and at a deep, perhaps Jungian, level negotiate male anxieties about sexual adequacy, property and succession. Restorations are of the essence of romance. Pastoral is a common reference point, the more useful because it is common.

Perhaps building on the successful experience of counterpointed plots in *Lear*, Shakespeare has three plots which ultimately integrate. First, the challenge to Cymbeline's power and royalty by Rome and his wife respectively. The consequences are the assumed loss of his child, the movement towards the critical battle, and the child's final restoration. Second, the 'Wager plot', where Iachimo echoes the subtleties of Iago as Posthumus faintly echoes Othello. The difference is that Iachimo is interested in money, not Innogen or power, and comparing himself to 'our Tarquin' only underlines the differences. Third, the Belarius plot: Belarius, the sequestered wise man who educates the young in a pastoral setting, anticipates Prospero. This pastoral plot where noble youths in nature contrast with the corruption of the civilized, underlines the corruption of court. Indeed, Innogen, even when in court, is still of the pastoral: the imagery attached to her is flowers, and as Posthumus moves to the corrupting urbanity of Italy she moves to the pastoral realm. The characters in pastoral return to reform and redeem other characters, and suggest a future of fruitful growth.

This seems in analysis a hopelessly varied multiplicity of motifs, yet it moves towards a great act of union: Posthumus and Innogen; Innogen reunited with Cymbeline; Innogen reunited with her brothers; Cymbeline united with his sons, and his lost *male* heirs; Cymbeline reunited with his old counsellor Belarius; and Britain and Rome united in amity. This triumphant vision of unity may well reflect metaphorically some of King James's ambitions. At the climax of the multiple *anagnorises* in 5.4 Cymbeline is a '*mother* to the birth of three' (5.4.369), a transgendering of his role as father of his kingdom to fulfil the part left sterile by his 'wicked Queen' (461) who fitly brought forth only her clottish son. Future fruitfulness and peace – the motifs stressed in Cranmer's prophecy of the reign of the infant Elizabeth in *Henry VIII* – are underlined by the importance of the tree image in the union of husband and wife – 'hang there like fruit my soul/ till the tree die' – and the soothsayer's interpreting the vision: for in the reuniting of the nation the 'lofty cedar, royal Cymbeline, personates thee' (452). The overtones of rebirth, of new life, of a future strengthened by the trials of the past, underline that the final restoration is not simply familial but also political, and divinely sanctioned.

The play's metaphoric, symbolic, iconographic discourse signifies far more than its expression in a narrative says. For in *Cymbeline* and *Pericles*, Shakespeare is developing a new theatrical language, which accepts the possibility of the supernatural, the marvellous, lying just beyond the borders of vision. In *All's Well that Ends Well*, Lafew says, 'They say miracles are past; and we have our philosophical persons, to make modern and familiar, things supernatural and causeless. Hence is it that we make trifles of terrors, ensconcing ourselves into seeming knowledge, when we should submit our-selves to an unknown fear'. (2.3.1ff.) It is precisely the conviction that miracles may *not* be past, at least in art, that Shakespeare seems to be addressing, and the whole point of miracle is that it *is* miraculous, inexplic-able, numinous. Developing dramatic language in this direction will obviously require a treatment of narrative and character radically different to that he created in the histories and later the tragedies. The play is full, as Peggy Muñoz Simonds showed,[11] of allusions to Orphic rituals of death and resurrection, of neo-Platonic response to Ovidian mythology, as well as of a systematic equation between the iconography of birds, animals, plants, stones and the themes of doubt, repentance, reformation and regeneration. The dénouement of forgiveness and happy marriage is achieved through personal temperance and self-knowledge, a musical concord in individual, state and cosmos. *Cymbeline* thus signals a major step on the way to the dramatic economy of *The Winter's Tale* and *The Tempest*.

The Winter's Tale

The Winter's Tale is built like a diptych. Its two panels, held together by the hinge of Time, contrast in location, in theme, in language, in genre. Time's speech splits the play exactly. Like Rumour in 2 *Henry IV*, he is a figure straight out of emblematics, a figure visually precise at least since editions of Petrarch's *Trionfi*. The play's 'naturalistic' first movement, the trajectory of Leontes's mad jealousy and its consequence in his heir's death, Perdita's exposure, and the apparent death of Hermione, is suddenly in 4.1. jerked into a new perspective by Time, impresario, chorus and also, in a real sense, theme. His retrospect recalls a world dominated by an imagery of winter following spring, culminating in a storm, real as well as symbolic, and the beast that wants discourse of reason dining on the gentleman. His prospect looks to a spring expressed in flowers that promise fruit and harvest. His appearance immediately qualifies the way we can *now* understand the first three acts – this making our first response itself problematically of interest – and also frames how we may understand the second. The device also neatly gets over Shakspeare's structural problem of the 'wide gap of time' and the two locales, Bohemia and Sicilia, at the end of 'opposed winds'.

The first half, generically, is unquestionably 'tragic'. Equally clearly, the last notes, the language, of Act 3 which introduce the second half move us towards the comic and the pastoral. Leontes's language recalls in some detail the idiolect of Othello; the dignity of Hermione recalls Desdemona but also anticipates Catherine of Aragon in her trial. In Bohemia, by contrast, the clowns might be first cousin to Athenian mechanicals or Venetian Gobbos;

Florizel and Perdita step straight out of romantic comedy. The business of this subtle play is the integration of these two worlds. Indeed, there may be more going on than just a generic integration into a *tertium quid*, for James' international policy was to broker a European peace by marrying his daughter to the leader of Protestant Europe, Frederick, Elector Palatine, and his son Henry to the Infanta of Spain: Spain's dominions included Sicily. No one in the audience could not have known that Sicily was Catholic, Bohemia Protestant and a refuge for English Protestants under Mary Tudor. It is attractive to argue that a play roughly coincident with Prince Henry's investiture as Prince of Wales and the opening of negotiations for the marriages should use its generic signals, and its resolution of the sins of the fathers by the hopes vested in their children, to support the idea of a union of the conflicting confessions. Time may indeed bring such things forth, and find concords of discord. For there is no music in the first half, while the second is punctuated by the songs of Autolycus, the dance of the Satyrs – surely reusing the dance the company had earlier performed in the *Masque of Oberon* on 1 January 1611 – and the music that Paulina calls for as Hermione is called to 'descend'. The Music of the Spheres that Pericles hears is part of the *musica mundana* which often is discordant with the *musica humana*.[12] In respectable Renaissance theory such music may heal the sick, tame the savage, and help reason rule the passions. This second half moves us steadily, never abandoning the nervous interplay of real dialogue for the hieratic statement of masque or pantomime, into the sort of discourse that the symbolic structures of masque best compass. The theatrical shock, first time round, when it is unexpected, of Hermione's resurrection – we have no reasons to suppose it anything else – recalls Pygmalion and Galatea, but also the emblem of Truth the Daughter of Time, drawn forth from the cave or prison where she had been imprisoned by Slander and Strife: just that emblem had been wittily used in the City of London's pageant for Elizabeth in 1559. Hermione thus ceases to be simply a character, but becomes part of a symbolic economy transcendent of the characters, recollected and understood in our memory of the play. A memorial statue/portrait in Paulina's Long Gallery, already visually arresting, suddenly acquires new and daring connotations. Cleverly, too, the staging mirrors the earlier scene of her trial: there Leontes, in that parody of justice, occupies the central authority space, and she was suppliant, while here their positions and authority are exactly reversed.

Questions and irresolutions as there are at the end of the play, the source has a much darker ending. There Time does indeed triumph, but Leontes' crime nearly leads to incest, and, recognising his fault, he commits suicide. No regeneration, no grace, no 'great creating Nature' there, only a sort of justice. Here the thrust of the play moves beyond strict justice to a world where forgiveness

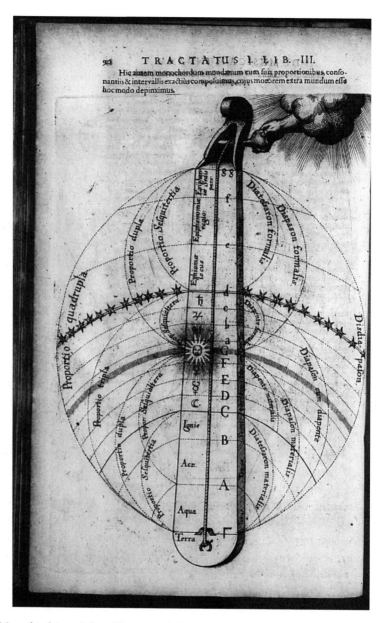

2. *Monochordum mundi*: an illustration from Robert Fludd's *Utriusque cosmi maioris scilicet et minoris metaphysica, physica atque technica historia* (Oppenheim: Johann Theodore de Bry, 1617–18). The universe is presented as a two-octave Pythagorean monochord, divided into the basic harmonic intervals. Fludd's caption reads 'I have set out the monochord of the universe with its harmonic proportions, very exactly, and I have shown that its driving force is from outside the universe.'

and mercy operate – if characters can bring themselves to accept them. This is a note first sounded in Shakespeare's canon by Portia, and it opens up a different conceptual and moral world, requiring a different dramatic language properly to express and explore it. These late plays explore ways in which that language might be articulated, and *The Winter's Tale*'s diachronic narrative offers one way of doing it.

The Tempest

The Tempest has strong links with pastoral, frequently used to highlight the corruption of court, as well as with the romantic comedic move from court to the educative wilderness and then back to the responsibilities of the everyday. By any standards, the structure is a *tour de force*. It is a play of delicate patterns, full of echoes and resonances exploring its main themes. For example, the providential storm that brought Prospero to the island figures the metaphorical storm(s) in the state, figures usurpation past or potential – of Prospero (twice), of Alonzo (once): destructive, in other words. The storm that Prospero raises, by contrast, figures the storm in Alonzo's and his supporters' minds, and is cleansing and purificatory. Characters too are patterned: Miranda/Caliban/Ferdinand invites us to consider the issues of Nature and Nurture; Alonzo, Antonio and Sebastian offer differing responses to misfortune and to grace; Prospero and Gonzalo, each apart, suggest uncorrupted moral judgement, while Caliban's responses to Prospero are paralleled in his response to Trinculo and Stephano – awe at first, then rejection. And with this second rejection comes acceptance of Prospero's goodness and a reconciliation that determines to 'seek for grace'. There are patterned motifs: Caliban as servant, showing his nature and Ferdinand as servant showing his nurture – and they speak exactly the same length of speech as they enter in consecutive scenes carrying their logs. Prospero's idea of right rule, which is the result of study and nurture, parallels Gonzalo's Utopian motif, relying on nature – which too likely might generate only 'whores and idlers'. Then there is the image of revolt: Caliban; Trinculo and Stephano; Antonio and Sebastian – each in their measure. True *Magia*, *theurgia*, is opposed to Witchcraft, *goetia*, Prospero to Sycorax. Sycorax validates Prospero (compare for contrast Paulina's clumsy protestation that what she does is 'lawful' in *The Winter's Tale*).[13] Ferdinand's and Caliban's responses to Miranda's beauty, where, as in all well-behaved heroines who obey Renaissance art theory, outward shape is an index of inner nature, leads to a view of chaste love mastered by reason and timeliness contrasted with Caliban's regret at his unsuccessful rape. Miranda's and Caliban's responses to education, to rule, to new experience, to new people, are clearly counterpointing each other. Moreover, this very visual play is self-referentially much concerned with appearances. There are three views of the storm, all different; of the banquet, again three – Alonso's, Prospero's, ours. The Masque of Goddesses, which must be the most elaborate speech of the father of the bride ever suffered by a bridegroom, seems like a heavenly blessing, but is in fact illusion and known to be illusion – like the play.

The play is built round several key spectacles, providing its climactic moments, all pregnant with symbolic meaning. First the storm: a shipwreck is frequently to be seen in the background of emblems of fortune, and the violence, even the detail of 'enter Mariners, wet', stresses disruption, punishment, violent change. Yet while this cacophony can be hurtful it may still be healing, and the antithesis of this is in the music with which the play resounds. Here art appears as nature. Second, the banquet: the close echoes of *Aeneid* III continue one of the sub-discourses of the play, but feasts, disrupted or not, are symbolic enough in Jacobethan drama – consider supper at the Macbeths'. Here in addition we have hints of food of which only those worthy can partake, of the Mass, and the metaphor of order is interrupted by the avenging figure of Ariel because the sinners – the Christian semantics are explicit – need to repent, to know themselves. Here art appears as art. Third, the Masque of Goddesses: a (conditional) promise of order, plenty, peace, acknowledged by impresario and by recipient to be art, an elaborate way of saying the unsayable in a memorable and experienced rather than merely verbal way. It is then interrupted by the recollection of sin and undivulged crime, highlighted by the antimasque spectacle of the clowns being hunted across the stage by the hounds. (We can be sure the King, when he saw it, would have appreciated the quality of the dogs.) Finally, the visual climax, using, like the dénouement of *The Winter's Tale*, a discovery space. Ferdinand and Miranda, seen in a tableau of order and right conduct, play the game of power and love and offer to those watching, sullied by the world's vagaries, the hope of a future that will put past suffering and crime behind it while yet acknowledging that Providentially that suffering has led to precisely this hope. That symbol, like the statue of Hermione, comes alive and comes out, active, into the play, as art can actively alter the reality we inhabit. The stage language of these nodal points exploits the tools of masque and antimasque in music, stage machinery, costume, dance and scenery. These high points of the play are flanked by orthodox dramatic writing which does provide, as was not the case in *Pericles*, a connected narrative sequence. Moreover, the play, as Mark Rose pointed out,[14] has a most interesting shape of nine scenes, with the plighting of Ferdinand and Miranda's troth – the turning from ancient grudge to hope for the future – at the centre of the design. Just so sits Time at the centre of *The Winter's Tale*.

In the Preface to *Hymenaei* (danced 5 January 1606) Jonson described his view of the poet's high function:

> It is a noble and just advantage that the things subjected to understanding have of those which are subjected to sense, that the one sort are but momentary, and merely taking; the other impressing, and lasting ... royal princes and greatest persons (who are commonly the personators of these actions) not only studious of riches and magnificence in the outward celebration or show ... but curious after the most high and hearty inventions to furnish the inward parts ... which should always lay hold on more removed mysteries.

His masques frequently suggest that moral reform results from the leadership of monarchs and courtiers whose natural virtues have been perfected by humanistic education, religion, and moral self-education – and art. Here, characters are indeed brought up against 'more removed mysteries', and, as Ferdinand and Prospero know, art is not simply decodable (a warning, indeed, for audiences and critics of the play). But what are those more removed mysteries? First, the ruler's duty to his people, and to take responsibility for the evil in his state for which he himself may be partly responsible. Second, the 'post-tragic' regeneration, driven by Providential purpose – and it would be difficult to find any Jacobean who did not have that view of Providence. This expresses itself beautifully in the Astraea myth – yet we have to make it happen by consent and belief, by as Paulina tells us, 'awaken [ing our] faith'.

The *Magus* – what Prospero makes himself – sought enlightenment, and the power to help all things in their process of becoming their fullest selves. But the greatest power, as wise Marsilio Ficino or Dr John Dee knew, is to renounce power: to break the staff, to drown the book. That is where Prospero is at the end of the play. So doing, he gives people back their freedom. They may use it wisely. They may not. But without that freedom, wisdom is nothing.

Henry VIII

Henry VIII, on which Shakespeare and Fletcher collaborated, deals with *very* recent events, perhaps still uncomfortably sensitive. It must have engaged with popular perceptions of Henry: Jacobeans were pretty familiar with his reign. After all, the folio calls it the '*Famous* Life of Henry VIII', and the King's person was familiar from images – in the Great Bible Frontispiece, in prints and printers' initial letters. The title page of Foxe's *Actes and Monuments*, aka *Book of Martyrs*, in every church in the land by law, has an imperial Henry trampling the ungodly Pope Clement under his feet.

Rowley's *When you see me you know me* (1613) has a disguised King Henry, and the quarto title-page has a version of the Holbein portrait. In 1601 the Admiral's Men had a play about Henry. So 'Shakespeare's' play is feeding into a mainstream interest. There is considerable irony in the play being watched when the Tudor line had died out and the Elizabeth in whom so much hope is placed in Cranmer's prophetic speech had died heirless. The stage demonstrates the shifts of power and Henry's failure to govern wisely. It is all very close to home.

Formally the play differs much from the earlier histories – which are generically inventive enough – and it relies heavily on spectacle, on a large cast, and on lots of gorgeously dressed pageantry. In this it goes a step further than *The Tempest*, which is built, as we have seen, round the nodal points of spectacle of the storm, the banquet and its masque, the masque of goddesses and its antimasque, and the epiphany of Ferdinand and Miranda. Like *Pericles*, *Henry VIII* is less interested in narrative than in dramatic visual effects, carefully composed. Indeed, the unusually detailed, precise stage directions – we have after all a 'reading' text – give a good idea of how important appearance and the silent body language was seen to be.[15] There is an emphasis on eyes, on seeing: consider stage directions in 1.2, 1.4, 2.4, 4.1.45ff., 4.2.70ff., 5.3, 5.5, and note too how the play's first scene starts with a detailed, almost lush, description of the Field of the Cloth of Gold as it would have been *seen*. Indeed, in the eighteenth century the spectacles of Anne's coronation and Elizabeth's christening were often detached from their play and became popular 'afterpieces'.

'Shakespeare' keeps very close to the sources. Several speeches are virtually verbatim from Holinshed, and the trial is set in the very Blackfriars where the play was staged before it fatally went to the Globe (where that cannon stopple set the thatch on fire). But there are some significant changes, not just in what is omitted – like Mary Tudor's existence – but in what is added, and which imply connections. The marriage to Anne (1536) comes *before* the fall of Wolsey (1526). Catherine's death (1536) is *before* Elizabeth's birth (1533). Anne's coronation procession is led by Thomas More, even though he refused to attend. Executed in 1535, he nevertheless presides over the trial of Cranmer (5.3) (ominously, watched by Henry unseen above). Cromwell's and Anne's trials and executions are both omitted, like More's. For those who knew even the outline of the events of the reign, this selectivity raises questions not only about the game of power and its dangers, but about how myths can come to be more powerful than that on which they were based.

Its subtitle, *All is True*, alerts us to the question of what *is* 'truth' in history. Shakespeare has handled the issue before of what we can know of past events, of what truth that knowledge can hold. Similarly, in *Henry V* the persuasive

Chorus presents us with a Henry who is unquestionably the Hero King, the myth; the scenes – tableaux, more accurately, for there is no plot to speak of – that follow show a much more problematic Henry and a much less united England, yet both elements of the play can claim, justly, to be 'true'.[16] The audience's collusion with *Henry VIII*'s Prologue's request makes its observation and judgement important, and there are many references to theatre and theatrical audiences watching and judging.

Henry is noticeably decentred. As the audience's knowledge can be relied on, Shakespeare can make him a marginal figure in a play less Henry's than about Henry's consequences. It is far more the play of Catherine and Wolsey, who might be seen as two tragic figures in a play culminating not, however, in their falls but in the promise of the reign of the young Elizabeth as the uncovenanted sequel to her father's questionable ability to govern wisely. Shakespeare gives Catherine huge dignity, and surrounds her with images of pastoral innocence and purity. (The lily image is also later applied to Elizabeth.) While Wolsey is figured as the over-reaching 'bad' Catholic – the play moves straight from the Cloth of Gold description into a very negative picture of him – Catherine is seen almost as a saint. Indeed, the Epilogue says

> ... All the expected good w'are like to hear,
> For this play at this time, is only in
> The merciful construction of good women,
> For such a one we showed 'em.

In 1.2, where Henry enters symbolically 'leaning on' Wolsey, she is interceding on behalf of Henry's subjects – a clear echo of the interceding Philippa in *Edward III*, but both remind of Mary, Queen of Heaven – and her voice is dominant in the scene, in her clash with the Machiavellian Wolsey. In 2.4, in a trial reminiscent of that in *The Winter's Tale*, her eloquent dignity emotionally dominates the scene. Her pity for her enemy in 4.2 is plangent, and her vision in the scene seems to echo the iconography of the Assumption of the Blessed Virgin. That may have had more associative weight than we now easily grasp, for there was an Assumption play in several of the mystery cycles.[17] This recollection of not just the old mystery drama but of a specifically Catholic element in it, denied by Protestants, is audacious indeed in a play 'about' the Reformation.

Cranmer's last speech (5.5.20ff.) predicts a future that is the audience's past and present, with a neat compliment to James as Elizabeth's Phoenix-like successor and as would-be broker of European peace. This again picks up the notion that runs like a leitmotif through these late plays of regeneration, restoration, rebirth, figured in the Phoenix, and in the Astraea motif of the Virgin's return: *iam redit et virgo, redeunt Saturnia regna*. Like Virgil's

Fourth Eclogue, this speech looks forward to an era of peace and plenitude – in fact, a far cry from what the later years of Elizabeth were like. But the *myth* is important – increasingly so, as the Queen's last years began to be coloured by a nostalgia that was a reaction to the present. Furthermore, at the back of the mind one hears echoes of Anchises' prophecy in *Aeneid* VI of the promise of the youth Marcellus, so soon cut off before his fullness of time. We never get quite this far with other plays of this group, where we stop with the promise of the young, not their eventual death. But the play is consonant with them in that like them it has a powerful father and redemptory daughter – as if Cordelia and Lear had been transposed into a major key – and each father has a flaw, the consequences of which are the means of the restoration by the daughter.

The Two Noble Kinsmen

The Two Noble Kinsmen has had varying theatrical and critical fortunes, and is often marginalised because of its shared authorship. Yet there is no reason why a collaboration should not be successful. The problem is not that it is a bad play badly plotted – it is neither—but that the languages of the characters do not quite 'join up': for example, the Arcite and Palamon of Fletcher do not think or *sound* like Shakespeare's, and the Jailer's Daughter (it is interesting that she is never named) whom Fletcher voiced in 2.5 is far more histrionically declaratory than the more active, interiorised, sensibility we hear in Shakespeare's 3.2. (Much of the mad scenes was Fletcher's work.) This is a problem, for Shakespeare's style goes off in directions typical of his later style, towards complexity and ellipsis, while Fletcher, more wordy, even florid, writes much more conventionally. But competent actors in this very visual play might make that gap less of a hindrance than we might think. The play moreover offers a clever vehicle for addressing certain values, issues and ideas fashionable at the time of its first performance. Further, a play dealing with wedding preparations interrupted by mourning for a noble knight's death could have seemed very, even tactlessly, topical when the sudden death in November 1612 of Henry Prince of Wales, on whom many hopes were pinned, was fresh in everyone's minds.

Just before the Admiral's Men separated from the Chamberlain's Men in 1594 they had acted a version[18] of *Palamon and Arcite* which as well as Chaucer's *Knight's Tale* may be behind *The Two Noble Kinsmen*. Even earlier, their story made a two-part play performed before the Queen on and 4 September 1566. Shakespeare's and Fletcher's decision to frame the story in a Prologue – like *Pericles* – acknowledging Chaucer as source claims an authorising ancestry, and, indeed, the more alert would recall other dramatic treatments of *The*

Knight's Tale as well as Shakespeare's own use of it in *A Midsummer Night's Dream*. There are striking similarities to *Dream*: the wedding frame, the wood, a woman lost in it at night, the countryfolks' Morris or the mechanicals' play complete with onstage backchat from the court. (In the last, similarities as well to *Love's Labour's Lost*: the Schoolmaster is first cousin to Holofernes.) But Shakespeare's response to Chaucer is never simple. *Lucrece* touches its hat to *Legend of Good Women*, but goes off in wholly new directions; *Troilus and Cressida* is deeply subversive of the greatest love poem in the language.[19] Here Shakespeare and Fletcher depoliticise the ending, for in Chaucer the marriage is not much to do with love but a lot to do with Theseus' determination to cement a peace with Thebes by marrying Emily to Palamon. They use neither the comedic trajectory of *Midsummer Night's Dream* nor the consolatory overview provided at the end of *Knight's Tale* by Theseus. The play closes with little joy in the marriage, and Theseus' final speech is closer to the resigned pessimism of Boccaccio's Egeo or Chaucer's Egeus than to the confident Boethian vision of a love that rules the universe, despite the vagaries of Fortune, with which Chaucer concludes *The Knight's Tale*. At the end, by contrast, they foreground the dire consequences of the clash between Love and Friendship in Arcite and Palamon. Though generically *Two Noble Kinsmen* must be classed as much a 'romance' as is Chaucer's own genre-bending poem, its avoidance of the romance comedic conclusion makes it far the darkest play in this group.

The play deploys the spectacular visual language and staging that was coming to be what audiences wanted:

1) the initial tableau of Theseus' grand entry and the mourning, suppliant queens;
2) the hunt;
3) the arming and the single combat – which must have been done with due regard to the right order to arm a knight (a slow business), while the single combat would have had to be at least as impressive as those exhibition bouts of skill at the weapon which often filled theatres when plays were not playing;
4) the Pageant of knights in 5.1, closely followed by the elaborate supplication before the altars;
5) the Morris, an antimasque reused from Beaumont's Masque for the Inner Temple and Gray's Inn (20 February 1613) just as *Winter's Tale* 4.4.340ff. reuses the dance of Satyrs;
6) and finally, Shakespeare's and Fletcher's last addition to the scenario, the stage set for the execution: perhaps a sight, like the fighting at the barriers, of which Jacobeans would have had connoisseurs' knowledge.

The remarkable revival of 'chivalry' and knightly combat at Elizabeth's court (consider the Accession Day tilts) when it had no conceivable military use intensified in the circle around Prince Henry.[20] Testing personal bravery in passages at arms was a frequent pastime, spectacle and ritual, and many prints show the young prince in armour, at the barriers, wielding lance or sword. The values of the *chevalier sans peur et sans reproche* cultivated, perhaps even followed, in this court culture are mapped into the play. With it go ideals of fidelity and friendship, and love or *fin amor*. Like *Merchant of Venice*, the play is built round Renaissance values of love and friendship – which are not ours. We do well to keep in mind the cliché 'The love of men to women is a thing common and of course: the friendship of man to man is infinite and immortal' (Lyly, *Endymion*, 3.4.114ff.). Such a view, with good classical antecedent, is influential in Renaissance thought and self-construction: consider, for example, Sidney's *Arcadia*'s Musidorus and Pyrocles, or romances like *Amis and Amiloun*, where indeed friends have all things in common, as Erasmus' adage said they should, or Montaigne's friendship with Etienne de la Boétie.[21] Such friendship is immediately challenged when love for a woman appears: consider how Musidorus' and Pyrocles' relationship, and the generosity of each to each, is under stress when they seek the love of a woman. *The Two Noble Kinsmen* plots in two pairs of friends, Arcite and Palamon, and Theseus and Pirithous, and then, oblique to that, the love between Theseus and Hippolyta, supported by mutual admiration and attraction, and the desires of Palamon and Arcite for Emily. In the one pair, love and friendship are balanced; in the other, love conflicts with friendship. This conflict, where each impulse is unquestionably noble and virtuous, is thematically central and is stressed in three scenes in Act 3.

Love itself – what it is, how to distinguish it from mere sex, how it should be 'performed' – is an issue. Its destructive potential, on one hand, is seen in the knights' conflict; on the other, it has baleful effects in the Jailer's Daughter. It is noticeable that the high sentiment, high language and high passion that is associated with the conventions of *fin amor*, which Chaucer left undiluted in his story, are here framed by the love grounded in marriage of the older Theseus and Hippolyta, and the inclusion of the non-noble Jailer's Daughter. Even the uncourtly can love and suffer almost unto death. This earths the high sentiment. Similarly, using the conventions of chivalric romance, the play makes all four principal characters strive to behave 'nobly': Theseus is asked for the 'pitee that renneth soone in gentil herte',[22] and to revise his doom; Emilia refuses to choose because she realises that to favour one would wrong the other; duty is put before personal desire, so Palamon and Arcite defend Thebes, and – again earthing the high sentiment – the Jailer's Daughter is torn between love for Palamon and her duty to her father, who could well be killed because of her action. It is also attractive to see the play as thoughtfully addressing again the issues about youth, growth, maturity we see in *Cymbeline, The Winter's Tale* and *The Tempest*: the knights' youth, their remembered playful follies ('twinned lambs', perhaps, 'frisking i'the sun'), their friendship, then the intrusion of sexual love, and its pain, highlighted by the Jailer's Daughter, and finally marriage – with its future stability indicated in Theseus and Hippolyta in responsible maturity and rule. (Creon the tyrant is set against the good ruler, Theseus, as Antiochus is against Pericles.) For in the end youth's a stuff will not endure. In several of these plays Shakespeare breaks the convention in romantic comedy of a world of *young* lovers to hint at 'what might happen next', in Pericles and Thaisa, Theseus and Hippolyta, Leontes and Hermione, Camillo and Paulina.

Shakespeare and Fletcher made another massive change to Chaucer's plot: the subplot of the Jailer's Daughter. Madness always seems to have gone well on stage and the vigorous writing for her, the staginess of her 'shipboard' fantasy, the number of her lines make her a curiously authoritative voice, expressing far from unattractive feminine sexual desire that neatly balances Emily's reticence and refusal to choose between her lovers, and the dignified (but certainly fully awakened) implications of Hippolyta. The Doctor's recognition of the effects of sexual frustration in his counsel to ignore social constraints in the interest of emotional cure is daring to say the least, and a necessary linking of the refined sentiment of the noble characters to what it is, at the end of the day, all about. This is a play replete with sexuality, repressed, sublimated, or overt.

These plays expected a lot of their audiences: critical alertness, readiness to make connections and willingness to explore the new. They work, as do the plays of the middle period (if in ways less obvious to us) in a world of symbol and metaphor. Yet they are emphatically not allegory, though they may use some of the tools of allegory. Nor, though they engage with contemporary worries, are they simply coded political discussions.[23] High art is not like that. High art transcends its context, it enables us to see the universal beneath the particular, and in communal experience like drama or film offers in a ritual space a dream from which we must wake into real time, but are changed, and cry to dream again.

NOTES

1. The term is first used by Edward Dowden in *Shakespeare: A Critical Study of His Mind and Art* (London: Henry S. King, 1875).

2. The 'Old *Arcadia*' dates from the 1570s; the 'New *Arcadia*' appears in the early 1580s, and the composite *Arcadia*, in 1593, seven years after Sidney's death. His sister wrote another romance, *Urania*.

3. *Compendio della poesia tragicomica, tratto dal duo Verati, per opera del Pastor Fido, colla guinti di molte cose spettanti all'arte* (Venice, 1601)

4. This point in Guarini is stressed by Michael J. Sidnell (ed.), *Sources of Dramatic Theory*, vol. I: *Plato to Congreve* (Cambridge: Cambridge University Press, 1991), p. 148

5. See G. Whitney, *A Choice of Emblems* (Leyden, 1586), Emblem iv.

6. As is fully discussed by F. A. Yates, *Astraea: The Imperial Theme in the Sixteenth Century* (Harmondsworth: Penguin, 1975); see also John Manning, *The Emblem* (London: Reaktion, 2004), p. 201.

7. C. A. Patrides, *Premises and Motifs in Renaissance Thought and Literature* (Princeton: Princeton University Press, 1982), and Patrides and Joseph A. Wittreich, *The Apocalypse in English Renaissance Thought and Literature* (Ithaca: Cornell University Press, 1985).

8. In *Pericles* 5.3.7, we are reminded that Cleon sought to murder Marina at 14, and time has elapsed since then. Sixteen may be a significant number – Time turns his glass in *The Winter's Tale* at line 16 of a 32-line speech; 16 is the square of 4, a number with universally favourable connotation in medieval and ancient number theory.

9. See the Introduction to Antony Parr, *Three Renaissance Travel Plays*, (Manchester: Manchester University Press, 1995).

10. Indeed, Speght's edition of 1598 adds a 'life' which suggests his intimate connection with the royal line of England.

11. Peggy Muñoz Simonds, *Myth, Emblem, and Music in Shakespeare's 'Cymbeline'* (London: Associated University Presses, 1993).

12. Medieval and Renaissance philosophers, drawing on Boethius, divided *musica* into three parts: the *musica universalis* or *musica mundana*, which is based on the mathematical proportions in the movements of the planets; the *musica mundana*, the internal music, again based on proportion and balance, of the human body and mind; and the lowest form of all, the *musica instrumentalis*, sounds made by singers and instrumentalists.

13.
> 'It is required
> You do awake your faith. Then all stand still;
> On: those that think it is unlawful business
> I am about, let them depart.' (5.3.94)

14. Mark Rose, *Shakespearean Design* (Cambridge, MA: Belknap Press of Harvard University Press, 1972).

15. See J. Bulwer, *Chirologia, Or the Natural Language of the Hand. Chironomia or the Art of Manual Rhetoric* (London, 1644) for illustrations of the precise signals, and see discussions in D. Bevington, *Shakespeare's Language of Gesture* (Harvard: Harvard University Press, 1984) and Mary E. Hazard, *Elizabethan Silent Language* (Lincoln and London: University of Nebraska Press, 2000).

16. See Andrew Gurr's discussion of the 'coercive chorus' in the Introduction to his edition (Cambridge: Cambridge University Press, 1992).

17. In the Coventry cycle, the Mercers probably played it. Laurence M. Clopper, *Drama, Play and Game: English Festive Culture in the Medieval and Early Modern Period* (Chicago: Chicago University Press, 2001), p. 173; see also Anna J. Mill, 'The York Plays of the Dying, Assumption, and Coronation of Our Lady' *Publications of the Modern Languages Association of America* 65, (1950), pp. 866–76. It forms part of the problematic N-town plays.

18. Philip Henslowe mentions it in his diary: *Henslowe's Diary*, ed. R. A. Foakes (Cambridge: Cambridge University Press, 2002), pp. 24–5.

19. See Ann Thompson, *Shakespeare and Chaucer* (Liverpool: Liverpool University Press, 1978), and E. T. Donaldson, *The Swan at the Well: Shakespeare Reading Chaucer* (New Haven and London: Princeton University Press, 1985), for detailed studies of Shakespeare's response to Chaucer.

20. Roy Strong, *Henry, Prince of Wales and England's Lost Renaissance* (New York: Thames and Hudson, 1986); Alan R. Young, *Tudor and Jacobean Tournaments* (London: Geo. Philip and Sons, 1987).

21. See the level-headed discussion in Eugene M. Waith's edition (Oxford: Oxford University Press, 1989) pp. 49ff.

22. Chaucer uses this line four times: *Knight's Tale*, I (A) 1761, *Merchant's Tale*, IV (E) 1986, *Squire's Tale*, V (F), 479, *Legend of Good Women*, Prologue F 503.

23. Frances A. Yates has an enlightening discussion of the political context in *Shakespeare's Last Plays: A New Approach* (London: Routledge and Kegan Paul, 1975).

4

KAREN BRITLAND

Politics, religion, geography and travel: historical contexts of the last plays

In the Newberry Library, there is a copy of a manuscript letter from a courtier to his 'sweete heart', describing his impressions of Scotland, a place he was visiting in the train of one of the Stuart kings. 'The countrey,' he noted, 'although itt be mountainous affoords no monsters but Women':

> The Ladies are of opinion yt Susanna could not bee chast because Shee bath'd so often. Pride is a thing bredd in theire Bones, and theire Flesh naturally abhorrs Cleanliness. Their Breath most commonly stinks of Pottage, their Linnen of Pisse, their Hands of Piggs turds, their Bodies of Sweate, and itt is a Position of Bellarmins to weare socks.[1]

Years after James VI of Scotland had travelled to England to take up Queen Elizabeth I's crown, bringing with him not only an entourage of Scots, but a determination to unite his two realms, an Englishman at court was still evincing humorously satirical reservations about his northern neighbours.[2] Such comments draw attention to tensions present from the start of James I's reign: the Scots were perceived by many in England as poor and backward and there was resistance on both sides to integration. Although a pamphlet poem such as the anonymous *Englands Wedding Garment, or a preparation to King James his Royall Coronation* (1603) might celebrate James's succession as a fortunate marriage, there was clear anxiety about the kind of baggage the new king would bring with him.

Englands Wedding Garment is a profoundly unaccomplished poem that nevertheless invokes the major iconographic themes of the start of the Jacobean reign. The poem's first lines ('Cease sad laments, King *Brutus* race, / Deplore no more your blessed Queene') allude to the Tudor myth that Elizabeth was descended from Brutus, and, through him, claimed ancestry with his great-grandfather Aeneas, a survivor of Troy and the founder of Rome. Edmund Spenser's epic Elizabethan poem, *The Faerie Queene*, had presented Tudor London as a new Troy, locating England as an empire fit to succeed the ancient Roman world. *Englands Wedding Garment* extends this iconography to James, emphasising the King's own descent from Brutus to generate a sense of continuity between the Tudor and Stuart reigns. The poem's nuptial imagery emphasises James's masculinity (he is described as a 'Sunne' and is aligned with 'mightie Ioue', father of the gods) at the same time as it foregrounds desires for peace and integration between his subjects.[3] In this it echoes the King's own assertions that he was the nation's husband and 'all the whole Isle' was his 'lawfull Wife'.[4] Mirroring James's own wishes for a united Great Britain, the poem calls on the English, Scots and Irish to join their hearts in loyalty to their king, while peers, court, church, city and country are exhorted to sing in harmonious celebration of the accession. This new, united nation is imagined to gladden friends, but to thwart foes: the Pope swells with fury; the Spanish Infanta fumes; 'Babel-Rome' fails in its plots to assassinate Elizabeth and James. The new king, like his predecessor, is presented as a 'patron stout of Christian faith', an 'English Lion' who will defeat the 'Horn'd beast' of popery, and yet he is also a *Salomon* of peace' whose reign will continue the Elizabethan 'golden-age'.

Despite its encomiastic intentions, however, the poem makes clear that there are unresolved tensions in the accession: it invokes the 'rebell Irish rout', commanding them to sheathe their blades and beg for mercy from their new king; it depicts Scottish eyes streaming with tears at James's absence; and, in its insistence that James is the champion of Protestantism and its persistent evocation of Catholic enemies, it rather obviously avoids acknowledging that James's mother was the Catholic Mary Queen of Scots executed in 1587 by the Protestant Elizabeth. In short, the poem seeks to allay fears about the change of regime, but this, in itself, is a clear indication that anxieties were rife. This chapter will investigate the political, geographical and religious issues prevalent in England during James's reign, examining how they were reflected in Shakespeare's late plays.

Politics

David Bergeron has suggested that Shakespeare's late plays all, in part, 're-present' King James and his family, and that they have a particular emphasis on succession through the female line because James's claim to the English and Scottish thrones was through his ancestor, the English Princess Margaret.[5] In a similar fashion, Philippa Berry has argued that, in several of Shakespeare's plays, 'the particular historical time of the play is implicitly paralleled or repeated by recent or near-contemporary political moments'.[6] Although Simon Palfrey has cautioned against assuming that playwrights followed 'a universal "court" line' to the detriment of the 'bustle and complexity' of early modern theatre, it is nonetheless possible, as he acknowledges, that

'Shakespeare's creative mind' was prompted by contemporary issues such as 'absolutism, Scottish union [and] conjugal diplomacy'.[7] In this section, I will explore these three political positions, showing how they influenced each other and how they were riven with internal conflicts.

James acceded to the English throne already a king. Only one year old at the time of his mother's abdication, by 1603 he had reigned as James VI of Scotland for thirty-six years; he had two male heirs and a daughter; and his opinions on kingship had been published in Scotland in a volume entitled *Basilikon Doron* (1599), addressed to Prince Henry, his eldest son. In 1603, demand for this volume in England was high and it was published by a number of printers working for the bookseller John Norton. In the same year, *Basilikon Doron* was reissued in Scotland and, in 1604, was translated into Welsh. It began with a sonnet detailing the work's argument, which declared:

> *God giues not Kings the stile of* Gods *in vaine,*
> *For on his throne his Scepter do they swey:*
> *And as their subiects ought them to obey,*
> *So Kings should fear and serue their God againe.*

For James, then, a king was God's representative on earth and ruled by divine right, placed at the top of a hierarchy that demanded obedience and submission from all his subjects. However, James clearly also considered his power to be circumscribed. The sonnet goes on to exhort a monarch to '*Obserue the statutes of your heauenly King, / And from his Lawe, make all your Lawes to spring*', drawing attention to the fact that a ruler was bound by God's laws and that he was constrained to mirror them on earth. Indeed, James reiterated this sentiment in a speech to the English parliament in March 1610 when he noted:

> I will not be content that my power be disputed upon, but I shall ever be willing to make the reason appear of all my doings and rule my actions according to my laws.[8]

As Michael Hattaway has observed, James here 'concedes that his authority is not absolute but subject to his ruling justly under the law' (110). Nevertheless, this kind of statement could be taken as advocating absolutism, an extremely contentious mode of leadership that could be conflated with tyranny. James clearly states that his subjects have no right to question his power; only God has the ability to direct a monarch's decisions. This clearly troubled those Englishmen who embraced the role of parliament within the English constitution. Indeed, as W. B. Patterson has pointed out, the MP Edwin Sandys, for example, 'evidently saw in the king's project of union between England and Scotland an ominous challenge' both to parliament and 'to the laws and liberties of English subjects'.[9]

The imagery of divine-right monarchy is shadowed in Shakespeare's late plays. Leah Marcus, for example, draws attention to the imagery of Jupiter in *Cymbeline*, noting that James was frequently associated with the god (as, indeed, he is, under the name of Jove, in *Englands Wedding Garment*). She describes how, in the play, Jupiter descends on an eagle to 'uplift' Posthumus and to 'presage the Union of the Kingdoms' in a manner that might be taken as an oblique reference to the King.[10] Similarly, in Act 1 of *Pericles*, the titular character announces that 'King's are earth's gods' (1.1.104) in a manner that resonates with James's own beliefs and which potentially associates him with Pericles. However, Margaret Healy has warned about making complete allegorical comparisons between characters in the plays and England's monarch. As she demonstrates, Pericles is not an exemplary ruler and, as the play progresses, his character accrues 'important negative implications'.[11] He is, she explains, 'a prince who is seldom in his own state', who 'flees from danger without confronting it' and who may, 'through neglect and poor government, be introducing "corruption" into the virgin body of his daughter and his kingdom' (104). Healy's careful analysis highlights the tension present in the portrayal of Pericles and draws attention to the dangers of reading Shakespeare's late plays as full of courtly praise. James, if these references alluded to him at all, could be obliquely criticised as well as complimented: monarchical absolutism could be conflated with paternal tyranny; the notion of Anglo-Scottish union did not have to be wholeheartedly endorsed.

James's desire to unite his two nations has been perceived as a controlling motif in several of Shakespeare's plays. For example, just as *Englands Wedding Garment* evoked the Tudor myth of monarchical descent from Troy and Rome, so *Cymbeline* has been seen as a play that draws on the same story of origins, particularly in the Soothsayer's words at the end of Act 5 which describe 'imperial Caesar' uniting his favour 'with the radiant Cymbeline, / Which shines here in the west' (5.4.475–6). In Martin Butler's words, the notion of union is foregrounded here and power is seen to pass 'from ancient Troy and Rome to James's new British *imperium*'.[12] However, this evocation of union is not straightforward for, as both Butler and Marcus have observed, it had become a contentious matter by the time *Cymbeline* was performed. As Marcus explains, both the English and Scottish parliaments balked at the idea of unifying the two kingdoms' legal systems, and, in 1607, James was forced to resort to the courts to decide 'whether a Scotsman born since the proclamation of union had the right to defend his ownership of English property held in England in a court of law' (p. 124). The case was decided in 1608 and established that Scots born after James's accession to the

English throne (who were known as *post nati*) had the same rights under English law as Englishmen. Marcus draws attention to Posthumus's name and his position in *Cymbeline*, presenting him as 'a dramatic figure whose alienation and restoration symbolically parallel the fortunes of James's subjects "born after" [1603]' (p. 125). As Butler observes, though, the decision in the legal case was established only on the basis of the *post nati*'s common allegiance to the King, and thus 'kept English and Scots law separate by stressing subjection rather than citizenship'. 'In 1610,' Butler continues, 'it was simply not possible for *Cymbeline* to endorse British union: politically, single nationhood was already dead, and would remain merely an aspiration until the realms were integrated by statute in 1707' (p. 39). To see *Cymbeline* as an unequivocal allegory of British union, then, is to simplify its relationship with its historical moment too completely.

The unification project, however, remained a favourite subject of royal panegyric, and was forcefully evoked in January 1607 in the celebrations surrounding the wedding of James Hay, one of the King's Scottish favourites, and Honora Denny, daughter of Sir Edward Denny, an Englishman initially opposed to the marriage. Thomas Campion's *The Lord Hay's Masque* presented Hay and Denny's union as a microcosm of James's larger project for unification, seeing it as a preparation for the 'high and everliving Union / 'Tween Scots and English'.[13] However, despite its overtly encomiastic tone, the masque encodes anxieties about James's project. For example, David Lindley's modern translation of a Latin sonnet from the start of the masque, begins:

> To the most Invincible, most Serene James, King of Great Britain. I am uncertain, O King, whether you be the father of England and of united Scotland, or the husband, or neither, or both at once. That one man should join to himself a pair of wives at the same time, this, by your own prohibition, we believe unlawful. And further, for a parent to violate daughters in a marital embrace, who does not think this to be a sin? But by divine good fortune both marry you; yet only one is your consort, one also the conjugal love. (p. 221)

This sonnet echoes James's own words to parliament in 1603/4 where, extending the analogy that saw him the husband of the nation, he asserted that he hoped 'no man will be so vnreasonable as to thinke that I that am a Christian King vnder Gospel, should be a Polygamist and husband to two wives' (Sommerville, p. 136). In James's hands, this was a forceful argument for union, yet, although the sonnet echoes this sentiment and closes with an attempt to reconcile its anomalies, the verses remain strangely disturbing, layering the ideas of bigamy and incest on to the concept of national unification.

The sentiments expressed in this sonnet resonate strongly with the opening plot of *Pericles* in which the King of Antioch is discovered to be the incestuous lover of his own daughter. Interestingly, Butler identifies a similar motif in *Cymbeline*, noting that Innogen's 'proposed marriage with her stepbrother has a whiff of incest that signals the dangers of endogamy and the need to marry beyond the tribe' (p. 7). Suzanne Gossett reads Antiochus's incest as a form of tyranny, aligning his actions with those of Cleon, whose weak acceptance of famine and murder shows him to be indifferent to his subjects and the law.[14] Susan Bruce, meanwhile, has noted of this motif that it draws attention to the geographic territories evoked by the plays, and that it presents Shakespeare's protagonists with a choice between endogamy and exogamy.[15] Pericles escapes endogamy by choosing to voyage beyond his kingdom to find a bride, but immediately encounters it in its most extreme form on his arrival in Antioch. Bruce interprets this as Pericles' bid to escape the constraints of noble inter-marriage, but, with Campion's poem in mind, it is also possible to read it as an expression of anxiety about the unification project. While Constance Jordan suggests that debates concerning the liberties of the subject and the Union of the Kingdoms were shadowed in *Pericles*, Butler notes that the Scots were worried about the precedent of Anglo-Welsh union, which had left Wales a colony of England.[16] As Campion's poem, like *Pericles*, suggests, close ties are not always healthy or lawful, even though Campion's verses subsequently attempt to justify the unification of the kingdoms as a 'wondrous marriage' (Lindley, *Masques*, p. 221).

As the Hay/Denny nuptial celebrations show, James's politics of marriage was not used just as a convenient conceit through which to discuss national union; it also extended to material unions between noble families undertaken to heal rifts or seal alliances. The most famous of these, perhaps, was the 1606 marriage between Frances Howard and Robert Devereux, third earl of Essex, which cemented a union between two ancient and antagonistic families only to see it broken seven years later by a controversial legal annulment and the bride's remarriage to Robert Carr, another of James I's favourites. Critics have identified references to this controversial second marriage in several plays from the period: Lindley, for example, sees echoes of it in Middleton's and Rowley's *The Changeling*, while Lois Potter sees Frances Howard shadowed in the Jailer's Daughter from *The Two Noble Kinsmen*, who, at the age of eighteen, 'may be' a virgin.[17] Gordon McMullan, in the same vein, notes that the divorce scene in *King Henry VIII* might have reminded a contemporary audience of Frances Howard's annulment.[18]

The most important marriages of the Jacobean reign were, however, those proposed for the royal children. Although, in *Basilikon Doron*, James had advised his son that he would 'rathest haue you to marie one that were fully of your own Religion' (2:78), negotiations were underway from as early as 1607 to marry Prince Henry to a Spanish Catholic princess. Indeed, in November 1608, the French ambassador to London expressed his anxieties about a secret mission he suspected was being carried out by a representative from the Hapsburg archdukes: 'It is possible,' he said, 'that it is to make inquiries about marriages between Spain and England.'[19] Although James liked to present himself as a *Rex pacificus*, smoothing national and international discord through dynastic alliances, such a marriage for Henry was controversial: it obviously perturbed the French ambassador, and it was also not welcomed by many English Protestants who saw in the young prince a new champion of their religion.

Henry was inaugurated as Prince of Wales on 5 June 1610, amid ceremonies that emphasised continuity with the Tudor reign. For example, Queen Anne's court masque, *Tethys' Festival*, performed the same day, placed particular emphasis on Milford Haven, the location of Henry Tudor's landing on his way to wrest the English throne from Richard III. Many critics have noted that this motif resounds strongly with *Cymbeline*'s emphasis on the Welsh port: Butler, for example, observes that 'the coincidence between the play's geography and the summer's political symbolism is very striking' (p. 5). More important, though, is the masque's deliberate evocation of the Elizabethan golden age, which culminates with the nymph, Tethys, performed by Queen Anne herself, passing Astraea's sword to Henry. Astraea, the goddess of justice, was one of Queen Elizabeth's favoured iconographical incarnations. Therefore, as Graham Parry has noted:

> The invocation of the sacred name and the passing of Astraea's sword to the new Prince of Wales indicates that Prince Henry was consciously trying to revive the semi-magical aura of golden majesty that had surrounded Elizabeth and transfer it to himself.[20]

This was Queen Anne's masque, so Henry cannot be assumed to have controlled its iconography. However, a strong strain of Elizabethan imagery certainly informed other entertainments undertaken for and by the prince, and his own masque, *Oberon, the Fairy Prince*, in which he danced the leading role on 1 January 1611, took its influence from Spenser's *The Faerie Queene*, constructing Henry as a fairy knight, with an affinity to King Arthur and the ancient world of chivalry.

The prince's court was renowned for its decorum and the prince for his love of arms and horses. He was interested in the navy, befriended Sir Walter Ralegh, and, as R. Malcolm Smuts has explained, 'rapidly gained a reputation as a champion of Protestant and national interests'.[21] Indeed, one of his admirers proclaimed of him:

The eyes, the hopes of all the Protestant world be fixed upon your Highness, all expecting your gracious faithfulness, and readiness in the extirpation of that man of sin [the Pope]. (Smuts, p. 30)

Unlike his father, whose pacific and arguably pro-Spanish policies frustrated the more militant Protestants at his court, Henry served as a rallying point for those who wanted to intervene actively in Europe's religious conflicts.

The choice of Frederick Henry from the House of Orange as his brother-in-law might then be deemed profoundly acceptable to the prince. Indeed, several critics, notably Richard Proudfoot and Muriel Bradbrook, have suggested that Frederick Henry and Henry Frederick might have provided inspiration for Shakespeare's heroes in *The Two Noble Kinsmen*. Pointing out that previous versions of the tale were published under the title *Palamon and Arcite*, Lois Potter has suggested that 'the choice of the unusual title *The Two Noble Kinsmen* may have been intended to recall the short-lived friendship and brotherhood of the young English and German princes' (p. 37). Frederick Henry arrived in London in October 1612 to be married to Elizabeth, James I's only surviving daughter. Although he was not a king's son, and despite being disparagingly perceived by John Chamberlain, a court observer, as 'much too young and small-timbered to undertake such a task', Frederick was generally regarded with favour because of his staunchly Protestant faith.[22] Indeed, in Parry's words, although he was young, he was 'widely regarded as the leader of continental Protestantism' (p. 95).

In early November 1612, before the marriage had taken place and to the great dismay of everyone, Prince Henry suddenly died, perhaps of typhoid fever. The wedding was immediately postponed and the nation was overtaken by a huge outpouring of grief. A great number of mourning pamphlets were published, eulogising Henry as, for example, 'The Prince of men' who 'Held all the eyes of Christendome intent / Vpon his youthfull hopes'.[23] His funeral was held on 7 December with a procession of 2,000 mourners. Two months later, on 14 February 1613, Princess Elizabeth finally married Frederick Henry. This quick succession of funeral and wedding has been seen as an influence on several plays. Potter, for example, suggests the 'dark tone' of *The Two Noble Kinsmen*'s ending might be accounted for by the royal funeral, while the royal wedding might seen an appropriate context for the first scene (p. 37). Similarly, McMullan notes that '*Henry VIII* shares in the mixed negative and positive emotions induced by this rapid succession of funeral and wedding' (p. 65). Although it should be remembered that the much earlier *Hamlet*, too, sees the funeral baked meats coldly furnishing forth the marriage tables, allusive connections between these events and *The Two Noble Kinsmen* are striking, particularly in the play's emphasis on its main characters' equestrian skills and in its choice of imagery, which J. R. Mulryne suggests echoes Prince Henry's interests in horses, armour and sailing.[24]

With Henry's death, the hopes of militant Protestants who wished to see England intervening in the religious wars of the continent became focused on Princess Elizabeth. Indeed, as McMullan notes, *Henry VIII*'s conclusion, which dramatises the birth of Elizabeth I, might draw oblique parallels with her namesake Elizabeth Stuart, upon whom English Protestants' hopes now rested (pp. 64, 70). Archbishop Cranmer's concluding prophecy in *Henry VIII*, which predicts James I's accession and sees 'the honour and the greatness of his name' creating 'new nations' (5.4.51–2), might not just be a reference to the union of the kingdoms, but also, perhaps, evokes hopes that the Stuart kings would promote colonialism and an active foreign policy. Elizabeth Stuart and her husband, supported by James I, would, in this context, become the heirs of Elizabeth I, actively encouraging the Protestant cause in Europe and beyond. In Willy Maley's words, the late plays see 'union and plantation supplanting succession as the touchstone of sovereignty'.[25] Nevertheless, as Margaret Healy has observed, James's management of his state was heavily criticised in this period as people wondered about his instincts to make peace with Spain, be lenient to recusants and to seek Spanish marriages for his children. James was, Healy notes, 'an expert purveyor of adages about kingship, but for many of his subjects he too seldom put them into action' (105).

Geography

On 15 February 1613, the night after Elizabeth and Frederick's wedding, gentlemen from the Middle Temple and Lincoln's Inn presented a masque at court whose main dancers were clothed as princes of Virginia. As Parry has noted, such a masque 'would have appealed to Prince Henry', who was interested in colonial projects, and 'might have veiled an anti-Spanish attitude' (98–9). Before his death, Henry's support was often requested by favourers of colonialism: for example, in 1610, Thomas Blenerhasset, an English gentleman involved in the plantation of Ulster, dedicated a book on the project to Henry, begging him to support its recommendations so that the plantation '*would be Peopled plentifully, yea fortified and replenished with such and so many goodly strong Corporations, as it would be a wonder to beholde*'.[26] Among Blenerhasset's aims were, 'The securing of that wilde Countrye to the Crowne of Englande'; increasing the Crown's revenue; establishing the 'Puritie of Religion there'; and ensuring that those involved in the project were enriched.

Maley has noted that 'Union and empire inevitably invoked images of amplification and expansion', pointing out that colonies shored up a deficiency in national identity, but could also become sites of resistance to an imagined or imposed unity (p. 152). An example of such resistance can be found in libellous verses criticising a 1612 lottery intended to raise funds for the Virginia Company. 'If either lotteryes or lottes / Could rid us of these rascall Scotts', the libel begins, 'Who would not venter then with thankes'. Virginia, it asserts, is 'made the toombe / For us, to make these rogues more roome', concluding 'Let them be gulld that list to bee; / Virginia getts no more of mee'.[27] Here, anti-union and anti-Scottish sentiments are linked with the colonial project: the Scots have taken over to such an extent that the indigenous English population is being forced to leave home for Virginia. Colonies could certainly help to confirm notions of English identity by securing a 'wilde Countrye to the Crowne of Englande', but they could also reveal the myth of union by emphasising the discord between its constituent parts. Indeed, such tensions have been identified in *Cymbeline*, which, as Butler notes, makes clearly evident the 'shortfalls between the rhetoric and reality of "Britain"': the Welsh are 'curiously absent from the play,' he points out; Wales is 'a place of mountains occupied by outlaws'; and Milford Haven is always referred to by its English name 'and never as Aberdaugleddyf or any other title more in keeping with the place or supposed period'. In sum, it is unclear 'whether Wales is part of Cymbeline's Britain or not' (p. 39).

The play most frequently associated with the colonial project, however, is *The Tempest*, the plot of which has been variously linked to the Virginia Company's experiences in the Americas, to the problems in Ireland, and to Africa and the Mediterranean. In the nineteenth century, Edmond Malone argued that the play was influenced by pamphlets detailing the wreck off Bermuda of one of the Virginia Company's ships and this interpretation has been widely embraced, with scholars suggesting that the play was informed by texts such as Sylvester Jourdan's *A Discovery of the Barmudas* and the Council of Virginia's *True Declaration of the State of the Colonie in Virginia*.[28] Jourdan's pamphlet, for example, begins with an account of a tempest that caused his ship to be 'so shaken, torne, and leaked' that its exhausted crew resolved, 'without any hope of their liues, to shut up the hatches, and to [commit] themselues to the mercy of the sea'.[29] Given fresh hope by the appearance of land, they were shipwrecked on the Bermudas, but were able to build a new vessel and finally arrived in Jamestown, Virginia, in June 1610. There are obvious similarities here with *The Tempest*, although it should be remembered that the shipwreck in the opening scene of Shakespeare's play is discovered, ultimately, to be the result of illusion and Ariel's magic, rather than of meteorological force.

Ariel, himself, like the coarser Caliban, has been interpreted from a colonial perspective as a native subjected to an usurping imperialism. Caliban, Barbara Fuchs suggests, recalls a model developed by the English to justify colonisation: the subject in need of civilising. Similarly, Ariel incarnates 'the colonizer's fantasy of a pliant, essentially accommodating, and useful subject'.[30] However, as Fuchs observes, '*The Tempest* makes sense only when viewed from the perspective of multiple contexts': its island should not be isolated 'somewhere in the Americas', but should be considered, for example, in the context of Ireland, the indigenous population of which (like the native Americans) was constructed by the English as savages and located 'at a stage of social development long since surpassed by England' (62, 52). This is certainly true of Blenerhasset's pamphlet, which makes no distinction between the Irish and beasts, conflating 'the cruell wood-kerne' and 'the deuowring Woolfe' with 'other suspitious Irish' (A3v). The Irish, Fuchs says, were perceived to require civilising by England 'in much the same way that England had required colonizing by Rome' (52). In other words, civilised themselves by prior Roman influence, Englishmen now set out to export their civilisation to more 'savage' peoples, often, as Blenerhasset intended to do, by simply taking over their lands and filling them with colonists. As Stephen Greenblatt has pointed out, Caliban's response to this process of civilisation comes in his famous lines to Miranda: 'You taught me language, and my profit on't / Is, I know how to curse' (1.2.363–4).[31]

Shakespeare's plays in this period, then, participate in discourses about nationhood and national identity in the context of colonial expansion, overseas travel and the state's relationship with foreign powers. James's kingdom, itself contentiously divided into English, Scots, Welsh and Irish, was located within a Europe where major Catholic powers were in constant conflict with each other and with the Protestant nations of the north. Hostilities between France and Spain had temporarily ceased with the signing of the Peace of Vervins in 1598, but, until 1609, Spain continued to wage war in the Netherlands. English soldiers, unemployed at home, hired themselves out as mercenaries in the foreign wars and it is this choice that confronts Bolt, the brothel servant in *Pericles*'s Mytilene. Castigated by Marina for his unsavoury profession, Bolt offers the riposte:

> What would you have me do? Go to the wars, would you, where a man may serve seven years for the loss of a leg and have not money enough in the end to buy him a wooden one? (4.5.173–6)

As Gossett has observed, 'Bolt blames his objectionable service on restricted employment opportunities that have more to do with London than Mytilene' (p. 123). *Pericles*'s exotic settings clearly shadow English concerns, evoking anxieties about international conflict and travel. Indeed, Gossett notes that *Pericles* was written at a time of debate about the purposes of travel, and draws attention to dramatic satires on unscrupulous, foolish and unrealistic voyagers in plays such as *Every Man Out of His Humour* (1600), *Eastward Ho!* (1605) and *The Knight of the Burning Pestle* (1607) (p. 132).

Travel can either confirm one in one's national identity or confound it. For example, in Ben Jonson's *Masque of Augurs* (1622), the ridiculous Vangoose, who appears to be a Dutchman, is discovered to be 'a *Britaine* borne, [who] learn'd to misuse his own tounge in travell, and now speakes all languages in ill *English*'.[32] Similarly, Lady Politic-Would-Be, in Jonson's *Volpone* (1606), travels to Venice, where she affects continental mannerisms and fashions to her own (and her nation's) embarrassment. However, undertaken with the proper instruction and within circumscribed limits, travel does not always have to disrupt identity and can be pursued for the benefit of the state. In the same year as *Volpone*, Sir Thomas Palmer published his *Essay of the Meanes how to make our Trauailes, into forraine Countries, the more profitable and honourable*, dedicating it to Prince Henry. Claiming that 'this subiect hath not worne an English habite heretofore', this work set out to help travellers make 'themselues more Compleat in all things' (sig. A2v). Foreign journeys, for Palmer, broadened the mind, provided beneficial knowledge for the nation and, above all, enabled travellers to 'liue a quiet, peaceable and godly life' on their return home (sig. A3v). In other words, travel, for Palmer, reinforced one's national identity, rather than challenging it.

The connection of travel with personal and national identities is clearly present in plays such as *Pericles*, *The Winter's Tale* and *The Tempest*, particularly in motifs of romanesque wandering and the recovery of lost children, wives and lands. Gossett, for example, suggests *Pericles's* voyages are metaphorical, and that he is searching for identity, inner peace and fulfilment (p. 126), while John Gillies suggests that the plays' settings are little more than geographic wraiths upon which are played out human narratives of exposure and return.[33] Just as the idea of Britain was presented to the Jacobean public as a return to a lost unity, so a play such as *Pericles* concludes with homecomings that return daughters to fathers and wives to husbands. However, as Gillies notes, by changing Pericles's daughter's name to Marina, 'Shakespeare connects her to the principal symbol of exposure, of spatial immensity and of ungrounded contingency – the sea' (p. 183). The play's conclusion, he implies, is partial, seeing 'two hopelessly ungrounded castaways "return" to each other'. In other words, as with *The Tempest*, there is, in *Pericles*, the possibility that there is 'no ground [and] no home' (p. 190).

Fuchs suggests that *The Tempest* is pervaded with the sense of an Eastern Empire encroaching on Europe, and most interestingly observes that 'the

European "center" of the text [is made] simultaneously the origin of colonial adventure and the target of another empire's expansionism' (p. 46). However strongly England (or the new, united Britain) was defined by panegyrists as a unified, imperialistic nation, this unity and its concomitant expansionism was constantly challenged and undermined. Nowhere is this conflict more pronounced than in England's relationship with its merchant navy, whose relationship with piracy was, as Fuchs points out, far from clear.[34] Conflict with Spanish ships on the high seas was seen by militant Protestants as an expression of English might and national pride, yet, particularly after James's peace with Spain in 1603, this kind of aggression was clearly a problem and undermined his conception of Britain as a harmonious nation whose pacific influence could be spread over the world.

After his accession, James made six proclamations about piracy and, in 1612, issued a general pardon to English pirates. That January, John Chamberlain wrote to his friend Dudley Carleton with the news:

> Many of our pirates come home upon their pardon for life and goods, but the greater part stand still aloof in Ireland, because they are not offered the same conditions, but only life; howsoever this course may serve the present turn, yet it is feared it may prove of ill consequence hereafter. (p. 124)

The association here of 'our pirates' with Ireland sees a conflation of identities that associates the lawless seamen with a lawless nation, at once complicating notions of British unity and obliquely registering the potential threat incarnated in the colony: it is no wonder that Chamberlain thought that ill consequences might follow from calling such wild men home.

Interestingly, around the same time, Carleton, who was stationed in Venice, received news that a Low Country ship had been 'set upon by three Tunis-men' who had fought with her for three days, but who had 'held it out stoutly though the master was slain in the fight'. The sea was 'so much molested with pirates', he explained, 'these Venetians have had the ill luck of late that they can no sooner peep out of the gulf but they are had by the backs'.[35] Earlier, in 1608, the Archdukes' representative in London had refused to set sail for Brussels because of a fear of pirates, presumably, this time, from the Protestant Netherlands (La Boderie, 4:63). The nationality of a pirate, in effect, could be used iconographically as a means to define the savagery and barbarism of an abhorred other against one's own civilised nation and its trading partners.

It is exactly this strategy that is invoked in *Pericles*, in which the 'great pirate Valdes' not only bears a Spanish name but, it has been suggested, recalls the historical figure of Don Pedro de Valdes, an admiral in the 1588 Spanish Armada fleet. Edmond Malone, for example, has observed that 'making one of this Spaniard's ancestors a pirate, was probably relished by the [play's] audience'.[36] It should be noted that two of the Armada commanders were named Valdes (the other was Diego Flores de Valdes) and that both had been involved in Spain's colonialist enterprises in America. Furthermore, both commanders' names were already current in theatrical circles for they were invoked in 1607 in Thomas Dekker's *Whore of Babylon* as admirals in the Babylonian fleet that was assembling to attack Fairy Land. In other words, nearly twenty years after the event, the Spaniards (here shadowed in the Babylonians) were still being aligned with a malignant, usurping religion (Babylon being commonly used as a figure for Catholic Rome) in a manner that shows how powerfully Elizabethan and Spenserian motifs could still be used to define a national Protestant identity.

Religion

While Prince Henry served as a focal point for anti-Spanish, militant Protestant aspirations, James I's religious policy, from the start of his reign, was one of conciliation. Although it has often been seen as an example of the King's intransigence towards Puritans, his Hampton Court Conference, held in January 1604, was conceived to deal with problems within the Church of England, and, in Patterson's words, to free it 'from any scandals which undermined its effectiveness or diminished its reputation' (p. 44). In other words, James was intent on creating a unified and peaceful church, just as he was set on creating a unified and peaceful nation, and hoped to walk a middle way between Protestant extremism and Catholicism. His most long-lasting and significant religious achievement was undoubtedly the publication of the Authorised Version (or King James) Bible in 1611, which was designed to replace both the Bishops' Bible and the Geneva Bible, and thus to provide a single, authoritative text that would ensure uniformity of worship throughout his kingdom. James also attempted to calm the troubled European religious scene by proposing an ecumenical council to the Pope, intended to 'ascertain the truth among "so many sects of religion"' (p. 69). This plan was first discussed in September 1605 by the papal nuncio in Flanders and the Earl of Arundel and, a little time later, some Spanish interest in such a council was forthcoming (pp. 69–74). However, the discovery of the Gunpowder Plot in November 1605 raised tensions between Protestant and Catholics to such a level that religious debate with Spain was rendered virtually impossible.

James described the Gunpowder Plot as 'an attempt by Roman Catholics to destroy both the place and the persons associated with the passage of "cruel Lawes (as they say) … against their Religion' (Patterson, p. 75), and reverberations from it echoed throughout the kingdom. Even Dudley Carleton,

John Chamberlain's correspondent, found himself implicated through his association with the Earl of Northumberland, whose cousin, Thomas Percy, was alleged to have been one of the plot's prime movers. In its aftermath, James and parliament instituted the controversial Oath of Allegiance, which compelled English Catholics, among other things, to acknowledge that the Pope had 'no power or authority to depose the King', and that 'neither the Pope nor any other person' had the power to absolve them of their oath (Patterson, pp. 79–80).

In *Cymbeline*, as Donna Hamilton persuasively argues, the Innogen plot can be seen to dramatise 'the struggles of the true church against the false church', using 'primitive history to argue that the true church originated in Britain' at a time before the Roman church brought christianity to England.[37] In other words, Hamilton reads *Cymbeline* as, in part, a debate about the legitimacy of Catholicism in England. However, rather than reading the play as straightforwardly endorsing a Protestant line, she draws attention to the character of Belarius, suggesting that he represents a threatened English Catholic subject. He is, she says, 'the conflicted subject who has good reason to withhold his allegiance from the king and yet who finally comes forward and gives support' (p. 130). Although this interpretation is perhaps a little unnuanced, it is nonetheless suggestive and shows how religious meanings could readily be uncovered in early modern plays.

The Oath of Allegiance caused storms of controversy in Catholic Europe with the Pope and Cardinal Bellarmine writing to English Catholics to forbid them from taking it. In 1607/8, James published the anonymous *An Apologie for the Oath of Allegiance*, refuting the Pope and the Cardinal's letters and calling into question what he called Bellarmine's 'strongest argument', that no Pope had ever 'either commanded to be killed, or allowed the slaughter of any Prince whatsoever'.[38] The exchange of opinions continued across the English Channel with Bellarmine and others publishing responses to James's work, and interested observers paying close attention to the debate. Carleton, for example, writing from Eton in September 1608, informed Chamberlain that the King was 'much troubled about an answer of his book, which is lately come over and done, as is thought, the most part by [the Jesuit, Robert] Parsons' (p. 105). The assassination of the French King Henri IV in May 1610 by a Catholic zealot gave these issues additional urgency: in Patterson's words, this 'one-time lay monk [was] believed to have been influenced by Roman Catholic theologians who justified tyrannicide' (p. 101). Indeed, it is possible that echoes of these crises can be perceived in Shakespeare's plays. For example, Butler draws attention in *Cymbeline* to 'Iachimo's claim that every touch of Innogen's hand would "force the feeler's soul / To th'oath of loyalty" (1.6.100–1)', adding that the Henri IV assassination might be reflected in Innogen's fierce words to Pisanio, her servant: 'O, get thee from my sight, / Thou gav'st me poison. Dangerous fellow, hence, / Breathe not where princes are' (5.4.236–8).

One of the most contentious questions surrounding the Oath of Allegiance was whether the Pope had secular as well as spiritual authority. According to James, Bellarmine had asserted that 'Church-men are exempted from the power of earthly Kings', continuing that they owed them 'no subiection euen in temporall matters'.[39] Suggestively, in *Henry VIII*, Wolsey's downfall is brought about because he is found to have been acting without the King's authority and also because he 'writ to th' Pope against the King' (3.2.287). In fact, as the Duke of Suffolk informs him, 'all those things you have done of late / By your power legative within this kingdom / Fall into th' compass *praemunire*' (3.2.338–40), or, in other words, they assert the jurisdiction of the Pope in England and deny Henry VIII's supremacy. The echoes here with contemporary Jacobean debates about the Oath of Allegiance are striking.

Donna Hamilton has also identified in Wolsey allusions to a topical Catholic threat. However, she sees this as one that was closer to home. The end of Henry VIII's reign, she points out, saw the fall from favour of the powerful Howard faction, represented in Shakespeare's play by Wolsey and the Duke of Suffolk (p. 11). The Howard family, who were known Catholic sympathisers, were in the ascendant for the first time since the end of Henry's reign, with the Frances Howard/Essex/Carr debacle being just one instance of James's patronage and approbation. Hamilton identifies an anti-Howard slant in *Henry VIII*, suggesting that the 'values and projects' of the Jacobean Howards were associated with the play's character of Wolsey 'and the values he represents' (p. 164). 'The play manages its assessment and criticism of certain court policies,' Hamilton suggests, 'by giving a presence to the one value of the group being criticised – their catholicism – that, in the England of the early seventeenth century, could virtually always be used to construct someone's influence as inimical to England' (p. 164). Drawing attention to the controversial fiscal measures introduced by the King and his council after the dissolution of parliament in 1610, she notes that Queen Katherine's speech against taxation resonates with the play's contemporary moment and points out that, after the death of Lord Treasurer Salisbury in the spring of 1612, the Treasury was run by commissioners who included the central figures in the Howard faction, Northampton, Suffolk and Somerset (pp. 169–70). *Henry VIII*'s religious and political messages certainly seem to combine to promote a strongly Protestant message and to discredit the ancient Howard family, presenting Wolsey as a man who 'Does buy and sell his honour as he pleases, / And for his own advantage' and whose 'ambitious finger' is to be found in every man's pie (1.1.51–2, 192–3).

Nevertheless, it is important to remember, as Palfrey does, that all early modern plays were subject to the 'bustle and complexity' of the theatre (p. 5). Although a play like *Henry VIII* might endorse a Protestant line, its meanings could be changed in performance. For example, as Gossett has remarked, *Pericles* was performed by a group of Catholic actors in the Christmas season of 1609–10 in the North Riding of Yorkshire alongside *King Lear*, a 'St Christopher play' and *The Travails of the Three English Brothers*, which included a scene in which the Pope was addressed as 'The stair of men's salvations and the key / That binds or looseth our transgressions' (p. 87). With its convent-like temple of Diana and its maiden priests, *Pericles* was ripe with possibilities for Catholic symbolism and Gossett suspects that the play was silently modified to promote a Catholic interpretation (88). This is certainly not to say that the play was written with Catholic symbolism in mind: like Queen Henrietta Maria's adoption of romance motifs twenty years later to promote her own brand of Catholicism at the Caroline court, this type of tale lent itself neatly to religious appropriation.

Ultimately, then, early modern plays were multivalent literary artefacts the meanings of which could be shifted by the intentions of an actor or the perception of an audience member. Nevertheless, it is possible to see in them allusions to contemporary anxieties and events. James I's scholarly, rather than military, approach to Europe's religious controversies, and his quest for religious and national unity were clearly not going to please everyone. His policies and his personal behaviour attracted censure, echoes of which can inevitably be found in the literature and drama of the period. As a Scottish king ruling a fragmented nation comprised of English, Welsh, Scots, as well as Irish and American colonists, his was quite clearly an invidious position. It was, in the end, just as likely to cause debate as the Roman Catholic opinions of Cardinal Bellarmine or the truly contentious prospect of socks.

NOTES

1. 'Lord Digbie's Letter, etc', Newberry Library, Case MS F 455.51, p. 16.
2. The letter must date from either 1617, when James I returned to Scotland, or from 1633, when Charles I travelled to Scotland to be crowned.
3. Anon., *Englands Wedding Garment, or a preparation to King IAMES his Royall Coronation* (London, 1603), sig. A2v.
4. James I, 'A Speach, as it was Delivered in the Vpper Hovse of the Parliament', in *King James VI and I: Political Writings*, ed. Johann P. Sommerville (Cambridge: Cambridge University Press, 1994), p. 136.
5. David M. Bergeron, *Shakespeare's Romances and the Royal Family* (Lawrence: University Press of Kansas, 1985), pp. 113–16.
6. Philippa Berry, 'Reversing History', *European Journal of English Studies* 1 (1997), pp. 367–87, at p. 385.

7. Simon Palfrey, *Late Shakespeare: A New World of Words* (Oxford, 1997), p. 5.

8. James's speech to parliament, 21 March 1610, quoted in Michael Hattaway, 'Tragedy and Political Authority', in Claire McEachern (ed.), *The Cambridge Companion to Shakespearean Tragedy* (Cambridge: Cambridge University Press, 2002), pp. 103–22, at p. 110.

9. W. B. Patterson, *King James VI and I and the Reunion of Christendom* (Cambridge: Cambridge University Press, 1997; repr. 2000), p. 67.

10. Leah S. Marcus, *Puzzling Shakespeare: Local Reading and Its Discontents* (Berkeley: University of California Press, 1988), pp. 110–19.

11. Margaret Healy, 'Pericles and the Pox', in Jennifer Richards and James Knowles (eds.), *Shakespeare's Late Plays: New Readings* (Edinburgh: Edinburgh University Press, 1999), pp. 92–107, at p. 94.

12. Martin Butler (ed.), *Cymbeline* (Cambridge: Cambridge University Press, 2005), p. 38.

13. See David Lindley (ed.), *Court Masques* (Oxford: Oxford University Press, 1995), p. 18, lines 18–19. See also p. 220.

14. Suzanne Gossett (ed.), *Pericles* (London: Thomson Learning, 2004; repr. 2006), p. 125.

15. I am grateful to Dr Bruce for sharing her views on this subject in a personal communication. See also Otto Rank, *The Incest Themes in Literature and Legend* (Baltimore: Johns Hopkins University Press, 1992), pp. 271–300.

16. Constance Jordan, *Shakespeare's Monarchies: Ruler and Subject in the Romances* (Ithaca: Cornell University Press, 1997), p. 53; Butler (ed.), *Cymbeline*, p. 39.

17. David Lindley, *The Trials of Frances Howard* (London: Routledge, 1993), p. 78; Lois Potter (ed.), *The Two Noble Kinsmen* (London: Thomson Learning, 1997; repr. 2002), p. 37.

18. Gordon McMullan (ed.), *King Henry VIII* (London: Thomson Learning, 2000; repr. 2007), p. 124.

19. La Boderie, *Ambassades de Monsieur de la Boderie*, 5 vols. (Paris, 1750), vol. IV, p. 83.

20. Graham Parry, *The Golden Age Restor'd: The Culture of the Stuart Court, 1603–42* (Manchester: Manchester University Press, 1981; repr. 1985), pp. 73–7.

21. R. Malcolm Smuts, *Court Culture and the Origins of a Royalist Tradition in Early Stuart England* (Philadelphia: University of Pennsylvania Press, 1987), p. 29.

22. John Chamberlain, *The Chamberlain Letters*, ed. Elizabeth McClure Thomson (New York: Putnam, 1965), p. 72.

23. Thomas Campion, *Songs of Mourning* (London, 1613), sig. A2r–v.

24. J. R. Mulryne, 'Shakespeare's *Knight's Tale*: *Two Noble Kinsmen* and the Tradition of Chivalry', in M. T. Jones-Davies (ed.), *Le Roman de chevalerie au temps de la Renaissance* (Paris: Jean Touzot, 1987), pp. 75–106, at pp. 77–8.

25. Willy Maley, 'Postcolonial Shakespeare: British Identity Formation and *Cymbeline*', in Richards and Knowles (eds.), *Shakespeare's Late Plays*, pp. 145–57, at p. 152.

26. Thomas Blenerhasset, *A Direction for the Plantation in Vlster* (London, 1610), sig. A2v.

27. Bodleian Library, MS Rawl. Poet. 26, fol. 1r. See also the 'Early Stuart Libels' database, http://www.earlystuartlibels.net/htdocs/index.html, accessed April 2008.

28. Edmond Malone, *An Account of the Incidents, from which the Title and Part of the Story of Shakespeare's Tempest Were Derived* (London: C. and R. Baldwin, 1808).

29. Sylvester Jourdan, *A Discovery of the Barmudas* (London, 1610), pp. 4–5.

30. Barbara Fuchs, 'Conquering Islands: Contextualizing *The Tempest*', *Shakespeare Quarterly* 48.1 (1997), pp. 45–62, at p. 53.

31. Stephen Greenblatt, *Learning to Curse: Essays in Early Modern Culture* (London: Routledge, 1990; repr. 1992), p. 25.

32. Ben Jonson, *The Masque of Augurs*, in C. H. Herford, Percy Simpson, and Evelyn Simpson (eds.), *Ben Jonson*, 11 vols. (Oxford: Oxford University Press, 1925–52), vol. VII, p. 633 (lines 111–13).

33. John Gillies, 'Place and Space in Three Late Plays', in Richard Dutton and Jean E. Howard (eds.), *A Companion to Shakespeare's Works: The Poems, Problem Comedies, Late Plays* (Oxford: Blackwell Publishing, 2003; repr. 2006), pp. 175–93.

34. Barbara Fuchs, 'Faithless Empires: Pirates, Renegadoes, and the English Nation', *Journal of English Literary History* 67 (2000), pp. 45–69.

35. Dudley Carleton, *Dudley Carleton to John Chamberlain, 1603–1624*, ed. Maurice Lee Jr. (New Brunswick: Rutgers University Press, 1972), p. 121.

36. Edmond Malone, *Supplement to the Edition of Shakespeare's Plays Published in 1778*, 2 vols. (London: C. Bathurst etc., 1780), vol. II, p. 105.

37. Donna B. Hamilton, *Shakespeare and the Politics of Protestant England* (Lexington: University Press of Kentucky, 1992), pp. 11, 129.

38. Anon., *Triplici nodo, triplex cuneus. Or An Apologie for the Oath of Allegiance* (London, 1607), p. 64.

39. James I, *An Apologie for the Oath of Allegiance ... with A Premonition* (London, 1609), p. 20.

5

RUSS McDONALD

'You speak a language that I understand not': listening to the last plays

Around 1608, Shakespeare changed direction. He had done so before, notably in taking up the tragic mode at the turn of the century.[1] After following that impulse through the sequence of major tragedies, he seems to have been drawn to a different kind of story, devising a new dramatic mode and giving his characters a new style of poetry to speak. When he had completed *Macbeth* and perhaps *Coriolanus* or *Antony and Cleopatra* (or perhaps both), he helped to finish *Pericles*, collaborating with George Wilkins or possibly rescuing an effort Wilkins had begun; between 1608 and 1611 he wrote three plays on his own, *Cymbeline*, *The Winter's Tale* and *The Tempest*; at the end of this phase, from about 1611 to 1613, he collaborated with John Fletcher on *Henry VIII*, *The Two Noble Kinsmen*, and *Cardenio*, now lost. Modern scholarship cannot decide what to call these seven plays, indeed can scarcely agree on what to call any one of them: Comedy? Romance? Pastoral? Tragicomedy?[2] Whatever the designation, Shakespeare's shift from tragedy to the new form coincided with, and is related to – both as cause and effect – his development of a poetic style like nothing he (or anybody else) had composed before: it is audacious, irregular, ostentatious, playful, and difficult. What follows amounts to a descriptive account of this late verse, especially its relation to the experimental form.

The last plays have provoked a wide range of responses, from Edward Dowden's reverential, Victorian picture of the playwright comfortably resting 'on the heights' after achieving spiritual victory and serenity, to Lytton Strachey's modernist view that Shakespeare was bored, 'bored with people, bored with real life, bored with drama, bored, in fact, with everything but poetical dreams'.[3] Whatever judgement one favours, the late plays are difficult to listen to and hard to read. With the aim of furnishing a kind of tool kit for attending to them, I begin by identifying some of the major stylistic features that differentiate this poetry from Shakespeare's earlier forms; this is followed by a demonstration of correspondences between the structure of the poetry and the shape of the dramas at large; and the essay concludes by

91

claiming that these poetic properties adumbrate their creator's ambivalent views of art, language, masculinity and femininity, the theatre, and his own professional career. The sovereignty of contextual study over the past three decades has threatened to make close analysis of poetic features seem tedious, but I hope that such scrutiny will be justified by its power to reveal the larger implications of style.

The technical features that make Shakespeare's late style distinctive can be enumerated in a few sentences.[4] Ellipsis exerts a constant pressure on sound and sense as the poet concentrates expression, omitting sounds and words that in an earlier phase of composition he would have retained. Connectives between clauses are sometimes removed, and thus the words and phrases that remain make the verse sound unusually 'distilled'. Syntax becomes convoluted, often confusingly so. The number of deformed phrases, directional shifts and intricately constructed sentences is exceptional for the period and exceptional for Shakespeare. Related to this grammatical complexity is the playwright's fondness for parenthesis and for extending sentences with strings of non-restrictive elements.[5] Repetition of various units – letters, words, phrases, rhythms – becomes more prominent and sometimes insistent, patterning forecast in the incantatory doublings in *Macbeth* and resounding most audibly in the extraordinary echoing effects of *The Tempest*. Blank verse, usually a guarantor of order and regularity, is now aggressively irregular, encompassing long lines, chopped lines, unruly lines, enjambed lines, light or weak endings, frequent stops or shifts of direction, and other threats to lineal integrity. Metaphors tend to be gestured at rather than articulated at length, and one figure often crowds after another. Crucially, language has been separated from speaker. That Shakespeare learned to make his persons sound like themselves, especially as he reached professional maturity in the mid-1590s, is recognized as one of the triumphs of his craft, but by about 1607 or so, he begins to attenuate the link between speech and speaker. Character becomes less important than the 'vivid and emotionally charged' action and 'some general design in the language of the play'.[6] Finally, governing all these technical features is a pervasive self-consciousness, an artist's playful delight in calling attention to his own virtuosity.

Elision

Shakespeare's late verse is frequently described figuratively as 'elliptical', meaning 'puzzling', but to take the term literally is to notice the technical effect of one of its cardinal features.[7] In seeking intensity, the mature poet experiments with a method based on distillation and reduction, on the suppression of certain grammatical elements (and the corresponding promotion of others), on subordination and casting away. The removal of disposable syllables and words consequently places intense pressure on those sounds and signs that remain and often troubles the poetic surface, playing havoc especially with metrical regularity.

Opening consonants increasingly tend to be dropped, as in "'em' for 'them'. Frequently phrases and words such as "of the" and "in the" and "it" are stripped of vowels or consonants and thus deprived of some syllabic weight so that, in metrical terms, a complete iamb or trochee is reduced to half its rhythmic status. Occasionally words may be deprived of auditory value altogether, as in Hermione's 'not a jar o' th' clock behind' (1.2.43).[8] Obviously those cases in which simple suffixes such as *ed* are reduced to *'d* should not be overemphasized since this is a conventional feature of normal English speech. Nor are contractions necessarily meaningful, although it is hard not to be impressed by Shakespeare's increasing freedom with such abbreviation: compared to the six contractions in *The Merchant of Venice*, the folio text of *The Winter's Tale* contains 154.[9] But any kind of omission, even the simplest and most familiar, assumes greater significance amid other forms of elision.

The impulse to abbreviate and distil often leads the mature poet to delete those parts of speech that normally tighten relations between parts of a sentence. Specifically, the relative pronouns 'that', 'which', and 'who' are often discarded, as in the Old Shepherd's wish 'To die upon the bed [*on which*] my father died' (4.4.456). In Hermione's plea for female companionship in prison, 'Beseech your highness / My women may be with me' (2.1.116–17), the pronominal subject ('I') is elided in the first clause, perhaps to make space for the unexpected 'Beseech'; also suppressed is the relative 'that' which would normally introduce the second clause. Conjunctions, as we might expect, are easily discarded. Participles and infinitives often stand in for more ample clauses, or for a longer, more specific phrase. *The Winter's Tale* abounds in such manoeuvres, as when Leontes shamefully confesses his attempt to make Camillo kill Polixenes:

> I with death and with
> Reward did threaten and encourage him,
> Not doing it and being done. (3.2.160–2)

To paraphrase: 'I threatened him with death if he refused to do it, and I encouraged him with the prospect of reward if he agreed to do it.' The logical integument between 'not doing' and the 'him' that governs it is initially vague, and the prepositional phrase that would explain 'being done' (i.e., 'by him') is dropped. Moreover, the shift of voice (from 'doing' to 'being done') is perplexing, violating as it does the parallelism established in the previous lines. One additional feature of these lines requires notice: although much is omitted, there is surplus as well. In this same example, the poet unnecessarily repeats the preposition *with* in the first line, creating a characteristic tension between omission and supplementation. At the same time that the verse is elliptical, it is also pleonastic, unnecessarily repetitious. Finally, as a reductive instrument, the participle frequently creates semantic difficulty: when normal relational pointers are eliminated, the listener must work harder to follow the speaker. As a result of such omissions, many passages sound as if an inattentive poet is merely piecing phrases together without regard for sequence or interrelation.

Syntax

Syntax, to put the matter only a little reductively, is another name for word order. Historical changes in the conventions of speech and writing require caution in generalising about 'normal' grammar and thus about Shakespeare's or anyone else's variations on it. Word order in early modern English was considerably more fluid than it has become. All of these difficulties notwithstanding, it is possible to generalise – carefully – and the way to begin is to say that the last plays exhibit what modern critics and editors have agreed to call 'loose syntax'. The relatively unregulated word order of early modern English is frequently exploited to the extreme: at one time or another most of the mobile components of the sentence, especially prepositional phrases, direct objects, and modifying phrases, are eccentrically placed. Interpolations, short and long, disrupt the process by which meaning is established. Some utterances break off and resume in another direction, while other sentences that would seem to have reached completion are extended, often to remarkable length, by the accretion of participial phrases and other modifiers. In many such sentences clause is piled upon clause, new ones correcting or reversing semantically those which have gone before, and such revision produces a sense of almost constant digression. As Keir Elam remarks, 'the dramatist's syntax tends to get trickier as he gets older', an understatement that covers a broad range of complex forms.[10]

Instead of assembling a group of tiny snippets that illustrate inversion, interpolation, breaking off, and shifts of direction, I present a single passage that exhibits the roundabout, unregulated quality of the late syntax: Cerimon's statement of his credo as he ministers to the apparently dead Thaisa in the third act of *Pericles*.

> 'Tis known, I ever
> Have studied physic: through which secret art,
> By turning o'er authorities, I have
> Together with my practice, made familiar,
> To me and to my aid, the blest infusions
> That dwells in vegetives, in metals, stones:
> And can speak of the disturbances that
> Nature works, and of her cures; which doth give me
> A more content in course of true delight
> Than to be thirsty after tottering honour,
> Or tie my treasure up in silken bags,
> To please the fool and death.   (3.2.31–42; quarto)

These lines display two major syntactical manoeuvres: interpolation and aggregation. While the urge to augment manifests itself in the interpolation of clauses and phrases, an equally common and meaningful form of accumulation is the piling up of appositional or elaborative phrases, usually at the end of a sentence. To some extent, aggregation is the mirror opposite of the elliptical impulse I have just examined. However punctuated, Cerimon's speech amounts to a single sentence built up gradually by the interpolation of prepositional phrases ('Together with my practice'), relative clauses ('That dwells in ...'), infinitives ('To please ...'), a second predicate introduced mid-speech ('And can speak'), as well as such extenders as supplementary examples ('in vegetives, in metals, stones'), comparatives ('more content ... / Than to be thirsty ...'), and alternatives ('Or tie my treasure up'). Usually the additional segments that so distend the sentence are, as linguists call them, 'continuative clauses'. Linguistically, such non-restrictive clauses form a separate tone-group, meaning that they were probably spoken in a distinctive, additive voice. If Shakespeare's actors provided such a tonal signifier for each of these added grammatical units, the auditory texture of these plays would have been even more various and complex than they seem to us now.

Sometimes a parenthesis will guide the reader (though not an audience member) through the semantic underbrush of a difficult passage. 'Round brackets', to use the modern printer's term, are especially plentiful in the printed texts of the late plays: *The Winter's Tale* contains 369 pairs, *Cymbeline* 158, *Henry VIII* 117 and *The Tempest* 97.[11] Some percentage of these relatively high numbers may be ascribed to the habits of Ralph Crane, the copyist who prepared at least three of the late plays for publication in the folio and who is known to have had a weakness for such markers.[12] But whether printed aids are available, and regardless of who supplied them, they attest to the digressive and incoherent tendencies of Shakespeare's late verse. Not 'bored' but confidently unconcerned with spelling out connections, Shakespeare has taken a deliberately 'careless' approach to construction and explanation, an insouciance in which the audience

with carelessness

is invited to share. Words, phrases, clauses, and sentences are less significant than the meanings beyond them, and the playwright seems to be pointing us to that mysterious region beyond.

To digression we must add its corollary, the second major syntactical feature, which is semantic postponement, or delayed understanding. Such a combination of delay and pay-off functions prominently in *The Winter's Tale*, as in Leontes' interrogation of Camillo:

> Ha' not you seen, Camillo
> (But that's past doubt; you have, or your eye-glass
> Is thicker than a cuckold's horn), or heard
> (For to a vision so apparent rumour
> Cannot be mute), or thought (for cogitation
> Resides not in that man that does not think)
> My wife is slippery? (1.2.267–73)

Leontes begins by posing a question, but before disclosing its substance he leads the auditor through a maze of parenthetical elements and qualifying material: a series of three verbs, 'seen', 'heard', and 'thought', alternates with a corresponding series of lengthy clauses asserting that Camillo must have seen, heard and thought. The interruptions here are comparatively regular, imposing a complementary or contrapuntal pattern of their own rather than simply deranging the sentence. The most telling feature is that Shakespeare has scrupulously controlled the grammar of the sentence to augment the force of the final clause. Without the last four words the sentence is meaningless, and yet getting to its end is no easy matter. The effect is that of a grammatical labyrinth in which we make our way through a series of baffles, then turn a corner, and find ourselves faced with the beast – 'My wife is slippery'. The mechanics of this construction leave us suspended in air, dangling through six circumlocutory lines, until we land with a jolt of understanding.

The grammatical suspension may be as familiar as a simple conditional sentence. The first line of *The Winter's Tale*, 'If you shall chance, Camillo, to visit Bohemia ...', is just such a construction, establishing the tone of conditionality characteristic of the mode in general and of this story in particular. According to the familiar form of such semantic structures, the mind's ear requires that the conditional beginning be resolved. Even the simplest construction beginning with an 'if' clause engages the listener in a rhythmic process of tension and release. In these last plays Shakespeare regularly elaborates and protracts the first term to such a degree that we risk losing our way before receiving syntactical and semantic satisfaction. Paulina's great aria at the end of the trial scene, 'What studied torments, tyrant, hast for me?' (3.2.175–202), in which she withholds the announcement of

Hermione's death until the last of twenty-eight lines, is a brilliant example of this tactic.

The conspicuously suspended sentence, we might say, represents a kind of gamble, a form of verbal play within the play, and Shakespeare's magnification of introductory phrases and clauses to extreme lengths entails a kind of authorial risk. He seems to be testing the listener's patience and acuity, pressing towards the limits of comprehensibility, and, what is more, he seems to be doing so playfully, as if the verbal medium were a kind of athletic bar to be continually raised.

Repetition

The late plays feel almost obsessively reiterative. A conspicuous source of this impression is the reappearance of many of the stories, character types and ideas that had occupied Shakespeare's imagination from the early 1590s: the separated family, the fraternal struggle for power, the slandered heroine, political usurpation and its consequences, the Virgilian concern with dynasty, an interest in familial reproduction, the destructive and redemptive sea, the restoration of that which was lost. In modern critical treatments, such structural and thematic repetition is a commonplace. Equally prominent, however, are the reiterative qualities of the poetry from which these familiar topoi emerge. The aural repetition characteristic of the late style creates a complex, artificial surface that gives these dramas a distinctive sonic texture, one that delights the ear and excites the mind. To listen carefully to the reiterative patterns that resound throughout these late texts is to perceive a primary source of their poetic power. The insistent repetition of vowels and consonants, words, phrases, syntactical forms and other verbal effects makes the dramatic texts uncommonly musical. These sounds also witness to an exceptional self-consciousness consistent with Shakespeare's turn from the representational to the presentational.

A plain example without detailed analysis will serve as a starting point, Polixenes's reference to Perdita as 'The queen of curds and cream' (*The Winter's Tale*, 4.4.161). This line appears in what is, relatively speaking, an unremarkable passage, a speech neither inordinately lyrical nor expressive of psychological stress. When the emotional temperature does rise, we should not be surprised at a corresponding increase in the poetic pressure. This is audible most clearly in the great recognition scene between Pericles and Marina (5.1), the most powerful exchange in the play, indeed one of those great scenes of discovery and reunion that make the romances so distinctively moving. The passion for duplicated sounds represents one of its most effective, if least remarked, poetic elements, the key to the music of the encounter:

> If I should tell my history, it would seem
> Like lies disdain'd in the reporting.   (118–19)

> Thou lookest
> Like one I loved indeed.   (124–5)

> What were thy friends?
> How lost thou them? Thy name, my most kind virgin?   (139–40)

> My name is Marina.
> O, I am mock'd.   (142)

> tell me if thou canst,
> What this maid is, or what is like to be,
> That thus hath made me weep.   (183–5)

Even in that simplest and most touching of declaratives, 'My name is Marina', the intensity of the plain truth is magnified by the musical syllables; literal repetition determines the beguiling sounds of the short sentence, obviously the echoing of the initial ms, but also the n in 'name' and 'Marina', the chiastic reversal of the m and n, and the vocalic repetition of the vowel sounds in the proper name. The hypnotic and transcendent power of the reunion resides to a large extent in the echoes that evoke an apparent pattern and thus seem to promise significance.

A sentence from John Hoskins's *Directions for Speech and Style*, a treatise written in 1599: 'The ears of men are not only delighted with store and exchange of divers words but feel great delight in repetition of the same.'[13] Lexical repetition is largely responsible for the incantatory appeal of all the romances, each play offering multiple instances of this ordering tactic. The aural effect of the repeated words is often intensified by other forms of echo, and two more instances from the opening of *The Winter's Tale* illustrate the extremes to which Shakespeare has taken the reiteration of words.

> Come, **captain,**
> We must be neat; not neat, but cleanly, **captain:**
> And yet the steer, the heckfer, and the *calf*
> Are all call'd neat. – Still virginalling
> Upon his palm? – How now, you wanton *calf,*
> Art thou my *calf*?   (1.2.122–7)

In the first speech to Mamillius, the several repeated words are also connected to each other and to other words by virtue of certain interlocking sounds: the opening 'c' sounds sharpen the effect of the first and second lines, and the syllable 'all' sounds both in and around 'calf'. This concentration on sounds should not, however, prevent us from noticing the semantic repetitions as

Leontes puns on and otherwise amplifies the word 'neat'. Here is the second speech.

> Go play, boy, play. Thy mother plays, and I
> Play too, but so disgrac'd a part, whose issue
> <u>Will</u> hiss me to *my* grave; contempt and clamour
> <u>Will</u> be *my* knell. Go play, boy, play.   (1.2.185–7)

In addition to the restatement of 'play', 'my', and 'will', the sonic integuments of the speech are created by the chiming of 'iss' in 'issue' and 'hiss'; by the consonantal reiteration of 's' sounds in 'so disgraced', of 'c' in 'contempt and clamour', of 'l' in 'will' and 'knell'; and by the assonance of 'play', '-graced', and 'grave'. Finally, although our grasp of early modern pronunciation is limited, the 'k' in 'knell' may well have been sounded as a hard consonant, making the music of the last clause even fiercer.

In *Pericles*, the most famous speech is similarly interlaced, studded with pairs and triplets of letters and with repeated words.

> O Helicanus, strike <u>me</u>, honoured sir,
> Give <u>me</u> a gash, put <u>me</u> to present pain,
> Lest this great <u>sea</u> of joys rushing upon <u>me</u>
> O'erbear the sho<u>res</u> of my <u>m</u>ortality,
> And drown <u>me</u> with their sweetness. O, come hither,
> <u>Thou</u> that <u>beget</u>'st him that did thee <u>beget</u>;
> <u>Thou</u> that wast born at sea, buried at Tharsus,
> And <u>found</u> at sea again! O Helicanus,
> <u>Down</u> on thy knees, thank the holy gods as <u>loud</u>   ·
> As thunder threaten<u>s</u> u<u>s</u>. Th<u>is</u> <u>is</u> Marina.   (190–9)

The starting point for comment on the musicality of this excerpt is the alliterative pattern of the second line, where the *g* and *p* sounds might serve as a textbook example. But the line is even more complicated than it seems for, as Kenneth Burke pointed out long ago, *b* and *p* sounds are closely related phonetically to *m* and constitute what he calls '*concealed* alliteration'.[14] He discerns another triad of such 'cognates' in *d*, *t*, and *n*, a group whose relations are clearly audible in the last line quoted. In addition to obvious and submerged instances of consonance, we should remark the sibilants in the first and third lines, and particularly the complex music of the fourth, in which the consonant of 'O'er' is repeated in 'bear' and then sounded again with the repeated vowel in 'shores'; and all these similar sounds exaggerate the shift to *m* in 'my mortality', which glances again at 'or' in the first syllable of the noun. The blizzard of repeated vowels and consonants is immediately audible even to a casual listener, although it is worth pointing out that the number of combinations is always greater than one thinks.

Such alliterative pleasures are enhanced by a high density of repeated words. The speech gains much of its musical power from the repetition of the pronominal 'me' after three different imperative verbs, each of them monosyllables ('strike me ... give me ... put me'). And as the passage continues, the recurrence of words and phrases intensifies into a kind of chant. Of course the emotional release of this climactic reunion accounts for the effect of these few lines, but the content is coloured, made more vivid, by the rhythmic duplication of simple sounds, words, and phrases. In addition to the obvious reiteration of 'Thou that' and 'beget', the pattern of repetition is subtly extended by the parallel series of verbs and prepositions in the last two lines. Even articles do their part to create a sense of reverie and wonder. Much contemporary discussion of the value of repetition implies its capacity to beguile the listener by charming the senses, and Shakespeare harnesses that power in the late plays especially.

Metrics

Blank verse is arguably the dominant instrument of repetition in any Shakespeare play, in that the sub-structural sequence of iambic feet creates an inescapable rhythm to which the audience's ears become accustomed and upon which the dramatic poet performs multiple variations. By 1607 or so, his approach to the pentameter line is infinitely more flexible and original than when he first began to compose verse. Metre functions as a symbolic system, a sonic world that mimes in a general way the living, changing world of the play, which mirrors in a general way the living, changing world we inhabit. Rhythmically, we participate in a competition between the demands of unbroken regularity, the iambic framework on which the verse is founded and the countervailing forces of energy and deviation. And from *Pericles* forward the metrical patterns exhibit the hand of a craftsman who long ago mastered his medium and now delights in taking liberties with it, modifying its regularity and pushing the forces of metrical subversion to the limit. In other words, rhythm both does and undoes its ordering function.

Blank verse is built upon an inherent tension between the regularity of the familiar decasyllabic line, the forces of similitude and the idiosyncratic energies of the English sentences that have been shaped into verse, the forces of difference.[15] In the late plays Shakespeare allows far greater clout to the sentence at the expense of rhythmic consistency. In the early histories and comedies the semantic unit tends to coincide with the poetic segment; as he gains experience, however, the poet is increasingly willing to run the thought past the end of the line, regularly enjambing the verse so that clauses extend without pause over two or even more lines. In the first ten plays or so, to about

→ *hypermetrics* (handwritten annotation)

1595, only about 10 per cent of the lines are extra-metrical: in other words, only one line in ten has an extra syllable or a feminine ending. In the late plays, however, one in every three lines is exceptional, some containing as many as twelve or thirteen syllables. To compare two texts of relatively equal length, one from the beginning and one from the end of the career, is to find that the late play will contain about 1,000 extra syllables, sounds that must be delivered by the actor and integrated into the pattern of pentameter. Such additional syllables alter the music of the verse and transform the sound of the play as a whole. As with syllables, so with stops: Shakespeare has become much more liberal and varied in his use of caesurae, employing the mid-line pause as a major source of aural variety. Unwilling to wait for the end of the line, he arranges that his speakers stop early and stop often.

The power of these hypermetrical, enjambed, fractured lines to create instability and uncertainty in the metrical frame is felt in Pericles' shipboard address to the elements, a rejoinder to the tempest in which Marina is born.

>   o, STILL
> Thy DEAF'ning DREADful THUNders; GENtly QUENCH
> Thy NIMble SULphurous FLAshes! – o, HOW, LyCHOridA,
> How DOES my QUEEN? – Thou STORM, VENomously
> Wilt thou SPIT all thySELF? The SEAman's WHIStle
> Is AS a WHISper in the EARS of DEATH,
> UnHEARD.   (3.1.4–10)

Although I have indicated a pattern, this passage might be spoken in a variety of different ways. Whatever the particular emphases chosen, the contest between similitude and difference is always audible.

The subtlety of the metrical system in the late plays corresponds to the complex understanding of experience represented on the stage. The delicate emotional balance achieved at the end of *The Winter's Tale* requires the audience to entertain conflicting feelings at the same time: joy at the recovery of Perdita and sorrow at the loss of Mamillius; regret at the loss of Antigonus and surprised pleasure at the marriage of Paulina and Camillo; delight at the bumpkins' social elevation and scorn at their misunderstandings. Sometimes the emotions are even mutually exclusive. Satisfaction at the reunion of Leontes and Hermione is diminished by our unresolved contempt for his destructive passion. The inescapable pain and bitter ironies of the preceding acts mitigate the joy and harmony of the reunion; and yet at the same time the joy and harmony of the reunion mitigate the inescapable pain and bitter ironies of the previous acts. So it is with the metre: the regularity of the beat controls the rhythmic adventurism of the verse. Even in its sound patterns, the Shakespearean system of values implies its own opposites.

Style and story

William Hazlitt, the nineteenth-century essayist and perceptive commentator on Shakespeare, remarked of *Cymbeline* that 'the reading of this play is like going on a journey with some uncertain object at the end of it'.[16] His statement has stylistic as well as narrative applications. Treating the sentence as a plot and the plot as a sentence is a standard critical tactic, one which has proved especially useful in the analysis of nineteenth-century prose fiction,[17] and here it is justified by the centrality of the journey as a structural device. Traditionally the quest has always been the backbone of romance fiction.[18] Characters in other modes do not invariably stay at home, of course, but travel forms the skeleton of romance in ways that it does not for the other major dramatic kinds. Indeed, the 'adventure' upon which romance is structured is a term etymologically derived (*ad-venire*) from the Latin for 'travel'. Tyre, for example, sees little of its Prince: *Pericles* is almost all journey, beginning with the hero's visit to Antioch, moving to various sites throughout the Mediterranean and ending in the temple of Diana at Ephesus. Shakespeare has magnified the adventure of getting to the end of the sentence and attaining semantic comprehension into the larger emotional experience of following characters on their way to safety, familial reunion and joy.

Romance depends upon certain narrative staples: adventures, journeys and wandering, shipwrecks, divided families, desert places, temporal leaps, apparent death, providential intervention, joy after despair.[19] These properties furnish the author with narrative material, whether he or she is Sir Philip Sidney or Barbara Cartland. For the study of verse style, two identifying organisational features of romance are especially helpful: narrative amplitude and structural looseness. As Shakespeare adapts his source materials to the task of telling stories on a stage, his arrangement of his dramatic materials corresponds, in shape and effect, to his ordering of the poetic constituents. Staging the unstable realm of romance produces narrative equivalents of those convolutions, reversals, ellipses, delayed grammatical units, repetitions, additives and other stylistic mannerisms to which the ear becomes attuned.

Many of the terms often used to describe the late style – 'extravagant', 'reckless', 'loose' – also pertain to the sprawling, episodic, casually organised dramatic structures that Shakespeare favoured from *Pericles* forward. Syntax offers an instructive example. As I have indicated, the difficulties of the loose syntax are attributable to the playwright's having weakened or suppressed certain normal relations among the parts of sentences, or between and among the several sentences in a larger speech or verse paragraph. This technique is a version of what the Renaissance rhetoricians referred to as 'asyndeton'.[20] A sentence coheres and delivers its meaning by virtue of its adherence to certain agreed-upon forms, but the liberty with which the speaker or writer distributes those syntactical units may stretch or even seem to defy the rules of coherence. Shakespeare's late style, comprising as it does hundreds of sentences very casually tied together, is recapitulated structurally in the episodic, disjointed unfolding of dramatic romance.

The unexpected juxtapositions, surprising turns of plot and temporal shifts characteristic of the action represent a mode of storytelling that might be called narrative asyndeton. Romance fiction is noted – and valued – for its neglect, even its defiance, of the canons of logic; in their place we are given magic, surprise, providential intervention and other manifestations of an alogical domain. Integuments among plots, relations among characters, motives of action or links among locations are by no means inevitable and are often puzzling, the conditions of the mode having relieved the storyteller of the obligation to clarify such connections and furnish background. We don't know why Leontes is possessed by jealousy; why Dionyza, the recipient of Pericles' compassion, suddenly turns on his child; why Florizel should happen upon the cottage of the beautiful Perdita; why Pericles' ship should fetch up in the harbour of Mytilene, site of the brothel where Marina languishes.

In responding to both poetic style and dramatic structure, the audience remains aware of the controlling hand of the dramatist. Chance would seem to govern the unpredictable course of events, but the theophanies or oracular interventions that mark each play suggest providential agency. The appearance of Diana in Act 5 of *Pericles* is one such intercession. Through a complicated network of ironies the effect of such a divine agent is, paradoxically, to highlight the supervisory role of the playwright. Throughout most of the late plays the audience remains conscious of (and indeed enjoys being conscious of) the managerial virtuosity of the dramatist, particularly his skill at concealing, diverting, revealing and above all controlling the multiple strands of the action. The managed complexity generates a feeling of pleasurable uncertainty. Likewise, the listener often feels the same combination of perceptual anxiety and security about the semantic direction of the verse sentences. It is as if, for the purposes of the theatrical experience, the providential agent is the poet, delaying comprehension and finally delighting the listener with clarification.

This correspondence between smaller and larger units is more than an analogy, however, something greater than a simple parallel between style and structure. Rather, noticing the correspondence between minute grammatical particulars and broad organisational principles helps to show how style makes meaning. As patterned sound passing from actor's throat to listener's ear, verse constitutes one of the primary conduits of transaction between playwright and audience, the actor serving as intermediary. In fact, the early modern terms for actor, *persona*, and for the creation of character, 'personation', derive from the Latin for 'speaking through'. The kind of language spoken determines how the audience experiences the story and thus controls its perception of events and their significance. Metrically, for example, the contest between the order of the blank verse pattern and the threats to that order posed by the energies of the sentence imparts to the listener a physical apprehension of the fictional conflicts that the structure of romance is calculated to emphasise. This stylistic recapitulation is most obvious in a speech like Leontes' 'Too hot, too hot', but the same principle obtains throughout each of the late works. And at all times the audience is granted the safety of virtuality.

Style and meaning

'*Euphues* had rather lie shut up in a lady's casket, than open in a scholar's study'.
  John Lyly, 'To the Ladies and Gentlewomen of England', Preface to *Euphues*

We now come to the question that all stylistic analysis must face. How does a detailed acquaintance with the technical features of Shakespeare's late style help us to comprehend the plays, both collectively and individually? If the scrutiny of verbal particulars is to offer more than a dry accounting of poetic turns, metrical eccentricities and sentence shapes, then it ought to elucidate larger topics of meaning and purpose. Shakespeare's sophisticated verse, like the romance form and the interest in reconciliation and artifice, is the product of an altered, complex understanding of human experience, and the poetic technique produces audible traces of that thinking. The verse is new because the way of thinking is new. Many of the tragedies immediately preceding the final phase – especially *King Lear*, *Timon of Athens*, *Macbeth* and *Coriolanus*, all fiercely anti-romantic – advance a profound critique of masculinity while presenting the most negative, even grotesque, portrayals of female sexuality in the entire canon. Shakespeare's rejection of tragedy for romance is accompanied by an imaginative recuperation of the female and a concentration on the redemptive associations of femininity. The late verse is intimately allied to this revised point of view. His embrace of the delights of romance and cultivation of an appropriate poetic style declare a conversion to new values, ideals often coded by his culture as feminine and secondary: art, stories, ornament, pleasure, fantasy, patience, forgiveness. The re-conception of his poetic medium bespeaks a renewed commitment to the compensatory power of illusion, a new theatrical realm that cheerfully confesses its status as a rhetorical construction.

The association of romance with the feminine, an affinity declared in the quotation from Lyly, is also articulated by the modern critic Rosalie Colie, who refers to 'the frippery of the mode's metaphor and attitude'.[21] Moreover, there is, as 'frippery' implies, something old-fashioned about romance, notwithstanding that the mode was *au courant* in London, circa 1609. Thus it is instructive to notice that as he began writing the romances Shakespeare seems to have been rereading fiction that had given him pleasure in his twenties. The last plays are shot through with characters, episodes, language and themes from the works of Sir Philip Sidney, Robert Greene, Edmund Spenser, John Lyly, Christopher Marlowe and other late Elizabethan writers. Significantly, in composing *The Winter's Tale* the dramatist used the original 1588 edition of *Pandosto*, even though the novella had been reprinted in 1607: this detail implies physical contact with a favourite book from an earlier age. It may also be relevant that *Shakespeare's Sonnets* appeared for sale in quarto in 1609. Not only do the poems look back to a form that reached its apogee in the 1580s and 1590s, but the extreme formality of this sub-genre of lyric seems consistent with the poet's rediscovered pleasure in artifice and verbal delights.

Whether Shakespeare's rereading of old favourites helped to prompt the romantic turn in 1607–8 or whether a change in his thinking then sent him back to sources of past pleasure, his return to old favourites apparently shaped his creative energies during the last phase of his professional life. In the books of his youth, he seems to have rediscovered the pleasures of fiction, acquired a refreshed attitude towards language, and renewed his faith in the possibilities of the theatre. The extreme artifice in Lyly's court comedies (not to mention in practically every sentence of *Euphues*), or the poetic formality and prodigal ornamentation of *The Faerie Queene*, or the narrative patterns of Sidney's *Arcadia* – each of these represents aspects of a style he and his Jacobean contemporaries had left behind. It also seems clear that he was fascinated by the self-conscious artfulness of these works, and it was his particular gift to recognize the pleasurable patterns on which they depend, to appropriate and play with those patterns, and thus to convert them into a 'modern', sophisticated kind of artifice.

The prominent artifice of the late work – in style, in structure, in presentation – attests to a striking turn in Shakespeare's thinking, a devotion to ornament consistent with his passage from tragedy to romance. This commitment to surface and style is surprising given his verifiable movement away from the heavy patterning of the early plays. It also runs counter to a powerful cultural strain, fed by the burgeoning Puritan ideology and widespread anti-Catholicism, according to which decoration is wicked and apt to obscure the truth. Artifice was identified with the external or inessential, clothing and cosmetics being the most familiar objects of censure. Misogynistic attacks on decoration are part of a larger cultural fear, a suspicion of the imagination and all its expressive products. Many of the anti-theatrical tracts issued throughout the 1580s and 1590s equate ornament and cosmetics with rhetoric (the 'harlot rhetoric') and language, and most of these implicitly constitute an attack on women, specifically on the ills traditionally attributed to Eve. Frequently the polemicists, concerned as they are with cross-dressing and sexual licence, direct their aim at the effeminising effects of theatrical performance. A late example of this discourse, William Prynne's *Histriomastix* (1633), rehearses at practically psychopathic length (the book runs to some 1,000 pages) the misogynistic views of his predecessors, attacking

> Dancing, Musicke, Apparell, Effeminacy, Lascivious Songs, Laughter, Adultery, obscene Pictures, Bonefires, New-yeares gifts, Grand Christmasses, Health-drinking, Long haire, Lordsdayes, Dicing, with sundry Pagan customes ... *you shall finde them ... either the concomitants of Stage-playes, or having such neare affinity with them, that the unlawfulnesse of the one are necessary mediums to evince the sinfulnesse of the other.*[22]

Reaching back to Augustine and even the Greeks, Prynne avails himself of the traditional identification of the stage, effeminacy, music, festivity and other forms of imaginative pleasure. Throughout his screed the theatre is denounced not only because of its power to emasculate but also because it perverts language for the iniquity and frivolity of fiction: 'the subject matter of our stage-Playes, is for the most part, *false and fabulous;* consarcinated [patched together] of sundry merry, ludicrous, officious artificial lies ... But such is the subject matter of most Comicall, of many Tragicall Enterludes. Therefore they must needs be odious and unlawfull unto Christians.'[23] Prynne also specifically attacks prose romance, scorning 'Arcadias, and fained histories that are now so much in admiration'.[24] Images, imagination, illusion, fictions, cosmetics, idleness, theatre – all these topics, vulnerable to charges of triviality and effeminacy, are also fundamental elements of Shakespeare's late plays.

Shakespeare's renewed affirmation of the feminine helps to account for his reconceived attitude towards language, his altered attraction to dramatic forms and his view of the theatrical enterprise itself. Ornament, indirection, disguise, words, and fiction generally, all figured as potentially lethal in the sequence of great tragedies, no longer seem mainly threatening. Rather, they are acknowledged and exploited as sources of consolation and creativity. And the new prominence of repetition, rhyme, assonance and consonance, and other forms of auditory ornament embodies this changed attitude poetically: what had been considered meretricious, excessive, even embarrassing, becomes pleasing and unifying. It is surely meaningful that the dramatic experience of separation and recovery is dramatised in language characterised by aural harmony and coherence. The auditory atmosphere of concordant sounds intensifies the sense of relation and familial reordering that gives the romances their extraordinary emotional power. The recuperation of the female, in other words, is heard not only in the eloquence of the female tongue but also in the poetic consonance that constitutes the virtual realm.

The return to artifice and virtuosity heard in Shakespeare's late verse is a token of the playwright's reconceived attitude towards his art, the exchange of mimesis for poesis. No longer content merely to represent the conflicts of this world, he has instead imagined new worlds. Embracing the metatheatrical style of presentational theatre, Shakespeare dissolves the conventions of representational drama that he had more or less observed in the tragedies. Now he toys with his theatrical instruments, frequently acknowledges the audience with Choruses, narrators, epilogues and abundant asides, mirrors his own dramatic actions in plays within plays, enriches his fictional world with gods and goddesses, dream landscapes, oracles and masques, and assumes the role of a player, a mediator, an 'interpreter' in the strict sense of a go-between. It might be said that the senior playwright of the King's Men begins to act again, not literally but virtually. One of the most telling signs of this reconsidered approach to drama is his new commitment to the delights of romance fiction. That he should have taken up romance at all, as Ben Jonson's notorious jibes at *Pericles* and *The Tempest* indicate, was something of a transgressive act, a discarding of a classically sanctioned form (Sidney's 'high and excellent tragedy') for an old-fashioned, popular mode associated with naive audiences and with women in particular. For the Elizabethans and Jacobeans, tragedy, with its historical authority, was evidently masculine. This prejudice survives in the long-standing privileging of tragedy over comedy: love stories are merely pleasurable tales, useless fictions for and about women; real men read tragedies. These commonplaces form the backdrop against which Shakespeare exchanges what Janet Adelman has called the 'end-stopped form' of tragedy for the more 'open' form of romance.[25]

The late commitment to the pleasures of artifice also betokens a refreshed view of the affirmative capacities of language, an endorsement of words as a medium for constructing an alternative reality. Throughout the first years of the seventeenth century Shakespeare's estimation of language seems to have deteriorated. From *Hamlet* and *Othello* to *Timon* and *King Lear*, human speech seems predominantly an instrument of deception, eloquence becomes what Cordelia refers to as a 'glib and oily art'; theatre is mainly an empty, misleading spectacle. Implicit in all these tragedies is the positive understanding that the creator's way with words paradoxically exposes the danger of language misused. In other words, Iago's vicious gift for misrepresentation is finally inferior to his creator's talent for representing that misrepresentation. But Shakespearean tragedy rarely makes such artistic confidence explicit, and always the theme emerging from the narrative is the capacity of language to destroy: in the hypocritical professions of Lear's daughters, the flattery of Timon's parasitical 'friends', the duplicitous punning of the weird sisters in *Macbeth*. Just at the end of the tragic sequence Shakespeare seems to oscillate between doubts about language and attraction to it in the twin Roman tragedies, *Coriolanus* and *Antony and Cleopatra*.

The turn to romance attests to his devotion to the compensatory value of the word. His retrospective appreciation of Elizabethan fiction, his late re-engagement with Sidney, Spenser, Greene and others, seems to have reminded him of the consolatory and diverting capacities of language. He invites the audience to relish the words themselves, not only for their power to illuminate but for their power to delight. In this respect the romances take a position in the early modern debate between form and content, indicating a preference for Ciceronian over Senecan values. Bacon admonishes his readers against 'the first distemper of learning, when men studie words, and not matter ... It seemes to me that *Pigmalions* frenzie is a good embleme or portraiture of this vanitie: for wordes are but the Images of matter, and except they haue life of reason and inuention: to fall in loue with them, is all one, as to fall in loue with a Picture.'[26] The emblematic use of Pygmalion is especially apt for understanding Shakespeare's thinking about his own role as a maker of art. *The Winter's Tale* famously blurs the distinction between the actual and the artistic by inviting us to fall in love with various forms of illusion, above all with Hermione's statue and, that which it represents, the play itself. For the mature Shakespeare, to fall in love with a picture is not self-evidently a fault: the artistic illusion, in the case of theatre a mingling of the verbal and the visual, is not a secondary endeavour, not an inferior form of experience. On the contrary, verbal illusion is a heightened form of human life, even more vivid and no less valid than the illusion it copies and of which it is a legitimate part.

By turning at the end of his career to stories of fantasy and magic, Shakespeare commits himself not only to the value of illusion but to the beneficent power of fiction in general. The tragedies record a profound abhorrence of the perils and deceits of illusion, a fear that exposes the playwright's serious doubt about his own profession. The turn to romance implies a reversal of this dubious view, an embrace of the illusory and the poetic. Shakespeare's professional doubts, if not dismissed, appear to have been at least allayed or balanced with renewed faith. Thus in the last plays the effects of spectacle, like the power of words, tend to be affirmative rather than threatening, a point best demonstrated in the last scene of *The Winter's Tale*. The moving statue could be terrifying: as Paulina puts it, 'you'll think / (Which I protest against) I am assisted / By wicked powers' (5.2.89–91). But instead of a demonic show, the on- and offstage audience confronts what amounts to a miracle – or a cheap trick. A work of art, an imitation of life, suddenly becomes 'real', and this miracle occurs in a play which is itself an imitation of life, a fiction in which imaginary persons come to life for the pleasure of a credulous audience. Shakespeare relishes the indistinguishability of the illusory and the 'actual'. We are mocked with art, as the play puts it. We can't tell if the statue is an actor or a monument – audiences take pride in noting how still the actress is as she impersonates the statue – and we can't tell if the resurrection is a miracle or a gimmick. The artificiality of all experience, with Providence as the artist, the divine play-wright, is the great theme of Shakespeare's last phase.

Now is the moment for Prospero's revels speech. Rather than quote it, however, I conclude by denying the positive description I have just presented: the last plays are just as full of doubt, subversion and ironic challenge as they are of affirmation and harmony. The poetic and generic hybridity I have been exploring is a stylistic manifestation of the ambivalence Shakespeare encourages his audience to consider and to relish. This recognition of a doubly ironic tone throughout the last plays should be extended to the style as well. Conflicting impulses govern Shakespeare's newly casual approach to poetic speech, specifically his disregard for syntactical connection in the sentence, his tolerance for metrical irregularity, and his heterogeneous mixture of the artificial and the naturalistic. Thus the style helps to confirm and to validate these competing attitudes towards romance and teaches us to read the apparently antithetical conclusions that the action of the plays suggests.

Those readers who have felt that Shakespeare is reaching 'beyond the words' describe a phenomenon that audiences notice every time one of the romances is performed. Each of the last plays offers its audience the promise of something beyond. Tantalizing verbal patterns, which seem to promise profundity or hint at elusive meaning, faithfully represent the fictional realms of Pericles' Mediterranean or the worlds of Sicilia and Bohemia. Some magical agency, some providential force seems to stand beyond the characters and their actions: there is something numinous about the world of Shakespearean romance. The style points us towards it.

NOTES

1. This essay reproduces, in abbreviated and altered form, material from my *Shakespeare's Late Style* (Cambridge: Cambridge University Press, 2006). In preparing this adaptation I recognise again my debts to many scholars and friends and wish to thank especially Cynthia Lewis (who solicited an oral version for a symposium at Davidson College), Sarah Stanton and Catherine M. S. Alexander.

2. The most recent thinking on the problem of nomenclature for the late plays is found in Barbara Mowat, 'What's in a Name? Tragicomedy, Romance, or Late Comedy?' in *A Companion to Shakespeare's Works*, ed. Richard Dutton and Jean Howard (Oxford: Blackwell, 2003), vol. IV, pp. 129–49.

3. The two passages are found in Edward Dowden, *Shakspere* (London: Macmillan, 1877), p. 60, and Lytton Strachey, 'Shakespeare's Final Period', *Independent Review* 3 (August 1904), pp. 414–15.

4. Critical works concerned specifically with the poetic style of the late plays, a relatively small number, include F. E. Halliday, *The Poetry of Shakespeare's Plays* (London: House of Stratus, repr. 2001); Ifor Evans, *The Language of Shakespeare's Plays* (London: Methuen, 1952); Frank Kermode, *Shakespeare's Language* (Harmondsworth: Penguin, 2000); James Sutherland, 'The Language of the Last Plays', in *More Talking of Shakespeare*, ed. John Garrett (London: Longmans, 1959), pp. 144–58; the Arden 2 editions of *Cymbeline* by J. M. Nosworthy (London: Methuen, 1955), *The Winter's Tale* by J. H. P. Pafford (London: Methuen, 1963), and *The Tempest* by Frank Kermode (London: Methuen, 1954); and Simon Palfrey, *Late Shakespeare: A New World of Words* (Oxford: Oxford University Press, 1997). Stephen Orgel, in his Oxford editions of *The Winter's Tale* (1996) and *The Tempest* (1987), addresses the problem of comprehension, proposing that the early modern audience didn't understand the extremely convoluted passages any better than we do.

5. Keir Elam refers to this phenomenon as 'parenthomania, the alarming outbreak of brackets'. See 'Early Modern Syntax and Late Shakespearean Rhetoric', in C. Nocera Avila, N. Pantaleo and D. Pezzini (eds.), *Early Modern English: Trends, Forms and Texts* (Fasano: Schena Editore, 1992), p. 65.

6. The phrase is from Anne Barton's seminal study, 'Leontes and the Spider: Language and Speaker in the Late Plays', in *Essays, Mainly Shakespearean* (Cambridge: Cambridge University Press, 1994), pp. 161–81, at pp. 180–81.

7. The term was first used by A. C. Bradley, referring to the complex sound of some of the late tragedies: see *Shakespearean Tragedy: Lectures on 'Hamlet', 'Othello', 'King Lear' and 'Macbeth'*, (London: Macmillan, 1972), p. 68.

8. All quotations, unless otherwise indicated, are from *The Riverside Shakespeare*, ed. G. Blakemore Evans (Boston: Houghton Mifflin, 1974).

9. Willard Farnham, 'Colloquial Contractions in Beaumont, Fletcher, Massinger, and Shakespeare as a Test of Authorship', *Publications of the Modern Languages Association of America* 31 (1916), pp. 326–58, at pp. 342–44.

10. Elam, 'Early Modern Syntax and Late Shakespearean Rhetoric', p. 64.

11. These figures derive from Ashley Thorndike, 'Parentheses in Shakespeare', *Shakespeare Association Bulletin* 9 (1934), pp. 31–37, at p. 33.

12. MacDonald P. Jackson, 'The Transmission of Shakespeare's Text', in Stanley Wells (ed.), *The Cambridge Companion to Shakespeare Studies* (Cambridge: Cambridge University Press, 1986), pp. 163–85, at p. 17. See also Stanley Wells and Gary Taylor, with John Jowett and William Montgomery, *Shakespeare: A Textual Companion* (Oxford: Oxford University Press, 1987).

13. Hoyt H. Hudson (ed.), *Directions for Speech and Style* (Princeton: Princeton University Press, n.d.), p. 12.

14. Kenneth Burke, 'On Musicality in Verse', in which he demonstrates the complex effects of assonance and consonance in some poems of Coleridge, in *The*

Philosophy of Literary Form (Baton Rouge: Louisiana State University Press, 1941), pp. 369–79.

15. For a thorough discussion of this tension, see George T. Wright's magisterial study of Shakespearean rhythm, *Shakespeare's Metrical Art* (Berkeley: University of California Press, 1988), especially Chapter 14, 'The Play of Phrase and Line'. See also Russ McDonald, *Shakespeare and the Arts of Language* (Oxford: Oxford University Press, 2001), especially Chapter 5, 'Loosening the Line'.

16. William Hazlitt, *Characters of Shakspeare's Plays* (London: C. H. Reynell, 1817), p. 1.

17. Peter Brooks, *Reading for the Plot: Design and Intention in Narrative* (New York: Alfred A. Knopf, 1984).

18. See, to begin with, Northrop Frye, *The Secular Scripture* (Cambridge, MA: Harvard University Press, 1976). Also helpful are Patricia Parker, *Inescapable Romance* (Princeton: Princeton University Press, 1979) and Helen Cooper, *The English Romance in Time: Transforming Motifs from Geoffrey of Monmouth to the Death of Shakespeare* (Oxford: Oxford University Press, 2004).

19. A comprehensive treatment of these devices is found in Cooper, *The English Romance in Time*. See also an earlier, more focused study, Howard Felperin, *Shakespearean Romance* (Princeton: Princeton University Press, 1972).

20. A helpful study of this device is that of John Porter Houston, *Shakespearean Sentences: A Study in Style and Syntax* (Baton Rouge: Louisiana State University Press, 1988), especially pp. 216ff.

21. Rosalie Colie, *Shakespeare's Living Art* (Princeton: Princeton University Press, 1974), p. 278.

22. William Prynne, 'To the Christian Reader', in *Histrio-mastix, or The Player's Scourge* (London, 1633).

23. Ibid., p. 106.

24. Ibid., p. 913.

25. Janet Adelman, *Suffocating Mothers: Fantasies of Maternal from 'Hamlet' to 'The Tempest'* (London: Routledge, 1992), pp. 73–4, 190.

26. Francis Bacon, *The Advancement of Learning*, ed. Arthur Johnston (Oxford: Clarendon Press, 1974), pp. 17–18.

6

PATRICIA TATSPAUGH

The Winter's Tale: shifts in staging and status

Strange as it may seem today, *The Winter's Tale* has not always been perceived as one of Shakespeare's most compelling, powerful and ingenious plays, one that dares to mix comedy and tragedy in unlikely combinations, to employ language at the extremes of extraordinarily demanding syntax and heart-stoppingly simple statement, to jump sixteen years, the leap eased by Time as chorus, and to introduce an oracle from Apollo, a bear, and, most bold and wonderful of all, a statue that moves after the command 'be stone no more' (5.3.99). For many years, however, these and other traits were treated as Shakespeare's apparent lapses or misunderstood because they did not meet prevailing critical standards: *The Winter's Tale* did not fulfil the unities; it mixed two, or even three, genres; it provided insufficient motivations for Leontes' jealousy and assigned him some incomprehensible lines; it introduced errors – such as a sea coast in Bohemia – as well as anachronisms and distractions, including Time, a bear and Autolycus. Looking for a coherent plot in *The Winter's Tale*, novelist Charlotte Lennox (1753) claimed that the 'incidents' of Shakespeare's source, Robert Greene's 'old paltry story of *Dorastus and Faunia*', were 'much less absurd and ridiculous'. It was, for example, inconceivable that Hermione, knowing that Leontes was repentant, chose 'to live in such a miserable confinement when she might have been happy in the possession of her husband's affection and have shared his throne'. As Lennox read it, the statue scene was 'a mean and absurd contrivance'. Completely missing the point, she argued that it was 'ridiculous … in a great Queen, on so interesting an occasion, to submit to such buffoonery as standing on a pedestal, motionless, her eyes fixed, and at last to be conjured down by a magical command of Paulina'.[1] But in the 1950s the theatrical and critical status of *The Winter's Tale* began the improvement that has culminated in the recognition it enjoys today. This essay traces first its theatrical fortunes in England between Simon Forman's afternoon at the Globe in May 1611 and Herbert Beerbohm Tree's

I am grateful to Robert Smallwood for his helpful comments on an early draft of this essay.

production in 1906; it introduces Harley Granville-Barker's seminal production; and it illustrates through six other productions something of the variety of stagings since 1951. With specific attention to topics raised by the performance history, the second section concentrates on criticism selected for its sensitivity to performance and explores Leontes' jealousy and the statue scene, two of the topics that have provoked the most intense debate of a play much debated in the rehearsal room and the study.

Performance history

About the reception of *The Winter's Tale* in Jacobean England we know very little. In his oft-quoted diary entry of 15 May 1611 Forman records his visit to see *The Winter's Tale* but does not mention the bear, Time, or the statue, three of Shakespeare's most-often commented-on additions to Robert Greene's *Pandosto*, his major source. Forman does, however, describe Autolycus, another of Shakespeare's creations, whose thievery provokes a warning: 'Beware of trusting feigned beggars or fawning fellowes'. *The Winter's Tale* was performed not only at the Globe but also at Blackfriars, the King's Men's indoor theatre, and at Whitehall Palace. Court records confirm five performances and suggest the possibility of two other performances at the First and Second Banqueting Houses between November 1611 and January 1633/4, when it was 'lik'd'.[2] The most accidentally topical of these performances took place during winter 1612/13 in the season of fourteen plays in honour of the marriage of Princess Elizabeth and Frederick, the Elector Palatine, a union effectively separating the sixteen-year-old from England and her family and resulting in her becoming Queen of Bohemia in 1619. More immediately, the death of her elder brother, the Prince of Wales, in November 1612 had robbed James and his queen of 'a gentleman of the greatest promise' (1.1.30).

The first reference to *The Winter's Tale* after the Restoration does not occur until January 1668/9, when it appears on the Lord Chamberlain's list of 108 plays performed at the Blackfriars and is assigned to Thomas Killigrew, proprietor of the King's Company and one of two men licensed to present plays.[3] There is, however, no record of its having been performed during the Restoration period – and therefore, alas, no witty entry about it in Samuel Pepys's diary. Advertised (apparently correctly) as 'Not Acted these Hundred Years', *The Winter's Tale* was revived on 15 January 1741 at Goodman's Fields and played a further eight times. It transferred to the larger Theatre Royal, Covent Garden the next season, where at its fifth and final appearance, commanded by the Prince and Princess of Wales, playbills promised 'A New Grand Ballet call'd the *Rural Assembly* ... With all new Habits and other Decorations proper to the Entertainment' and with a company expanded to include a huntsman, six 'Pastors', five 'Shepherdesses', an 'Old Herdsman', a 'Nymph of the Plain', a 'Cottage Nymph', two 'Nymphs of the Vale' and a 'Sylvan'. Although the production was not revived, its embellishment of the Bohemian scenes anticipated the three adaptations that form the next phase of the play's performance history.

In the second half of the eighteenth century, adaptations accounted for all but two of the ninety-eight performances in twenty-nine London seasons and gained audiences in provincial towns as well as Dublin and New York. From the Bohemian scenes Macnamara Morgan crafted *Florizel and Perdita* (1754), an afterpiece with music by Thomas Arne. Interpolated characters included Pan, who sang 'Shepherds hear the voice of Pan', and a priest, who married Florizel and Perdita. David Garrick's more popular adaptation (1756), announced as either *The Winter's Tale* or *Florizel and Perdita* and also set in Bohemia, drew on Acts 3, 4 and 5, played as a main piece, and featured music by Arne's son, Michael. 'The Sheep-shearing song', sung originally by Perdita, remained a popular feature of productions until William Charles Macready banished it in 1837. Garrick's adaptation created one gentleman from Shakespeare's three gentlemen and played a truncated statue scene into which Garrick inserted new lines. Instead of Shakespeare's silent reunion of Hermione and Leontes, Garrick has Hermione address Leontes as 'My lord, my king, – there's distance in those names, – / My husband! – '. After he professes his penitence and offers his thanks to the 'Most bounteous gods', she responds:

> No more my best lov'd lord; be all that's past
> Buried in this enfolding, and forgiven.[4]

Garrick's adaptation is the first production for which we have contemporary evidence revealing playhouse decisions. When the statue moved from the pedestal, Garrick stepped back.[5] '[S]tone no more' (5.3.99), Hannah Pritchard's Hermione was 'serene and composed'. Pritchard established the tradition of associating the statue with Christian iconography: Hermione descended from a 'temple' and wore a cross (*Universal Museum*, February 1762). The 1770s saw the third and least successful adaptation, *The Sheep-Shearing; or, Florizel and Perdita*, by George Colman the Elder (1777), as well as two performances heralding the next stage: for the evening of 24 April 1771 Covent Garden announced Shakespeare's 'unaltered *Winter's Tale*' as 'not acted for 30 years'.

Two contradictory artistic creeds dominate the years between 1802 and 1906.[6] In the first half of the nineteenth century, when theatre-going essayists such as William Hazlitt added their considerable voices to the growing body of descriptions and evaluations of performance, actor-managers concentrated on restoring Shakespeare's words. From mid-century increasingly elaborate scenic effects took precedence over Shakespeare's text.

John Philip Kemble, who had presented three performances of Garrick's adaptation in his first season as manager of the Theatre Royal, Drury Lane (1788), initiated in 1802 the first stages in the restoration of Shakespeare's text. But Kemble did not reinstate Time and retained Garrick's cuts and additions to the statue scene. Kemble also initiated the search for design based on historical accuracy and the introduction of extras to swell some of the Sicilian scenes. Apparently drawing heavily on stock sets, Kemble mixed historical periods and introduced anachronistic properties. He set some Sicilian scenes, such as the opening dialogue and the statue scene, against a classical Grecian background and others before Tudor Gothic architecture. Sketches in Kemble's promptbooks suggest that blocking in the trial scene underscored the futility of Hermione's case by placing the King centre stage and surrounding him with regal accoutrements and at least forty-eight attendants and by confining Hermione to a corner downstage right and limiting her to four attendants and two officers (see illustration 3). The promptbook also reveals that Kemble broke the trial scene after Hermione is borne off and continued it at 'Apollo, pardon / My great profaneness 'gainst thine oracle' (3.2.150–1). Playing the scene before a drop curtain, Kemble reinforced the shift from Leontes' public display of authority to his private remorse. For an insight into Kemble's Leontes, we have not only his promptbooks with their cuts, sketches and stage directions – such as the annotation that Leontes enters 2.1 with seventeen attendants and throws 'Mamillius over to Thasius' – but also reviews and Hazlitt's essays in the periodical press. Theatre-goers expected Kemble and his successors to convey both 'the dignity of the King' and 'the emotions of the man' (*Daily Advertiser and Oracle*, 12 May 1807). Hazlitt praised Kemble's portrayal of 'the growing jealousy of the King, and the exclusive possession which this passion gradually obtains over his mind' (*Times*, 25 June 1817). Sarah Siddons, playing Hermione to her brother's Leontes, was less successful in the first two acts, where she imbued Hermione with 'too much of unbending and freezing dignity', than she was in the trial scene, where the outstanding tragic actor of her generation embodied 'indignation at the groundless charge' (*Daily Advertiser and Oracle*, 26 March 1802) and defended herself with 'the eloquence of dignified and insulted innocence' (*Morning Advertiser*, 12 November 1807). Establishing the tradition of wearing Grecian drapery in the statue scene, Siddons moved her head suddenly when Paulina called for music.[7]

Between 3 November 1823 and 30 May 1843, actor-manager Macready revived *The Winter's Tale* during seven seasons at Drury Lane and three at Covent Garden. Less dignified than Kemble's, Macready's Leontes had a restless energy: the promptbook indicates many changes in his stage position

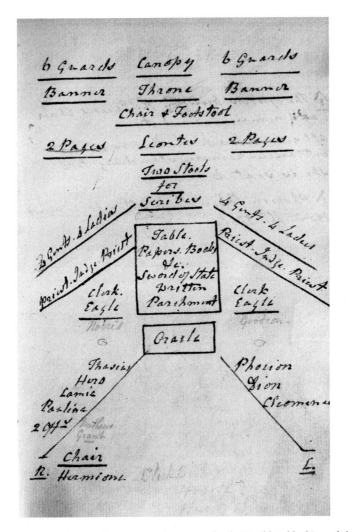

3. Hermione's trial, from William Creswick's promptbook. Kemble's blocking of the trial scene focuses attention on Leontes, who sits on a throne shielded by a canopy and surrounded by forty-eight attendants, and places Hermione on a chair downstage right, with four attendants and two officers.

when he imagines Hermione has been unfaithful. Leontes' 'incipient jealousy', records *The Times* (4 November 1823), which

> gradually ripen[ed] into a conviction of his consort's guilt, and finally terminat[ed] in bitter hatred, was traced through all its tortuous ramifications with the skill of one who had been no inattentive observer of human nature.

Macready's playing of Shakespeare's statue scene, which he restored, was much admired, especially from 1837, when Helena Faucit, the most successful of his four queens, assumed the role and became the first actor to win praise for each of Hermione's scenes. Whereas Garrick had stepped back when Hermione moved, Macready stepped back when Paulina said she could awaken the statue and when Hermione moved he 'appeared for a time annihilated; lost in amazement, and love, and joy' (*Morning Post*, 2 October 1837). In her essay on playing Hermione, Faucit recalled that nothing could have prepared her for Macready's 'display of uncontrollable rapture ... the finest burst of passionate speechless emotion I ever saw, or could have conceived'. Even when Faucit knew what to expect, she admitted 'the intensity of Mr Macready's passion was so real, that I could never help being moved by it, and feeling much exhausted afterwards'.[8] Costumed as a living queen, not in the Siddons' tradition of a marble statue, Faucit 'descended from the pedestal, with a slow and gliding motion, and wearing the look of a being consecrated by long years of prayer and sorrow and seclusion' (*Scotchman*, 3 March 1847).

Between 1845 and 1862, Samuel Phelps staged 137 performances of *The Winter's Tale* in nine seasons at Sadler's Wells, a theatre more intimate than Drury Lane and Covent Garden. Phelps, who played the statue scene and reinstated other lines, was 'evidently' the first to give *The Winter's Tale* a 'wholly Grecian setting' (Bartholomeusz, p. 65). As Leontes, Phelps made a 'gradual transition from one state of mind to another'[9] and embodied Coleridge's view that Leontes possessed 'a genuine jealousy of disposition' (Muir, p. 30).

But mid-century productions saw not only this restoration of words and characters but also the start of a new process of drastic cutting to allow for grand scenic effects made possible by advances in stage machinery. In the preface to his acting edition, Charles Kean (Princess's, 1856), the abettor of this pictorial realism, claimed that Shakespeare's text was 'carefully preserved throughout' his production,[10] but it omitted 62 per cent[11] to accommodate the shifting of scenery and placing of numerous extras. Neither Kemble's innovative, but inconsistent – today we might call it 'eclectic' – historical design nor Phelps's Grecian setting could have anticipated Kean's determination to stage the Sicilian scenes as '*tableaux vivants* of the private and public life of the ancient Greeks' (Kean, p. vi) Leontes honoured Polixenes with a splendid banquet, where the guests 'crowned with Chaplets [were] discovered reclining on Couches, after the manner of the Ancient Greeks'. Some of the seventy extras – 'cup bearers, slaves, female water carriers, and boys [were] variously employed'; others played 'the Hymn to Apollo' on replicas of Grecian instruments; and thirty-six youths 'in complete armour' performed an energetic pyrrhic dance (p. 12). Having chosen the theatre at Syracuse as an appropriate setting for the trial, Kean filled the stage with more than 170 extras, including forty-five children, and had still more silent observers painted on the backcloth. Four attendants bore the couch on which Hermione rested, and Paulina helped her to stand. Kean's acting version describes his elaborate presentation of Time:

> A classical allegory, representing the course of Time. Luna in her car, accompanied by the stars (personified), sinking before the approach of Phoebus. Cronos, as Time, surmounting the globe, describes the events of the sixteen years supposed to have elapsed. Ascent of Phoebus in the chariot of the sun. (p. 64)

For the statue scene Kean employed more than a hundred extras to swell the 'procession by torchlight'[12] to 'the peristyle of Paulina's house [w]ith part of the sculpture gallery' (p. 96). Kean relied on visual effects for his innovative characterization of Leontes as jealous from the beginning of 1.2. During the long, interpolated banquet Leontes 'anxiously' watched Hermione 'in earnest conversation' with Polixenes; the banquet over, Leontes addressed Polixenes 'at intervals cold though courteous, studied but not warm, diplomatic more than affectionate, an effort of the tongue rather than a desire of the heart' (Bartholomeusz, p. 87). The promptbook cues him to faint when Paulina announced Hermione's death. Ellen Kean, who undermined her husband's meticulous historical research by wearing starched petticoats beneath her Grecian costume, continued the tradition of playing Hermione as a decorous Victorian upper-class woman for whom public admissions such as 'The childbed privilege denied' (3.2.101) were an anathema. With an eye on posterity as well as the box office (the production ran 102 consecutive performances in 1856) Kean and his associates produced playbills carefully detailing the scenic effects, lavish souvenir booklets, numerous pages of drawing for props and costumes and the text 'arranged for representation at The Princess's Theatre, with historical and explanatory notes'.

Working in the same tradition, Charles and Adelaide Calvert (Prince's, Manchester, 1869) and Edward Saker (Alexander, Liverpool, 1876) borrowed from and adapted Kean's script and added individual touches of spectacle. When Calvert's Leontes defied the oracle, 'a sudden storm, with thunder, &c – great consternation' broke.[13] To the Calverts' thunderbolt, Saker added a lighting effect: 'a pale, steel-blue radiance ... [of] ghastly but intense light'.[14] In another departure from Kean's staging, the Calverts extended to the entire fifth act the religious tone that Pritchard had introduced into Garrick's statue scene. Their acting edition calls for an incense-bearing servant and other mourners to sing 'a hymn in praise of the dead' and to accompany Leontes, who offered 'oblations of incense and flowers' at 'the Mausoleum of Hermione and Mamillius' set in 'A Sacred Grove'. The Calverts placed the statue scene in 'a small temple' and closed the production with 'a paean of rejoicing … played and sung' by the court, whose entrance Paulina had signalled.

Believing, as she argued in the preface to her edition, that 'No audience of these days would desire to have the *Winter's Tale* produced in its entirety',[15] Mary Anderson (Lyceum, 1887) played a heavily cut text and reduced the running time to two hours and eight minutes. She might also have acknowledged that a number of her cuts and rearrangements, as well as stage business, helped to call attention to Hermione and Perdita, roles she was the first actor to double. Thus, Anderson added business to establish her fondness for Mamillius (typically business in 1.2 had worked to Leontes' advantage) and cut not only the troublesome appearances of Cleomenes and Dion (3.1), the bear, and Time, but also approximately 60 per cent of the trial scene. James Agate describes Hermione at the close of the scene:

> The crouching at the altar during the thunderstorm, the lowering, hunted, terror-stricken attitude, were excellent preludes to that glare of terror with the averted veil, concluding with the covered face and the tall white figure that falls prone with a crash upon the marble floor.
>
> (*Daily Telegraph*, 12 September 1887)

Against this visual image Paulina spoke just five of her lines before the promptbook cued her to 'Moan till Curtain'. To solve the problem of playing both mother and daughter in the statue scene, Anderson cut all of Perdita's lines and introduced a 'strange, veiled, speechless figure, who keeps her back to the audience and who is addressed as Perdita' (*Times*, 12 September 1887). A popular, but not a critical success, Anderson's production was the longest-running production of *The Winter's Tale* in the nineteenth century (Bartholomeusz, pp. 116–17).

The last production of *The Winter's Tale* in the tradition of pictorial realism was that of Herbert Beerbohm Tree (His Majesty's, 1906), who, as had his predecessors, played a heavily cut script and introduced unscripted business: Autolycus, for example, washed in a stream to which the Young Shepherd would later lead a donkey to drink. Three unifying devices, of the sort still employed, underscored points: theme music for Perdita and the reading of the oracle, interpolated allusions to Apollo, and thunder to mark the stages of Leontes' jealousy.

Producing *The Winter's Tale* (1912) as the first of his three Shakespearean plays at the Savoy, Harley Granville-Barker departed from nineteenth-century traditions by restoring almost all of Shakespeare's text and by

[margin note: charged so actress could double]

banishing elaborate stage effects and the heavy reliance on interpolated business and unscripted characters. Time was not transfigured into an allegory and all three gentlemen reported what little they knew about the amazing off-stage reunions. Granville-Barker sought not only to restore Shakespeare's script to the stage but also to explore Elizabethan playing conditions. By extending the platform beyond the proscenium arch and concentrating action on the new acting space, Granville-Barker made possible a more intimate relationship between actor and audience. Just two sets (the interior of Leontes' palace and exterior of the Old Shepherd's cottage), minimal props, and drop curtains resulted in a swiftly moving performance, with no time lost for shifting scenery and dressing the stage. Eclectic costumes evoked a 'world of fancy, fantasy, and romance'.[16] When Shakespeare's text called for music or dance, the production drew upon traditional English music and authentic folk dances.

Henry Ainley and Lillah McCarthy offered new readings of Leontes and Hermione. Ainley's delivery 'blurred' some of his lines, an effect which conveyed 'the King's fevered, irrational, or … neurotic mood and temperament' (*Nation*, 28 September 1912). His 'displays of physical frenzy' and his 'disagreeable-looking' appearance helped one reviewer understand why Hermione had taken three months to accept his proposal and why she 'exhibited a comparative coldness' in the statue scene and 'hardly' earned Camillo's observation that 'She hangs about his neck' (*Westminster Gazette*, 23 September 1912). Portraying the man rather than the monarch and exploring the nature of the reunion would become theatrical and critical motifs in the second half of the century.

Although Granville-Barker's *Winter's Tale* has been called one of the four or five most important twentieth-century productions of Shakespeare (Kennedy, p. 136), political and economic conditions mitigated against its immediate influence. The next significant production was not until 1951, when Peter Brook directed John Gielgud and Diana Wynyard as the monarchs at the Phoenix. Brook also sought to play a full script and to achieve continuous action on a set of 'modified upper and inner stages'.[17] Gielgud's Leontes, who 'both terrifie[d] and move[d]', contradicted received opinion that Leontes was 'unplayable'.[18] Gielgud 'turned [the] gnarled verse'[19] into 'wild hurtling music' and 'as the king repentant used all his emotional grandeur in the remembrance of his queen: "Stars, stars / And all eyes else dead coals!"'[20] Unlike Granville-Barker, who saw it as a stage effect, Brook believed that Hermione's resurrection 'held the whole truth of the play'.[21]

In the decades since Brook's staging, numerous productions have proved the versatility and powerful appeal of *The Winter's Tale*. Directors and designers have sought to rediscover Jacobean playing conditions; incorporated nineteenth-century business; presented *The Winter's Tale* in seasons of late plays and plays about love; set it in various historical periods and unusual geographical locations; introduced a unifying character or design motif; explored a concept or theme; and read the play in light of contemporary society and critical theses. It has been staged in theatres resembling the amphitheatre and hall theatres where the King's Men performed; in intimate, medium-sized, and large theatres; in the round; in the open air; and, on tour, in spaces as widely divergent as sports halls and Lincoln Cathedral. As had their predecessors, directors have altered the text and seemed to value design or music more than speaking the text.

Trevor Nunn's production for the Royal Shakespeare Company (RSC) in 1969 was one of the most influential post-war productions. Nunn cast Judi Dench as Hermione and Perdita; opened the production with a dumbshow that called attention to Time; set the stage with symbolic nursery toys – a rocking horse and blocks, which replicated the white box-like set; costumed the Sicilians in white, with its conflicting suggestions of the innocence of Hermione and Mamillius, the harshness of winter, and superficial stylishness of Sicilia; introduced strobe lighting effects, during which Hermione and Polixenes enacted Leontes' jealous fantasies; and found, in a hippy Bohemia, a setting with contemporary resonances as well as an exuberant contrast with Leontes' Sicilia. Nunn did not, as had Anderson, cut Perdita's lines in the statue scene, but his solution – and the solutions of those who followed him in doubling the roles – still required that Hermione address a stand-in, not the young woman who had enchanted Florizel, charmed as 'mistress o'th'feast' (4.4.68), and suffered reversals of fortune. Nunn's influence may be seen not only in productions that double Hermione and Perdita but also in those that use lighting or other technical effects to help explain the onset of Leontes' jealousy, portray Sicilia with white sets and costumes, dress the stage with nursery toys, place Bohemia in a hippy commune and introduce dumbshows involving Time.

At the National's Cottesloe Theatre (1988; tour and transfer to NT Olivier), Peter Hall placed *The Winter's Tale* in Caroline England. Hall and his designer sought to replicate the characteristics of a seventeenth-century hall stage: central double doors upstage with a discovery space, a set of exits on each side, a raked thrust stage, a ramp that led onto the central aisle. Above, a large tilting disc presented Copernicus' version of the heavens. The Sicilians wore handsome costumes of rich fabrics: lace collars and cuffs on garments in autumnal and wintry shades, silks, linens, brocades, and velvets (see illustration 4). In humbler styles, with vernal greens predominating, the Bohemians staged their sheep-shearing feast on a circular patch of grass beneath the Copernican heavens. Tim Pigott-Smith's Leontes was 'a

4. Costumed as Caroline aristocracy, Leontes (Tim Pigott-Smith),
Polixenes (Peter Woodward) and Hermione (Sally Dexter) share a convivial
moment before *tremor cordis* consumes Leontes.

radical rethinking of the role'. The *tremor cordis*, for example, was 'a physical symptom, recurring later in the action at moments of especial stress'.[22] Hall 'drew out the darker elements' of the sheep-shearing festival. Autolycus had 'a wolfish menace' and was 'contemptuous of those he fooled' (Wells, p. 144). Thunder and flashes of lightning, traditionally associated with the trial and the sea-coast of Bohemia, recurred at the close of the sexually threatening satyrs' dance. Polixenes' disowning of Florizel was 'like a rerun of Leontes' destructive violence'.[23] His furious threat to have Perdita's 'beauty scratched with briars' (4.4.405) also recalled Leontes' irrational behaviour. Reversing the image of the trial, Hall placed Hermione downstage centre with her back to the audience and focused attention on the responses of Leontes, upstage of her and with the other witnesses to Paulina's magic. Roger Warren describes the 'chastened, delicate, painful' moments that closed the production: 'After the final speech, Leontes and Hermione stood alone on stage looking at one another, before he ushered her off through the audience. They did not take hands' (p. 152).

Four years later Adrian Noble's production for the RSC celebrated the healing power of *The Winter's Tale*. As had Hall, Noble blocked the statue scene to concentrate attention on Leontes and the court, who gazed at the statue, downstage centre and with its back to the audience. His staging,

5. By placing the statue of Hermione (Samantha Bond) downstage centre with its back to the audience, Noble (RSC, 1992) concentrated attention on the responses of the stage audience, especially Leontes (John Nettles), whom Polixenes (Paul Jesson) comforts. Perdita (Phyllida Hancock) kneels to her mother's left; Paulina (Gemma Jones) is upstage of her.

however, suggested parallels with the opening image of a more carefree time. Then Mamillius, at the same spot, spun a top and the Edwardian court, dressed for a festive party, froze upstage of him within the large gauze box that would symbolize the damaging psychological and emotional isolation soon to erupt in Sicilia. When jealousy struck, Leontes prowled around the edges of the box, a self-imposed exile from the festivities. In 2.1 Leontes and his attendants stood motionless within it while downstage of them Mamillius whispered his tale of sprites and goblins. In 5.3 Leontes and the court were again clustered within the box, which was flown out when they faced the statue (see illustration 5). In contrast with Hall's, the overriding tone of Bohemia was restorative. Presented as a village fête and influenced by Stanley Spencer's paintings of his native Cookham, the sheep-shearing feast was a communal celebration. Villagers set the stage decorated with bunting, lights and balloons with mismatched chairs and tables and danced enthusiastically, if not always skilfully, to tunes played by the amateur band. Although a sudden storm broke up the festivities, it seemed characteristic of an English summer fête, not the harbinger of a cool reunion. In 1992, the wholesomeness of Bohemia set the stage for the reconciliations in Sicilia.

Greg Doran (RSC, 1999) chose the more sombre setting of a late nineteenth-century Eastern European court. Costumes were in shades of black and grey; and the set, which narrowed gradually as it approached upstage and which closed in as Leontes' isolating jealousy intensified, was overhung with a white cloud-like drapery. Sound effects of faint whispers suggested that Leontes' jealousy predated the interpolated business that opened the production: servants attended to their duties; Hermione, Leontes and Polixenes robed themselves in ermine-trimmed cloaks and acknowledged the cheering offstage crowds. Antony Sher's Leontes gave credence to the possibility of whispering servants: public duties attended to, he removed his crown and cloak and settled down to some serious document-signing, leaving Hermione (Alexandra Gilbreath) to entertain his childhood friend and refusing to join their dance. He taunted their wheelchair-bound son (Emily Bruni, doubling Mamillius and Perdita) as the sharp grip of 'morbid' or 'psychotic' jealousy took hold.[24] Accusing Hermione of adultery in 2.1, he mocked her voice and pushed her to the floor, his eyes starting. After her exit, he lit a cigarette, searched her bag for evidence, and Ford-like sniffed her shawl for tell-tale scents. Dishevelled, he complained, 'Nor night, nor day, no rest' (2.3.1), but the attending physician could not minister to this mind diseased. His memory seeming to have failed him, Leontes faltered and consulted his notes to open his prosecution of Hermione. Sixteen years later, the penitent, coaxed by Estelle Kohler's Paulina, pored over a religious text. The statue scene reintroduced images from the earlier Sicilian scenes. Witnesses included the servants, whose whispering Leontes had imagined and whose expressions had signalled their distress at palace events. There was an emblematic resemblance between the trial scene, where Hermione in filthy prison shift and chains defended herself from a railed dock, and the statue scene, where she stood Madonna-like on the same railed platform, now encircled by burning candles (see illustration 6). In both scenes Hermione 'extend[ed] her arms in yearning for reconciliation with her husband'.[25]

The unifying image of Edward Hall's production (Watermill, 2005, and tour) with its all-male ensemble company of twelve actors was Mamillius, who witnessed the 'nightmare of family disintegration' (*Guardian*, 28 January 2005). With doubling and trebling essential, only Tam Williams as Mamillius, Time, and Perdita held any significance. Pyjama-clad, Mamillius opened the production, playing with toys and lighting a candle, and was a silent observer of scenes Shakespeare excludes him from. He exited angrily and earlier than scripted, when Leontes commanded, 'Go play, boy, play' (1.2.185), but he re-entered above to overhear Leontes reveal his jealousy to Camillo. On stage throughout the accusation, he tried to break free from Emilia to intervene when Leontes kicked and spat at Hermione. Touching him gently, Hermione addressed 'This action I now go on / Is for my better grace' (2.1.121–2) to Mamillius instead of directing the line to her attendants, as is usual. Just as the

6. Doran's staging (RSC, 1999) of 5.3 allowed the audience to study the faces of Leontes (Antony Sher), Hermione (Alexandra Gilbreath) and Paulina (Estelle Kohler), as well as attendants; placed the statue on the same platform, now filled with candles, that had served as Hermione's dock in the trial scene; and reinforced the religious imagery introduced in earlier scenes.

boy had started the action, sometimes he moved it along. In interpolated business that alluded to the opening image and Leontes' command to 'play', Mamillius 'sailed' his toy ship to create the storm-tossed voyage to Bohemia and with his teddy bear pursued Antigonus. He spoke Time's lines, enacted Time's effects by ageing the beards and hair of Polixenes and Camillo and portrayed Perdita, whose foster father so sharply contrasted with Leontes. With its various restorations and reunions and especially the long embraces of Hermione and Leontes and of Hermione and Perdita, the statue scene seemed to be building to a harmonious resolution. But Hall, as have other directors, introduced as a framing device a visual reminder of the irrecoverable loss. Williams made a quick change, returned as Mamillius and found Leontes alone. Unaltered by the passage of sixteen years, Mamillius lit a candle, a music box played, and Leontes reached out toward his son, who blew out the candle.

Over the last decades directors and actors, such as those associated with these productions, have explored the lines, scenes and characters that their predecessors had perceived as problems and chosen to cut or smother in design. Because Gielgud had proved Leontes playable, the role was more attractive to other actors, some of whom consulted mental health professionals to help them understand Leontes' jealousy. Whatever the diagnosis, actors usually found Leontes' language a help, not a hindrance. The restoration of lines once deemed too indiscreet or risqué for Hermione, Paulina and Perdita to speak has revealed the women as strong, witty and compassionate. Actors, such as Estelle Kohler (RSC, 1999) and Linda Bassett (RSC, 2006), who understand the structure and imagery of Paulina's great speech at the close of the trial, have made it a thrilling theatrical moment. Recent Hermiones have played the trial scene in ways unthinkable in the nineteenth century: not only have they spoken a full or nearly full text, they have entered in chains, in prison shifts stained from childbirth. The statue scene usually closes in the reconciliation of Hermione and Leontes and his call for Paulina to 'Lead us from hence, where we may leisurely / Each one demand and answer to his part / Performed in this wide gap of time since first / We were disseverd' (5.3.152–5) seems a formality or a technical device for clearing the stage. But some productions have made clear that intense discussions will follow their tentative or chilly reunion, and other productions hold out little or no hope that Hermione will forgive Leontes. The wide range of emotions on the shores of Bohemia – including the Old Shepherd's description of the child and the Clown's 'two such sights, by sea and by land!' (3.3.77) and his determination to bury anything left of Antigonus – have seldom failed in performance. In the theatre even the apparently dispensable little scene in which Cleomenes and Dion recount their impression of Delphos seems perfectly judged, as does the excitement – the one-upmanship – of the three gentlemen, each of whom enters with a little more information than the previous gentleman had. Time and the bear seem to be the greatest challenges. They have tempted some directors toward symbolic interpretations. Time has assumed other characters' lines, appeared in the guise of, say, a gardener, or recurred as an aural or visual motif. So too the bear – although almost always best represented by an actor in bear costume – has been presented as a visual motif or been associated with another character in the play.

Critical afterlife

Fifty years on from Philip Edwards, who argued in 'Shakespeare's Romances: 1900–1957', that there is 'little progress to report' in support of claims for the excellence of the romances,[26] we no longer lament that criticism has failed to demonstrate claims for the excellence of the group of plays he called romances. Nor do we side with the decades of derision directed at the crafts-manship of *The Winter's Tale*. For this shift in critical perspective, three essays, as well as several twentieth-century productions, are central.

The first of these essays, in Granville-Barker's *Prefaces to Shakespeare*, claims the authority of a successful producer, as 'directors' were known until mid-twentieth century. Unlike the widely disseminated prefaces by nineteenth-century directors, who concentrated on visual aspects of their own productions and, in Kean's case, on historical and archaeological sources for their staging, Granville-Barker's *Preface* examines *The Winter's Tale* 'as in action and on the stage' and places Shakespeare's craftsmanship in the context of his earlier work and of the 'three chief opportunities' he found in Greene's story.[27] The *Preface* offers performance-based insight into aspects of the play that had proved stumbling blocks – and that would continue to attract directorial intervention and scholarly debate: the mixture of tragedy and comedy (Granville-Barker classifies the play as tragi-comedy); Leontes' jealousy and his challenging syntax, 'a most daring piece of technique by which twice or three times an actual obscurity of words (their meaning could never have been plain to any immediate listener) is used to express the turmoil of his mind' (pp. 95–6); the introduction of Cleomenes and Dion's return from the oracle as a bridging scene between 'the raucous revilings of Leontes' and 'the dignity … of the trial' (p. 96); Shakespeare's handling of the passage of sixteen years; the sheep-shearing; and his careful preparation for the statue scene and 'the perfect sufficiency of Hermione's eight lines' (p. 94). To Granville-Barker we may also trace the twentieth-century reinves-tigation of the female characters. Hermione not only possesses the 'goodness' nineteenth-century actors portrayed but also is 'an exquisitely sensitive woman, high-minded, witty too, and tactful' (p. 95). Presaging feminist criticism, he concludes, 'No play of Shakespeare's boasts three such women as Hermione, Perdita, Paulina' (p. 95).

The next important contribution, Nevill Coghill's 'Six Points of Stage-Craft in *The Winter's Tale*,' appeared in *Shakespeare Survey* (1958) as a compa-nion piece to Edwards's survey of criticism. Coghill asserted with little fear of contradiction that, 'It is a critical commonplace that *The Winter's Tale* is an ill-made play.' Urging its deriders to consider that Shakespeare 'may well have had some special, and perhaps discernible, intention' in employing the alleged 'creaking dramaturgy', Coghill argues that an examination of how something works might reveal its purpose.[28] A director of plays, as well as a teacher at Oxford (he had directed *The Winter's Tale* in 1946), Coghill explores three of the topics Granville-Barker had singled out – Leontes' sudden jealousy, Time and the statue scene – and three passages cavilling critics often cited: the bear's pursuit of Antigonus; 'The Crude Shifts' that follow Camillo's plan for the escape to Sicilia (4.4.486–594); and the penultimate scene, in which three gentlemen compare notes about the offstage reunions.

The third contribution in this series on craftsmanship is William Matchett's 'Some Dramatic Techniques in "The Winter's Tale"'.[29] Matchett looks at three dramatic techniques the emergence of Leontes' jealousy, the bear – and the statue scene – 'to call particular attention to the way in which Shakespeare, thus late in his career, had learned both to trust his actors and to manipulate audience response' (p. 93). Matchett's argument contradicts critics who discover Shakespeare's declining power in *The Winter's Tale*, places, as had Granville-Barker, the play in the context of Shakespeare's earlier works and acknowledges a debt to Coghill's insights.

Of the points of stagecraft treated above in the performance history and these three essays, Leontes' jealousy and the statue scene have attracted the most considerable attention. Critics, actors and directors have offered many answers to the three basic questions about Leontes' jealousy: When does it strike? What is its root cause? How is it manifested? Solutions that may seem insightful in the library often prove dead ends in the rehearsal room. How, for example, might an actor convey that diet causes Leontes' 'apparently motive-less jealousy'?[30] Despite sharing an approach to perceived difficulties and problems (both men placed the play in the contexts of Shakespeare's other plays and of his chief source and drew upon their directing experience) Granville-Barker and Coghill reached different conclusions about Leontes' jealousy. To Granville-Barker it was sudden and inexplicable. He described it as 'a nervous weakness, a mere hysteria', a 'wanton malice ... [found] in his own heart' (pp. 92, 93). Leontes has 'hardly the shadow of an excuse for his suspicion' (p. 93). Coghill's explanation, on the other hand, relies on an attentive audience, a close reading of the script and the stage picture as he imagines it. The opening dialogue, in which Camillo and Archidamus describe an amiable friendship, does not prepare the audience for the scene Coghill stages: Leontes and Polixenes enter separately, Leontes 'wears a look of barely controlled hostility', and Polixenes stands beside Hermione, whose pregnancy the audience notices. Coghill contrasts Polixenes' 'flowery language' with the 'one-syllabled two-edged utterances of his host' (pp. 32–3). Matchett visualises the scene a third way. Taking the conversation of Camillo and Archidamus at face value, he argues that Leontes is not jealous when he enters the second scene. As Matchett reads the scene, Shakespeare leads the audience to believe that Hermione might be guilty –she's visibly pregnant, Polixenes' first words reveal that he has been in Sicilia for nine months, and images of 'conception, fertility and gratitude' characterise his speech (p. 96). Attentive to the stage picture, the audience would find irony in Leontes' 'Is he won yet?' (1.2.85). Shakespeare's method, Matchett posits, lets 'his audience participate directly in the fall of Leontes, by leading us to mistake innocence for guilt' (p. 98). Norman Nathan also argues that Leontes 'jealousy is sudden *and* well-motivated', but he builds a different case.[31] Hermione's silence is a dramatic necessity: propriety demands that she remain silent until Polixenes has refused all of Leontes' entreaties; and when she speaks, her 'excellent wit' contrasts with Leontes' 'chiding' (p. 21). Her repartee is skilful, and her bantering includes ambiguities with sexual connotations. Whereas editors insert stage directions and directors interpolate business to distract Leontes, such as Sher's signing documents, or even to take him offstage during their conversation, Nathan believes Leontes is present. He presents three possible explanations for Leontes re-entering the dialogue with the question 'Is he won yet?': he wants to change the tone of the conversation; he wonders what else Hermione has to say before Polixenes agrees; Polixenes has not said a clear 'yes' or 'no' (p. 22). The point at which Leontes' jealousy strikes is 'At my request he would not' (1.2.86).

In a pair of insightful essays for *Players of Shakespeare 5*[32] Antony Sher and Alexandra Gilbreath have recorded their preparation for, and playing of, Leontes and Hermione (RSC, 1999). Sher was struck at first by the fact that only ten minutes into performance Leontes must reveal himself as a 'very disturbed, very dangerous man' with only one clue to guide him: the 'three crabbed months' (1.2.100–5) he waited for Hermione's response to his proposal of marriage (Sher, p. 94). The first helpful clue he found was 'Inch-thick, knee-deep, o'er head and ears a forked one!' (1.2.184), with its imagery 'of flesh, of sewage, of devils and cuckholds' (p. 94). Delving into his own experience as well as Shakespeare's image, Sher came to understand that Leontes' behaviour was not 'evil'; he was 'someone in trouble, in pain' (p. 94). For the next step, identifying the illness, Sher consulted experts in the field of mental health. He rejected the first three diagnoses (schizophrenia, manic-depression, Leontes as a portrait of the ageing dramatist) and pursed the fourth: Leontes suffered from 'morbid' or 'psychotic jealousy', for which the 'dominant characteristic is a delusion that the patient's partner is betraying him' (p. 95). Sher then found in the text symptoms of the 'wildly obsessive behaviour' of the morbidly jealous and turned to the challenge of presenting Leontes as ill and therefore 'as much a victim … as those whose lives he wrecks' (p. 95). One solution was to use soliloquies to confront the audience. Sometimes he directed painful lines, such as those beginning 'And many a man there is' (1.2.192–4), to individuals in the audience. At other times he 'implored the audience to guide [him]: 'I don't want to kill her, but do you think it might be best – to cure this torment? – please help me' (2.3.7–9; p. 96). The iambic pentameter, which Shakespeare used 'like a master jazz musician', also guided Sher. 'Leontes does,' Sher concludes, 'become incoherent, yet he is struggling to make sense of a world which has become unrecognizable. And this is absolutely exhilarating to play' (p. 99).

Whereas Sher's goal was to play Leontes as a victim, Gilbreath determined that Hermione was 'not a victim: incapable of shaping her own destiny, not passive and submissive, but someone who places her trust in fate ...' (p. 76). In Hermione's speeches Gilbreath found an 'informality ... a rather gentle, teasing quality'; she is 'gently persuasive and very, very charming'. But Gilbreath also wanted to convey that Hermione 'was consciously aware of the subtle sexual overtones' in the dialogue with Polixenes, 'yet graceful and dignified enough not to yield to them' (p. 79).

The contributions of set and costume design to the course of Leontes' jealousy, which Sher and Gilbreath consider briefly, is a major topic in Inga-Stina Ewbank's essay 'From Narrative to Dramatic Language: *The Winter's Tale* and Its Source'.[33] She describes the extent to which both Trevor Nunn (RSC, 1969) and John Barton with Nunn (RSC, 1976) relied on visual language to prepare the audience for the emergence of Leontes' jealousy. In 1969, the nursery setting 'explained Leontes's psychology and motivated his jealousy' (p. 31). In stark contrast with the contemporary society of the 1969 production, the design in 1976 placed Sicilia in 'a kind of "Lapland" decor'. The 'primitive symbols', which decorated the curtains and the 'rugs and furs', which covered the floor and furniture 'established for the audience a tribal world in which behaviour might well be incalculable' (p. 31). Losses ensue, Ewbank argues, when visual symbolism replaces language:

> if the audience's response to Leontes is controlled by external ... means, then we run the risk of losing that closeness to his specific, self-engendered agony which Shakespeare's language creates. And language is Shakespeare's main dramatic tool in these early scenes where we watch how the jealousy grows.   (p. 40)

Disagreeing with those who label the statue a contrivance, who believe it is 'not prepared for' and therefore 'appears to have been a change of plan',[34] or who find a religious meaning in Hermione's 'resurrection', a number of critics buttress Granville-Barker's sensitivity to the theatrical power of the scene. Although they approach the scene from different angles, each critic praises the careful dramaturgy, as revealed especially in 3.2 and 5.2, with which Shakespeare anticipated the final scene. Turning to *Pandosto*, Adrien Bonjour looks at two of the major changes Shakespeare made to his source, changes that gave 'a unity of theme' absent from Greene.[35] The first, that Camillo does not, like Greene's Franion, disappear from the plot; it is Camillo's ingenuity that gets the major Bohemian characters to Sicilia and makes possible the offstage reunions of Act 5. The jubilant conversation of the three gentlemen, together with the close of the trial scene, prepares the audience for the second major change: Hermione, unlike Greene's Bellaria, is restored to the King. Paulina's long speech in 3.2, the climax of which is her announcement that the Queen is dead, convinces Leontes, as subsequent lines make clear, and must convince the audience, although some might mutter that the lady doth protest too much. The three gentlemen's comments about the statue, its likeness to Hermione, and Paulina's visits to the 'removed house', for example, may also, Bonjour argues, make the audience suspicious. Suspicion does not creep into Coghill's audience, for whom Shakespeare's 'stage-craft' has achieved the two dramatic necessities: that we believe Hermione dead; that we believe the statue real. Paulina's announcement of, and subsequent references to, Hermione's death convince Coghill, as does the three gentlemen's revelation that Paulina has commissioned a statue. Coghill, moreover, looks closely at the skill with which Shakespeare created the statue's 'long stillness' – Coghill times it at four minutes – and the suspense created by Paulina's 'long, pausing entreaty' that it 'be stone no more' (p. 40). In Paulina's five lines, 'the most heavily punctuated passage' Coghill could find in the folio, he calls attention to twelve colons, to which we may add the further pauses indicated by two commas, a semi-colon and a parenthetical sentence (p. 40). Matchett's analysis of the statue scene, which he finds illustrative of Shakespeare's faith in his actors, picks up where Coghill stopped. Just as the audience expected to see Leontes' reunions with his daughter and his childhood friend, so it expects 'his poetry to reach an emotional climax' (p. 103) when Leontes and Hermione are reunited. But they speak 'the eloquence of silence' (p. 107). Matchett traces 'the limitations of language' to the first scene, where words fail Archidamus (1.1.11–12), and sketches its course to the final scene, where, in Shakespeare's hands, the reunion is 'a carefully constructed thematic triumph' (p. 104).

NOTES

1. Kenneth Muir (ed.), *Shakespeare: 'The Winter's Tale': A Casebook* (London: Macmillan, 1969), p. 25.
2. E. K. Chambers, *William Shakespeare: A Study of Facts and Problems* (Oxford: Oxford University Press, 1930), vol. II, p. 352. His *The Elizabethan Stage*, 4 vols. (Oxford: Oxford University Press, 1923) is the source for the record of performances.
3. Unless otherwise noted, the source for the period 1660–1800 is the five parts of *The London Stage 1660–1800*, eds. William Van Lennep *et al.* (Carbondale: University of Southern Illinois, 1960–8).
4. Robert Kean Turner and Virginia Westling Haas (eds.), *A New Variorum Edition of 'The Winter's Tale'* (New York: The Modern Language Association of America, 2005), p. 848.

5. Thomas Davies, *Memoirs of the Life of David Garrick* (London: Longman, Hurst, Rees and Orme, 1808), vol. I, p. 314.
6. The sources for performances between 1800 and 1951 are Dennis Bartholomeusz, *'The Winter's Tale' in Performance in England and America 1611–1976* (Cambridge: Cambridge University Press, 1982); and my *'The Winter's Tale* on the Stage: Performances', in Turner and Haas (eds.), *A New Variorum*.
7. James Boaden (ed.), *Memoirs of the Life of John Philip Kemble, Esq.* (London: Longman *et al.*, 1825), vol. II, p. 314.
8. Helena Faucit, Lady Martin, *On Some of Shakespeare's Female Characters* (London: William Blackwood and Sons, 1891), p. 391.
9. Shirley S. Allen, *Samuel Phelps and Sadler's Wells* (Middleton, CT: Wesleyan University Press, 1971), p. 178.
10. Charles Kean (ed.), *The Winter's Tale* (London: John K. Chapman and Co., [1856]), p. ix.
11. M. Glen Wilson, 'Charles Kean's Production of *The Winter's Tale*', *Theatre Studies* 5 (1985), pp. 1–15, at p. 2.
12. W. Moelwyn Merchant, *Shakespeare and the Artist* (London: Oxford University Press, 1959), p. 214.
13. Charles Calvert (ed.), *The Winter's Tale* (Manchester: John Heywood, 1869).
14. Russell Jackson, 'Shakespeare in Liverpool: Edward Saker's Revivals, 1876–81', *Theatre Notebook* 32 (1978), pp. 100–9, at p. 103.
15. Mary Anderson (ed.), *The Winter's Tale* (London: W. S. Johnson, 1887).
16. Dennis Kennedy, *Granville Barker and the Dream of Theatre* (Cambridge: Cambridge University Press, 1985), p. 128.
17. Alice Venezky, 'Current Shakespearian Productions in England and France', *Shakespeare Quarterly* 2 (1951), pp. 335–42, at p. 335.
18. J. C. Trewin, 'Town and Country', *Illustrated London News* (15 September 1951), p. 418.
19. J. C. Trewin, 'Raising a Storm', *Illustrated London News* (21 July 1951), p. 110.
20. J. C. Trewin, *Peter Brook* (London: Macdonald, 1971), p. 60.
21. Robert Speaight, *Shakespeare on Stage* (London: Collins, 1973), p. 275.
22. Stanley Wells, 'Shakespeare Performances in England, 1987–8', *Shakespeare Survey* 42 (1990), pp. 129–48, at p. 144.
23. Roger Warren, *Staging Shakespeare's Late Plays* (Oxford: Clarendon Press, 1990), p. 136.
24. Antony Sher, 'Leontes in *The Winter's Tale*, and *Macbeth*', in *Players of Shakespeare 5*, ed. Robert Smallwood (Cambridge: Cambridge University Press, 2003), pp. 90–112, at p. 95.
25. Robert Smallwood, 'Shakespeare Performances in England, 1999', *Shakespeare Survey* 53 (2000), pp. 244–73, at p. 265.
26. Philip Edwards, 'Shakespeare's Romances: 1900–1957', *Shakespeare Survey* 11 (1958), pp. 1–18, at p. 1.
27. Harley Granville-Barker, *Prefaces to Shakespeare* (London: William Heinemann, 1912; rpr. London: Batsford, 1984), pp. 91, 92.
28. Nevill Coghill, 'Six Points of Stage-Craft in *The Winter's Tale*', *Shakespeare Survey* 11 (1958), pp. 31–41, at p. 31.
29. William Matchett, 'Some Dramatic Techniques in *The Winter's Tale*', *Shakespeare Survey* 22 (1971), pp. 93–108.

30. Joan Fitzpatrick, *Food in Shakespeare: Early Modern Dietaries and the Plays.* (Aldershot: Ashgate, 2007), p. 67.
31. Norman Nathan, 'Leontes' Provocation', *Shakespeare Quarterly* 19 (1968), pp. 19–24, at p. 20.
32. Sher, in Smallwood (ed.), *Players 5*, pp. 91–112; Alexandra Gilbreath, 'Hermione in *The Winter's Tale*', in Smallwood, (ed.), *Players 5*, pp. 74–90.
33. Inga-Stina Ewbank, 'From Narrative to Dramatic Language: *The Winter's Tale* and Its Source', in Marvin Thompson and Ruth Thompson (eds.), *Shakespeare and the Sense of Performance* (Newark: University of Delaware, 1989), pp. 29–47.
34. Clifford Leech, 'The Structure of the Last Plays', *Shakespeare Survey* 11 (1958), pp. 19–30, at pp. 24, 25.
35. Adrien Bonjour, 'The Final Scene of *The Winter's Tale*', *English Studies* 33 (1952), pp. 193–208, at p. 197.

7

CATHERINE M. S. ALEXANDER

Cymbeline: the afterlife

Reading the play

Two anecdotes attest to the emotional power of *Cymbeline*. Charles Cowden Clarke recalls seeing a young John Keats in the early 1800s reading the play aloud and noticing his eyes filling with tears, 'And for some moments he was unable to proceed, when he came to the departure of Posthumus, and Imogen's saying she would have watched him … "till he had melted from / The smallness of a gnat to air"' (1.3.21–2),[1] and it is often said that Tennyson felt such affection for the play that at his death in October 1892 he was buried with a copy of *Cymbeline* in his hand. A letter to the *New York Times* of 23 April 1910 from William M. St John went further and insisted, with no evidence at all, that 'in the poet's last moments his finger rested on "Fear no more the heat o' the sun."' The afterlife and reception of the play, however, is characterised less by such testimonials to affect than the enduring, critical reaction of Samuel Johnson (and his commentary will recur throughout this essay). In the *Notes* that he compiled between 1745 and 1765 and added to his edition of Shakespeare Johnson acknowledged that *Cymbeline* has 'many just sentiments, some natural dialogues and some pleasing scenes, but they are obtained at the expense of much incongruity' and concluded, 'To remark the folly of the fiction, the absurdity of the conduct, the confusion of the names and manners of different times, and the impossibility of events in any system of life, were to waste criticism upon unresisting imbecility, upon faults too evident for detection, and too gross for aggravation'.[2] The play clearly falls far short of Johnson's expectations (which would seem to be for the Enlightenment values of wisdom, rationality, lucidity, plausibility and consistency) and, for him, places Shakespeare in the position of the 'writers of barbarous romances' who 'can only gain attention by hyperbolical or aggravated characters, by fabulous and unexampled excellence or depravity', and whom he condemned in the Preface to his edition, adding 'and he that should form his expectations of human affairs from the play, or the tale, would be equally deceived'.³ It has been suggested that Johnson may have assisted Charlotte Lennox with *Shakespear Illustrated*,⁴ her account, with critical commentary, of Shakespeare's source material, and certainly her response to *Cymbeline* displays similar assumptions about the constituents of effective drama. She explained Shakespeare's use of Boccaccio and retold much of the plot of the play (giving up the struggle when Innogen, disguised, becomes Lucius' page) and pointed to what she saw as its many weaknesses: 'It would be an endless task to take notice of all the absurdities in the plot, and unnatural manners in the characters of this play ... with inconsistencies like these it every where abounds; the whole conduct of the play is absurd and ridiculous to the last degree, and with all the liberties Shakespear has taken with time, place and action, the story, as he has managed it, is more improbable than a fairy tale' (vol. I, p. 166). In highlighting what she sees as a particularly gross inconsistency Lennox uses a telling phrase: 'Shakespear no doubt foresaw his *readers* would ask this question ...' (vol. I, p. 162), a reminder that neither she, whose comparative method is likely to privilege continuous narrative, nor Johnson have had the opportunity to see the play performed as Shakespeare wrote it and are responding to the read rather than the staged play and with expectations that the author will provide a 'Map of life, a faithful miniature of human transactions' (vol. I, p. x). The earliest record of performance, possibly of 1611 at the Globe, is the account written by Simon Forman in his 'The Book of Plays and Notes Thereof', and is concerned solely with the main elements of the plot. There is nothing to suggest that Forman – and, by extension, others in the audience – were concerned with improbable actions or unfaithful representations of character; indeed, his rather breathless style with many repetitions conveys a strong sense of engagement and excitement:

> And how the Italian that came from her love conveyed himself into a chest, and said it was a chest of plate sent from her love and others to be presented to the King. And in the deepest of the night, she being asleep, he opened the chest and came forth of it. And viewed her in bed and the marks of her body and took away her bracelet, and after accused her of adultery to her love, etc. ...⁵

There is no doubt that Johnson was a careful reader of the play, albeit an unappreciative one: his personal copy of the text survives (Warburton's edition of Shakespeare, 1747), marked to indicate the words and phrases that he mined for etymological and illustrative purposes in his Dictionary. He quotes from *Cymbeline* almost as often as from *Othello* and more frequently than from *The Tempest*, *Romeo and Juliet* and *Antony and Cleopatra*, amongst others, an acknowledgement, perhaps, that he found more in the language of the play than just 'some natural dialogues'. William Warburton himself had a higher estimation of *Cymbeline* than Johnson: in the introductory material to his edition he established a league table of the plays: 'It seemed not amiss to introduce the following observations with one general criticism on our author's dramatick works, by dividing them into four classes, and so giving an estimate of each play reduced to its proper class.'[6] Distinguishing only between tragedy and comedy, he placed *Cymbeline* as the last play in the second division of the tragedies, giving it a higher 'estimate' than *Richard II*, *Coriolanus*, *Troilus*, *Romeo and Juliet* and the four plays he dismissed into the fourth class as not authored by Shakespeare: the three parts of *Henry VI* and *Titus*.

Other eighteenth-century readers saw value in the work too. William Dodd's popular *The Beauties of Shakespeare*, the first anthology of Shakespeare,[7] used passages of *Cymbeline* to illustrate aspects of romantic married love using headings such as 'A Wife's Innocency', 'Parting Lovers' and 'A Wife's Impatience to meet her Husband' and making moral commentary: he glosses Iachimo's 'Had I this cheek ...' (1.6.99–112) and 'To be partnered / With tomboys' (1.6.121–6) with the observation:

> These lines are well worthy the reflection of all those gentlemen, who stile themselves *Men of pleasure*; if they would duly weigh the truth of them: their own pride sure would be the first thing to *drum them*, as *Shakespear* says, from their lascivious sports. (pp. 199–210)

Others subsequently used passages from the play in the growing body of literature that employed passages of Shakespeare's text to illustrate commentary on moral or critical worth: Henry Homes, Lord Kames, as evidence that 'Bad news gain also credit upon the slightest evidence',[8] for example, and Joseph Priestley quoting 'No tis slander, / Whose tongues / out venom all the worms of Nile ...' as a specimen of the personification of the passions.[9] Yet at a time when writers were appropriating portions of Shakespeare and allusions to specific characters for parody, illustration and to inform *new* writing few borrowed from *Cymbeline*. William Collins, a writer of odes who was subsequently admired by the Romantics, borrowed 'Dirge in *Cymbeline* sung by Guiderius and Arviragus over Fidele, supposed to be dead' in 1744 and while his choice of text suggests early interest in 'Fear no more the heat of the sun' it is an isolated example of textual reworking and little more than paraphrase: 'No wailing ghost shall dare appear / To vex with shrieks this quiet grove, / But shepherd lads assemble here, / And melting virgins own their love ...'[10] *Cymbeline* lacked the visibility, in new print, of better-known or more popular texts until the early 1800s when, prompted perhaps by the greater accessibility of texts after the end of perpetual copyright,[11] a shift in popular taste, minor appropriations by Gothic novelists and the attempts at reclamation by the Romantics, there was a greater appreciation of the imagination, the supernatural and the sublime. Matthew Lewis, for example, in his extravagantly Gothic *The Monk* (1796) used Iachimo's lines as the epigraph for the racy chapter (vol. III, chap. 1), that owes much to *Cymbeline*, in which the 'lusty monk' Ambrosio attempts to rape Antonia:

> The crickets sing, and man's o'er-laboured sense
> Repairs itself by rest. Our Tarquin thus
> Did softly press the rushes, ere he wakened
> The chastity he wounded. Cytherea,
> How bravely thou becom'st thy bed! Fresh lily,
> And whiter than the sheets!   (2.2.11–16)

William Hazlitt, who much preferred the critical writings of Pope on Shakespeare, tried to refute Johnson's method: his 'general powers of reasoning overlaid his critical susceptibility. All his ideas were in a set form: they were made out by rule and system ... He reduced everything to the common standard of conventional propriety ... he seized only on the permanent and tangible.'[12] Hazlitt himself, who privileged the play by placing it first in *Characters of Shakespeare's Plays* and beginning his account with the assertion that it 'is one of the most delightful of Shakespeare's historical plays' (p. 1), saw very different qualities in it. Keats-like he admired its pathos and its tender gloom (p. 2) and while he, too, was responding to it as a text to be read he found excitement in the reader's journey, sustained suspense and 'the most complete development of the catastrophe' (p. 1). Hazlitt's German contemporary August Schlegel shared his pleasure: '*Cymbeline* is also one of Shakespeare's most wonderful compositions,' and while his account of the play is largely character-driven he saw value in the last scene, 'Where all the numerous threads of the knot are untied [and] he has again given its full development, that he might collect together into one focus the scattered impressions of the whole'.[13] While the Romantics made much less use of *Cymbeline* as an inspirational source than *The Tempest*, there is evidence of some influence: Coleridge borrowed the plot for his play *Zapolyta*; there are signs of appropriation in the songs and poems of William Blake; and Keats made use of the same passage that Lewis had borrowed for the threatening bedroom scene of 'The Eve of St Agnes'.[14]

Yet it remained Johnson's 'hold of the mechanical and commonplace' (Hazlitt, p. xxxvi) – reason rather than the imagination – that continued to inform and influence the critical response to the play on the page and the stage for many years. He lurks in the background of a great deal of commentary. J. M. Nosworthy, in the Arden edition first published in 1955, suggested that, 'It may cheerfully be admitted that even Johnson did not realize exactly how great a tissue of incongruities the thing is' before arguing for the strength of the whole rather than its parts, which he believed 'seldom rise above a certain modest standard' (p. lxxvii). Howard Taubman, reviewing William Gaskill's RSC *Cymbeline* in the *New York Times*, 18 July 1962, both quoted from and endorsed the prejudices: 'Dr Samuel Johnson was not too harsh when he called the plot "imbecile," and perhaps too generous when he applauded the play's "many just sentiments"', and Sheridan Morley opened his review of David Jones's 1979 RSC production with '*Cymbeline* is the impossible one' (*Punch*, 25 April 1979). Reviewing Elijah Moshinsky's 1983 BBC *Cymbeline* in *The Times Literary Supplement* (22 July 1983, p. 773), Katherine Duncan-Jones began: 'While few modern readers of *Cymbeline* would go the whole way with Johnson in his refusal to "waste criticism upon unresisting imbecility", it is undeniable that any modern director of the play must make some positive decisions about how to deal with this clogged, often obscure and highly complicated romance.'

Performing the play

Clearly the play has become problematised and *Cymbeline* remains the least performed of the single-authored last plays. Johnson apart, the difficulties begin, perhaps, with the slippery genre of the play. Directors and actors may be little exercised by Heminges and Condell's placement of the play in the tragedy section (and the list of contents, the 'Catalogue'), of the 1623 First Folio, the distinction endorsed by Warburton, but they will still question the nature and tone of the play. They may well find a drama which begins remarkably like the tragedy of *King Lear* (Shakespeare's other play set in ancient Britain) with a dialogue about a monarch, daughters and the succession, and subsequently concludes, via a pick and mix of history, pastoral, romance, masque and comedy, with the sequence of revelations, restorations and reconciliations that Lennox dismissed as a fairytale, disconcertingly uneven. Many productions, striving for generic consistency and aesthetic symmetry, have tinkered with the opening of the play. J. P. Kemble who presented *Shakespeare's Cymbeline, King of Britain* as *An Historical Play* at the Theatres Royal in 1815 and published his text in the same year,[15] strove for a more convincing beginning than the dialogue of Shakespeare's bald dramatic device. He reattributes the opening lines to Pisanio (the First Gentleman's role), who is in conversation with 'Madan', and gives him additional comments – 'Are you so fresh a stranger to ask that?' for example – to contribute to a more realistic exchange. Other productions have chosen to establish a sense of 'story', with its different conventions of narrative and audience expectations, rather than dramatic verisimilitude. John Barton's production for the RSC in 1974 expanded the role of Cornelius to create a narrator, like Gower in *Pericles*, who presented the story, indicated scene location and described the battle scenes using the stage directions, dispensing with the dialogue. Adrian Noble's 1997 RSC *Cymbeline* rewrote the opening dialogue to create a prologue for a single actor who tells his story to an onstage audience, a group gathered round a camp-fire. As he names a character in his tale an actor stands and identifies his role, a device which achieves some clarity but at the expense of revealing that the king's lost sons have survived. Although, as Ann Thompson has pointed out, 'What auditor or reader is so naïve as not to realize that if missing children are mentioned in the first scene of a play they will be found before the last one?',[16] delaying the revelation of identity, when handled skillfully, can add to the delight of the play. The sense of 'story' was reinforced in Noble's production by oriental costume, hairstyle and set and the production was well received even though, for some, Johnson remained the critical yardstick:

> Some great critics have had a high old time trashing *Cymbeline*. Dr Johnson complained of its "imbecility", while Shaw declared it "stagy trash of the lowest melodramatic order".
>
> Watching Adrian Noble's fine production one finds oneself thinking that if this is stagy trash, let's have more of it.[17]

Mike Alfred's simplified *Cymbeline* at the Globe in 2000 was presented by just six actors, all of whom, from the start of the play, functioned as narrators, setting up the plot and identifying character and place. The imposition of metatheatre in these examples establishes a tone that goes some way towards accommodating the episodic nature of the play, its apparent generic incongruities and the difficulties of the ending as well as the beginning. There are expectations of the heroes and heroines of tragedy that this play does not, clearly, fulfil: at its conclusion *Cymbeline* forgives the morally culpable and audiences may find this more acceptable, ethically and aesthetically, in the context of the conventions of 'story'. Such an approach can exploit the stereotypical elements of fairytale – the wicked stepmother, the oafish son, the innocent princess, the lost boys, the poison – that are an ill fit in tragedy. Furthermore, if 'non-realism' has been established then the masque elements of 5.3 may be more easily accommodated. The ghosts of Posthumus' parents and two brothers whose appeals summon Jupiter, who 'descends in thunder and lightning, sitting upon an eagle' and throws a thunderbolt, are perhaps the least-anticipated appearances in the play. Structurally this is the moment when the play shifts from suffering to reconciliation; contextually this reinforces contemporary politics and links the play to the Stuart court masque, a connection identified by Graham Holderness, who points to the use of a device in which 'a group of characters appears to question, challenge or doubt the justice of existence, the equity of a sovereign's government, or the rationale of a divine providence'.[18] At the same time it is a reminder of the classical, Roman elements of the play: it is a multi-functional piece of stagecraft that adds further complexities to the debate about genre.

But the staging challenges of *Cymbeline* go beyond genre, particularly for those of the Johnson/Lennox mindset. There is the range of location and the different worlds of the play: an ancient British court, rural Wales, a sophisticated Italian city (much closer, surely, to Renaissance Rome than the world of Shakespeare's Roman plays), battlefields and interior and exterior scenes. The difficulty here lies not only with the accurate representation of place but in decisions about time. Shakespeare's knowing anachronisms resist some obvious answers to the question of when to set the play and both geography and history are potentially problematic. One of the sources, Holinshed's *Chronicles* (1587), provides a very specific date for the action:

> Kymbeline or Cimbeline the son of Theomantius was of the Britains made king after the deceasse of his father ... This man (as some write) was brought up at Rome, and there made knight by Augustus Caesar, under whom he served in the warres, and was in such favour with him that he was at libertie to pay his tribute or not. Little other mention is made of his dooings, except that during his reign, the Saviour of the world, our Lord Jesus Christ, the onelie sonne of God, was born of a virgine, about the 23 yeare of the reign of this Kymbeline.[19]

If the setting of year 0, give or take a year, presents staging challenges (and Shakespeare makes far less attempt in this play to return to the values and language of an earlier age than he does in *Lear*) then the obvious alternatives – the Jacobean world of the period of the play's composition or the imposition of a new, pre- or post-Shakespearian era – are no less difficult given the playwright's disregard for temporal consistency and the anachronisms of, say, the reading in bed and clock striking in 2.2. Add to this the practical difficulties of disguise, a vision or apparition, a headless body and the separated head and *Cymbeline* becomes a play that requires great ingenuity and skill to stage.

An examination of its performance history suggests that a number of strategies and approaches to the text have been employed, not necessarily as discrete responses, to stage the play and overcome Johnson's criticisms, the practical and aesthetic challenges, and to accord with contemporary taste and interests. The play has suffered major excisions, adaptations and, through setting, had its diversity replaced with a unity of time or place. The first strategy has been to avoid some of the perceived difficulties through cutting the text. Probably the most famous production of the play, by Henry Irving at the Lyceum Theatre in London in 1896, cut roughly a quarter of the text

7. The bedchamber scene: a much-praised moment at the Lyceum Theatre, 1896, with Henry Irving as Iachimo and Ellen Terry as Innogen (drawing by H. M. Paget in *The Graphic*).

including, as is not uncommon in productions seeking realism or consistency, Posthumus' vision of his parents and brothers and the descent of Jupiter (5.3). The enduring interest in the show rests largely on the performance of Ellen Terry as Innogen and her detailed correspondence with George Bernard Shaw as she prepared the role. He was unhappy with Irving's prepared text and on 8 September wrote to Terry:

> Generally speaking the cutting of the play is stupid to the last extremity. Even from the broadest popular point of view, the omission of the grandiose scene about England and Caesar for the queen, Cloten and the Roman, is a mistake ... Posthumus's exit on p. 32 is utterly spoiled by a fragment of another scene stuck in utterly the wrong place ... The prudery of the cutting is silly: Pisanio says 'disloyal' instead of adultery; Iachimo discreetly omits the lines 'where, I profess, I slept not etc.'[20]

Shaw is selective in his criticisms here; prudish though occasional excisions may have been 2.2 remained intact and Iachimo (played by Irving himself), leaning over Innogen in her bedchamber, was a much-praised scene and the subject of illustration in both *The Graphic* (by H. M. Paget) and *The Illustrated London News* (by S. Begg) in May 1896 (see illustration 7). Many years later,

Shaw heard that *Cymbeline* was to be revived in Stratford and in 1945 revisited his assumptions that the last act of the play was 'a cobbled affair by many hands' and recalled the Lyceum production:

> when Irving, as Iachimo, a statue of romantic melancholy, stood dumb on the stage for hours (as it seemed) whilst the others toiled through a series of *denouments* of crushing tedium, in which the characters lost all their vitality and individuality, and had nothing to do but identify themselves by moles on their necks, or explain why they were not dead. The vision and the verses were cut out as a matter of course ...[21]

So in part as a response to prevailing cutting and staging practice – and to further his own critical interest in character rather than plot – he rewrote the last act, retaining eighty-nine lines of Shakespeare and reducing the length of the whole by over 500 lines. He concluded with an offer to directors who may lack the 'courage and good sense to present the original word-for-word as Shakespeare left it, and the means to do justice to the masque': if they are 'halfhearted about it, and inclined to compromise by leaving out the masque and the comic jailer and mutilating the rest, as their manner is, I unhesitatingly recommend my version. The audience will not know the difference; and the few critics who have read *Cymbeline* will be too grateful for my shortening of the last act to complain' (p. 138). Irving's cuts, however, had been as much to do with prevailing stage practice as with concern with the plot or the status of the text. The Lyceum's house style and, in part, the basis of its popularity, was 'pictorial realism', the attempt to re-create historically accurate and visually pleasing scenery and costume. *Cymbeline*, however, is resistant to such an approach as the reviewer in *The Times* of 23 September, 1896 pointed out, 'any attempt to obtain archaeological consistency in such a hotch-potch of history, fiction and period must fail', and he questioned whether:

> it would not be well to adopt on the stage a more or less fantastic setting, with something of that indefiniteness of place, period, and costume, which the modern stage-manager for some reason will only allow in comic opera. Perhaps after all there is not much more reality in these picturesque kilted Britons who fill the Lyceum picture.

The problem was not simply one of aesthetic consistency in Irving's choice of period setting (identified in the published version of his cut text as 'First Century' although clearly more mock medieval Gothic than ancient Britain) but the result of practical considerations too. While much admired, the specific locations that were re-created (designed by Sir Lawrence Alma-Tadema and executed by Hawes Craven and Harker), such as 'Philario's

House, the Triclinium' and 'Philario's House, the Atrium', required seventeen complete scene changes and the time taken by this activity dictated the severe reduction of the spoken text.

Twentieth-century productions frequently cut the text of *Cymbeline* less for pragmatic staging concerns than to support a specific reading of the play. John Barton, while expanding Cornelius' role, cut 820 lines and, through some transpositions, narrowed the focus of the play to highlight British imperialism and kingship (an emphasis achieved in part through the shared staging and costuming with his contemporary productions of *Richard II* and *King John*) and the relationship between Innogen and Posthumus. 'Start Here Productions', a group of actors from the English Shakespeare Company directed by Tim Carroll, undertook much more severe cutting in 1991, reducing the play to one and a half hours, confining the plot to Posthumus, Innogen, Iachimo, Cloten and Pisario (with one actor doubling Iachimo and Pisanio) and retitling the work as *Cymbeline – The Wager*. Without the King, his wife or the lost sons and performed within a sand circle bounded by a rope – suggesting a space for physical conflict – the focus of this touring production was clearly narrowed to the politics of gender rather than nationalism.

While cutting has been a common device to make *Cymbeline* 'work' on stage the most frequently employed strategy during the late seventeenth and eighteenth centuries was to adapt the play. After the performance described by Simon Forman there is a record of just a single further staging of Shakespeare's play, at court for Charles I in 1634, and then the play becomes invisible until Thomas Durfey's adaptation published in 1682 (and, if the Epilogue is to be believed, written nine years earlier) as *The Injured Princess, or The Fatal Wager: as it was acted at the Theater-Royal by his Majesties Servants*.[22] Surprisingly, given the original's potential for exploitation as a nationalistic text with a concern for succession, Durfey's version is less politicised than other Shakespearian adaptations of the period. It clearly reflects, however, the Restoration taste for symmetry – Pisanio has a daughter, Clarina (an expansion of the role of Innogen's servant, Helen) – and exploits the presence of women on stage: Clarina, who like her mistress is innocent and virtuous, is threatened with rape by Cloten and Jachimo (here a drunken companion of Cloten; Shakespeare's Iachimo becomes Shattillion):

CLOT. ... Prithee art thou such a
Fool to think we fear the Devil? Jachimo, show
Her the contrary, rowze her, towze her, Boy, I'le
Do thee an honourable kindness, and pimp for thee,
For fear of disturbance.

JACHIMO.   A very friendly part, faith, my Lord: Come, Madam,
You and I must be more familiar; nay, nay, no
Struggling, my heart's a flame, and you must quench the fire. (4.3)

Pisanio attempts to rescue his daughter, kills Jachimo but is disarmed by Cloten who with actions and words that draw heavily on *King Lear* 'puts out his eyes' with the injunction:

So, now smell thy way out of the Wood, whilst
I follow thy Daughter, find her, and cut her piecemeal:
I'll sacrifice her to the Ghost of Jachimo.

The whole is similarly less subtle and lacks the variety of the original: the focus is on the story of Posthumus (here called Ursaces) and Innogen (Eugenia), Shakespeare's songs and visions are omitted, and while the revelations and reconciliations of the ending are maintained Ursaces kills Shattillion, here 'an opinionated Frenchman' rather than an Italian, and so named perhaps after the character in Fletcher's *The Noble Gentleman*, which Durfey altered and revived in 1688 under the title *The Fool's Preferment: or, the Three Dukes of Dunstable* and in which Shattillion is identified as 'a Lord, mad for love'.

The coarseness of Durfey's *Injured Princess* is signalled from the tone of the Prologue, addressed to the men in the audience, which likens old plays to 'Mistresses, long since enjoy'd' and extends the analogy:

… at new Plays you come so soon,
Like Bride-grooms, hot to go to Bed ere noon!
Or, if you are detain'd some little space,
The stinking Footman's sent to keep your place,

before suggesting that a revived play is like a 'Husband after absence' who will 'wait all day, / And decently for Spouse, till Bed-time stay.' Perhaps because of such raciness (reminiscent of the 'New plays and maidenheads are near akin' of the Prologue of *The Two Noble Kinsmen*) it had a remarkably long stage life, playing at Lincoln's Inn Fields fifteen times between 1702 and 1720 and being revived at Covent Garden in the late 1730s.[23]

Two further adaptations were published in 1759. Charles Marsh's version was never performed and is most memorable for the note on its title page, beneath the author's name, 'As it was agreed to be acted at the Theatre-Royal in Covent Garden', followed by a two-page explanatory Preface that described the rehearsal process with Spranger Barry and Susannah Cibber and the alleged broken promises over a five-year period, involving John Rich the theatre manager, that kept the play off the stage.[24] William Hawkins's version also struggled to get to performance: it was first offered 'to the manager of the other theatre' (David Garrick at Drury Lane) before being performed at Covent Garden, where he 'contended not only with the *usual* difficulties, but also with *others* of an *extraordinary* nature'.[25] At a time when the two playing houses licensed for legitimate theatre (Drury Lane and Covent Garden) were competing hard and sometimes unscrupulously for London audiences *Cymbeline* is caught in the crossfire. Hawkins drew on contemporary events for his audience appeal: Britain was fighting the French in the Seven Years War and he emphasised the patriotic elements of the play and exploited the nationalistic plot strand: he recast Cymbeline as a much stronger monarch, a lover of liberty fighting tyrannical Romans, and stressed his intentions in the Prologue spoken by Mr Ross, who played Leonatus (Posthumus), beginning 'BRITONS, the daring Author of to-night, / Attempts in Shakespear's manly stile to write' and, having identified some of his plot omissions, makes his nationalistic point:

> For what remains, the poet bids you see,
> From an old tale, what Britons ought to be;
> And in these restless days of war's alarms,
> Nor melts the soul to love, but fires the blood to arms.
> Your great forefathers scorn'd the foreign chain,
> Rome might invade, and Caesars rage in vain –
> Those glorious patterns with bold hearts pursue,
> To king, to country, and to honour true! (ix–x)

Military topicality is stressed further in the Epilogue spoken by Mrs Vincent (who played Innogen): she hopes 'there are no Frenchmen in the pit' and praises 'mighty Prussia', a close ally since the Treaty of Westminster the year before and linked to Britain through George II (xi). Hawkins had aesthetic considerations too; a former Professor of Poetry at Oxford, he found *Cymbeline* irregular, with what he called 'superfluities', and so imposed a new time frame on the play, condensing the action to two days and restricting its geography, bringing it closer, structurally, to the classical unities. He cuts the Queen, Italy, Iachimo, the wager, and the bedchamber scene and deals with them through report. The dirge set to music by Thomas Arne must have been one of the few bright moments in an otherwise dull play. Nevertheless, it ran for six nights with an additional command performance for the Prince of Wales. Garrick almost certainly saw this production and it may have prompted progress with his own adaptation first mooted as early as 1746 (and Hawkins's prefatory comments may indicate that, in rejecting his adaptation, Garrick was already working on his own) and performed for the first time at Drury Lane in November 1761. His was a very different version from those of Durfey, Marsh or Hawkins, although in cutting the promise to resume the tribute it may also be read as a patriotic piece, and is less an adaptation of Shakespeare than a revival or restoration with significant compressions and transpositions as his Advertisement in the published edition explains:

> The admirers of Shakespeare must not take it ill that there are some scenes, and consequently many fine passages, omitted in this edition of *Cymbeline*. It was impossible to retain more of the play and bring it within the compass of a night's entertainment. The chief alterations are in the division of the acts, in the shortening of many parts of the original, and transposing some scenes. As the play has met with so favourable a reception from the public, it is hoped that the alterations have not been made with great impropriety.[26]

His transpositions included shifting all the British scenes of the first act into the first scene of the play, so that the whole act only required a single set change, while the major act change was to compress Shakespeare's second and third acts into a single second act. As usual the prison scene was cut and overall 610 lines were lost, 524 from the last act,[27] but the plot survived relatively intact and led to some interest in the play as a performance text. Arthur Murphy, one of Garrick's earliest biographers, repeated Johnson's criticism but acknowledged that 'Garrick thought fit to revive the play, because he knew that amidst all its imperfections, a number of detached beauties would occur to surprise and charm the imagination,'[28] while Francis Gentleman, comparing Hawkins's and Garrick's versions, drew a clear distinction between the needs of the theatre audience and imaginative readers:

> Mr. Garrick's is, no doubt, best calculated for action, but Mr. Hawkins's will stand a chance of pleasing every fanciful reader better, because he has in many places harmonized the expression, and rendered the obscure passages more intelligible; however, we wish he had retained more of the original, and Mr. Garrick less.[29]

A much more audacious adaptation than the eighteenth-century versions and one that, through its explicit textual and physical allusions to sex and violence, was closer in tone to Durfey's, was created by Kneehigh Theatre, a Cornish-based company that brought its *Cymbeline* to the RSC's Complete Works season in 2007. A pre-text scene established the social realism of a world inhabited by hoodies, young graffiti-spraying outsiders, who scaled and hung mementoes on a large metal cage – evoking the 'disappeared' and creating a strong sense of loss – that was later revealed to be the security fence round Cymbeline's palace. The director Emma Rice largely dispensed with Shakespeare's lines, using a new text written by Carl Grose, that retained much of the plot but introduced new characters, one of whom, a pantomime dame figure (Mike Shepherd in drag) functioned as a narrator, speaking directly to the audience, sharing her holiday snaps, and dispensing with the need for the explication of the opening dialogue and subsequent plot twists. The show reflected the elements of the original that are concerned with dysfunctional families, with pointers to and reminders of childhood: a radio-controlled car carrying messages and helping to fix scene location; Posthumus's wooden boat, with fish attached, hanging from his shoulders on braces; war presented as a board game; the articulated wooden deer of the lost boys; and the closing scene (adhering to the structure and tone of the original) as the characters, childlike and safe at last, are tucked up in bed.

While Kneehigh's staging style reflected some of the eclectic and diverse elements of the original others have sought to create a credible whole through a third strategy: the superimposition of a single, new world. Sir Barry Jackson's 1923 *Cymbeline* at Birmingham Rep (directed by H. K. Ayliff) achieved some notoriety as 'Shakespeare in plus-fours', a reaction to Belarius's trousers and Imogen's disguise as Fidele, and asking the audience, as J. C. Trewin put it, 'To go the full distance, to accept the one major anachronism of modern dress.'[30] Court costume and army uniforms easily identified class and nationality for viewers only five years away from the First World War but some found Guiderius dressed as a hiker in shorts carrying Cloten's head in a pudding cloth risible. Almost sixty years later Elijah Moshinsky's heavily cut version for the BBC created a new, consistent world for the play by returning to the past and using tapestries, furnishings and convincing costumes to craft a Jacobean world that took a Rembrandt portrait as its starting point and continued to present scenes as a series of framed pictures based on old masters.

More recently, productions have chosen to celebrate rather than disguise the diversity of the play, a strategy that recognises the value of the constituent parts and demonstrates greater confidence in the performability of the text. The New York-based group Theatre for a New Audience, performing in The Other Place in Stratford in 2001, combined some elements of an Oriental setting with the Wild West: Guiderius, Arviragus and Belarius wore stetsons, cracked whips and sang country and western songs, and Cloten entered at the gallop with a plastic horse attached to his waist. Dominic Cooke's production for the RSC two years later was even more eclectic. Early in the rehearsal process the cast was invited to bring props and costumes that signified 'Britishness'. Umbrellas, bowler hats, 'bovver boots', horsetails and suggestions of Morrismen characterised the British scenes, and for battle the warriors smeared themselves in mud; white-suited lascivious Italians populated the Roman scenes; and, played with a full text, the descent of Jupiter was a remarkable *coup de théâtre*. There was no attempt to impose a single time frame or setting or diminish the variety of tone: the production revelled in its moments of pantomime, fairytale and romance and in exploiting the dramatic potential of the parts demonstrated the effectiveness of the whole. The staging devices did not give the patriotic focus on 'Britishness' that had been an element of eighteenth-century *Cymbelines* but a much less reverential, post-modern take on nationhood. There are almost fifty uses of the word 'Britain' or its adjectival or plural forms in *Cymbeline*, more than any other play in the canon, and late twentieth- and early twenty-first-century criticism of the play began to focus on the politics of nationhood often as an offshoot of post-colonial criticism, which was shifting its gaze from overseas colonialism to the constituent parts of the (now) United Kingdom. Such criticism (by Willy Maley, for example)[31] revisits and relocates the play in its Jacobean political and religious context or, as in the essay by Jodi Mikalachki,[32] explores the relationship between the construct of nationhood and gender as evidenced in the play.

Focusing the play

Sometimes as an intentional response to contemporary context and sometimes as a by-product of the staging strategies or the manipulation of text, approaches to the play have led to shifts in emphasis or a focus on one of the plot strands or, indeed, a focus on character achieved through the work of a skilled performer. It is generally agreed that in Garrick's version the best acting part – and a less ambiguous and more heroic role than in the original – was Posthumus, the part played by Garrick himself. It remained the lead role, and the subject of critical and audience attention, through the performances of the Kembles, Macready, Kean and Phelps until the mid-1800s, when attention began to shift to Innogen. The character, both in criticism and stage presentations, fulfilled a popular Victorian stereotype of woman: lusted after, victimised, suffering but, above all, innocent and faithful. Helena Faucit, who took the part opposite both Macready and Phelps, was to describe the character later in effusive terms: 'In drawing her [Shakespeare] has made his masterpiece; and of all heroines of poetry or romance, who can be named beside her?'[33] It is telling that Anna Jameson, in her 1832 biographical study of Shakespeare's heroines, *Characteristics of Women, Moral Poetical, and Historical*, had placed Innogen in her 'Characters of the Affections' section along with Hermione, Desdemona and Cordelia, rather than 'Characters of the Intellect' or 'Passion and Imagination' or 'Historical Characters', and wrote: 'of all his women, considered as individuals rather than heroines, Imogen is the most perfect … In her we have all the fervour of youthful tenderness, all the romance of youthful fancy, all the enchantment of ideal grace.'[34] The attachment to the character is epitomised in Barry Cornwall's Introductory Remarks to the play in his popular 1843 edition of Shakespeare which begin:

> Of all the loving female characters of Shakspere – although some may display a lustre more intense – there is not one that cheers the eye with a more mild and modest radiance than the spotless jewel, Imogen. Harsh and difficult as sometimes is the diction of the play, the sweetness of her nature o'erinforms it with delightful associations; we think of her as of the pine-apple in its prickly enclosure; or as of the delicious milk in one husky shell of the cocoa-nut. In the clear heaven of that unclouded mind, the wearied spirit obtains glimpses of human truth and unsuspecting gentleness that well, indeed, "may make us less forlorn." No impure thought can dwell in the atmosphere that is perfumed by her breath ...[35]

Kenny Meadows's illustrations reinforce this panegyric. The 'O' of the opening word 'Of' is formed by a bracelet held by a spider in the centre of its web. It is a gross, threatening insect with a human head that is clearly to be read as Iachimo. On the facing page, and preceding the text of the first scene, is Innogen, bent and careworn and trapped in a cleft of rock. Her way out is barred by tangles of briers that are the visual and metaphorical equivalent of both Iachimo's web and Cornwall's 'prickly enclosure'. A lowering cloud above her contains the capitalised legend 'Fear not slander' (a line from the 'Fear no more the heat o'th'sun' song of 4.2) and at the top of the composition is a giant hand (of God?), the source of shafts of sunlight that focus the composition on the bowed figure. Swinburne went further with the deification. Innogen is the dominant figure in his *Study of Shakespeare* and the object of his concluding remarks.[36] She is 'Above them all, and all others of his divine and human children' (p. 170) and 'the loveliest heaven-born sister' and the 'woman above all Shakespeare's women ... the immortal godhead of womanhood' (p. 227). What lurks in these descriptions is more than sentiment: there is the voyeuristic sex appeal in the faithful woman whose cross-dressed disguise is less a comedic, sexually ambiguous device than a rational response to threat. As a *married* woman Innogen can, for many, suffer without sexual insecurity.

On stage the popularity of the character – the 'Imogenolatry' in Ruth Nevo's term[37] – and the emotional affect that engaged Keats and Tennyson reached its height in Ellen Terry's 1896 performance where the confluence of charisma, physicality and focus on her body created a hagiography that was enhanced by the shift in the male lead role from Posthumus to Irving's Iachimo. Nevertheless, vestiges of the highly sentimental view of the character

8. A blonde Innogen. Vanessa Redgrave with Cloten's corpse in William Gaskill's production at Stratford-upon-Avon, 1962.

and its centrality in performance remained well into the twentieth century. Even as feminist criticism began to reassess the gender politics of the play and explore its underlying misogyny (frequently drawing on the 'woman's part ...' of Posthumus' rant in 2.5) there continued to be a surprising number of white-shifted, blonde Innogens (usually threatened by dark, saturnine men) on mawkish display: Vanessa Redgrave in 1962, Susan Fleetwood in 1974, Judi Dench in 1979, Joanne Pearce in 1997, Emma Fielding in 2003 (see illustration 8). In the 1980s, however, focus on the character became textual rather than sexual when the Oxford edition of the *Complete Works* adopted the spelling 'Innogen', used in Simon Forman's account of the play and some of its source material, in place of the former 'Imogen'. The 'Imogen' of the First Folio, assumed to be an error, has disappeared from recent editions, while the traditional idealised and centralising reading of this role has become less the focus of recent productions. In 2007 Cheek by Jowl's modern dress and determinedly anti-romantic touring production (arguably an adaptation given its extensive cuts, textual tinkerings and additions) redirected the gaze through some intriguing casting choices. The decision to double Posthumus and Cloten (played by Tom Hiddleston) had the potential to draw attention to the heroine's powerlessness but resisted that reading through a remarkably unsympathetic Innogen. Played by a younger actress (Jodie McNee) than is often the case, this was more petulant teenager than mature married woman and she inspired little sympathy. The doubling strategy of this cynical production highlighted the political strands of the plot, drawing attention to sons, daughters and inheritance (Innogen as 'the heir of's kingdom', 1.1.4) and Cymbeline's dual role – and inadequacy – as monarch and father.[38]

To return to, and to conclude then, with Samuel Johnson. He wrote disparagingly of *Cymbeline*'s 'folly', 'absurdity' and 'confusion' – and in a neo-classical critical tradition his judgement is accurate – but if his comments are transferred from the style and structure of the play to its tri-partite subject matter and scope (to family life, nationhood and international relations) then performance and criticism still has a great deal to interrogate. Its afterlife is assured.

NOTES

1. Jennifer Wallace (ed.), *Lives of the Great Romantics II: Keats, Coleridge and Scott by their Contemporaries* (London: Pickering and Chatto, 1997), vol. I, pp. 233–4. Throughout this essay I follow the name spelling from the Cambridge edition of the play, edited by Martin Butler (Cambridge: Cambridge University Press, 2005) except in quotations, where alternative spellings are retained.

2. Samuel Johnson (ed.), *The Plays of William Shakespeare* (London: J. and R. Tonson *et al.*, 1765), vol. VII, p. 403.

3. Donald Greene (ed.), *The Oxford Authors: Samuel Johnson* (Oxford: Oxford University Press, 1984), p. 442.

4. Charlotte Lennox, *Shakespear Illustrated: or the Novels and Histories on which the Plays of Shakespear Are Founded*, 3 vols. (London: A. Millar, 1753/4). Johnson's and Lennox's assessments sit oddly with their own literary outputs for neither Lennox's *Female Quixote* nor Johnson's *Rasselas* are characterised by realism (and indeed the former may be read as a satire on literal-minded readers of romance).

5. For the full text and an account of the manuscript see Martin Butler's edition of *Cymbeline* (Cambridge: Cambridge University Press, 2005) which is also the source text for all quotations from the play.

6. William Warburton (ed.), *The Works of Shakespear in Eight Volumes* (London: J. and P. Knapton, 1747), vol. I, n.p.n.

7. William Dodd, *The Beauties of Shakespeare: Regularly Sketched from Each Play*, 2nd edn, 2 vols. (London: T. Waller, 1757).

8. Henry Home (Lord Kames), *Elements of Criticism*, 2nd edn, 3 vols. (London: Miller; Edinburgh: Kincaid and Bell, 1763), vol. I, p. 152.

9. Joseph Priestley, *A Course of Lectures on Oratory and Criticism* (1777), p. 250. This example occurs in Part 3, 'Of Style'.

10. Roger Lonsdale (ed.), *The New Oxford Book of Eighteenth Century Verse* (Oxford: Oxford University Press, 1987), p. 376.

11. For sales figures and a discussion of copyright see William St Clair, *The Reading Nation in the Romantic Period* (Cambridge: Cambridge University Press, 2004).

12. William Hazlitt, *Characters of Shakespeare's Plays* (London: Oxford University Press, 1949 [1817]), p. xxxv.

13. August Schlegel, *Lectures on Art and Literature* (London: Bell, 1883), pp. 397 and 339.

14. See Jonathan Bate's discussion of these authors in *Shakespeare and the English Romantic Imagination* (Oxford: Oxford University Press, 1986).

15. London: John Millar, 1815.

16. 'Person and Office: the Case of Imogen, Princess of Britain', in Vincent Newey and Ann Thompson (eds.) *Literature and Nationalism* (Liverpool: Liverpool University Press, 1991), pp. 76–87, at p. 79.

17. Charles Spencer, *Daily Telegraph*, 28 February 1997, p. 25.

18. 'Late Romances: Magic, Majesty and Masque' in *Shakespeare, Out of Court: Dramatizations of Court Society*, ed. Graham Holderness *et al.* (London: Macmillan, 1990), pp. 127–235, at p. 185.

19. Geoffrey Bullough (ed.), *Narrative and Dramatic Sources of Shakespeare* (London: RKP, 1975), vol. VIII, p. 43.

20. Christopher St John (ed.), *Ellen Terry and Bernard Shaw: A Correspondence* (London: G. P. Putnam's Sons, 1931), p. 43.

21. George Bernard Shaw, *Geneva, Cymbeline Refinished, & Good King Charles* (London: Constable, 1946), p. 134.

22. Thomas Durfey, *The Injured Princess* … (London: Bentley and Magnes, 1682).

23. For an account of this play see Harry William Pedicord and Fredrick Louis Bergmann (eds.), *The Plays of David Garrick* (Carbondale and Edwardsville: Southern Illinois University Press, 1981), vol. IV, p. 413.

24. Charles Marsh, *Cymbeline: King of Britain. A Tragedy* (London: Charles Marsh, 1759).

25. William Hawkins, *Cymbeline a Tragedy; Altered from Shakespeare* (London: Rivington and Fletcher, 1759), p. vii.

26. David Garrick, *Cymbeline: A Tragedy by Shakespeare with Alterations* (London: J. and R. Tonson, 1762).

27. See Pedicord and Bergmann (eds.), *The Plays of David Garrick*, pp. 412–417, for details.

28. Arthur Murphy, *The Life of David Garrick* (London, 1801), vol. II, p. 358.

29. Francis Gentleman, *The Dramatic Censor* (London: J. Bell, 1770), vol. II, p. 95.

30. J. C. Trewin, *The Birmingham Repertory Theatre, 1913–1963* (London: Barrie and Rockliff, 1963), p. 71.

31. See Maley's essays: 'Postcolonial Shakespeare: British Identity Formation and *Cymbeline*', in Jennifer Richards and James Knowles (eds.), *Shakespeare's Late Plays: New Readings* (Edinburgh: Edinburgh University Press, 1999), pp. 145–57, and '*Cymbeline*, the Font of History, and the Matter of Britain', in Diana E. Henderson (ed.), *Alternative Shakespeares 3* (Abingdon: Routledge, 2008), pp. 119–37.

32. 'The Masculine Romance of Roman Britain: *Cymbeline* and Early Modern English Nationalism', *Shakespeare Quarterly* 46 (1995), pp. 301–22.

33. Helena Faucit, Lady Martin, *On Some of Shakespeare's Female Characters* (Edinburgh and London: Blackwood, 1891), p. 158.
34. *Shakespeare's Heroines: Characteristics of Women, Moral, Poetical, and Historical*, 2nd edn (London: George Bell, 1879), p. 210.
35. Barry Cornwall and Kenny Meadows (eds.), *The Complete Works of Shakespeare ... with a Memoir and Essay on His Genius by Barry Cornwall* (London Printing and Publishing Co., 1843), p. 204.
36. Algernon Charles Swinburne, *A Study of Shakespeare* (London: Chatto and Windus, 1880).
37. Ruth Nevo, *Shakespeare's Other Language* (London: Routledge, 1987), p. 67.
38. See the discussion of paternalism, patriarchy and power in Leonard Tennenhouse's *Power on Display: The Politics of Shakespeare's Genres* (London and New York: Methuen, 1986).

8

VIRGINIA MASON VAUGHAN

Literary invocations of *The Tempest*

Ever since John Dryden and William Davenant's *Enchanted Island* reshaped *The Tempest* in accord with Restoration notions of neo-classical decorum,[1] writers have appropriated the play's plot and characters, reshaping them according to changing literary tastes and differing political and social contexts. *The Tempest*, argued poet W. H. Auden, is 'a mythopoeic work ... [that] encourages adaptations' and inspires 'people to go on for themselves ... to make up episodes that [Shakespeare] as it were, forgot to tell us'.[2] *The Tempest*'s setting on an uncharted island somewhere between Naples and Tunis, its representation of public and personal power relationships (king and subject, master and servant, father and daughter), its elliptical action and indefinite ending and its pervasive use of stage spectacle have repeatedly spurred artists in every media – from music, film, theatre, literature and the art of high culture, to popular culture's comic books and cartoons – to reimagine the original within the context of new literary conventions and new circumstances.[3]

Hundreds if not thousands of *Tempest* adaptations and appropriations exist, coming from all eras and all parts of the globe, and no single essay could do justice to them all. The focus here is the ways poets, playwrights and novelists have responded to *The Tempest*'s unusual emphasis on the role of art in human consciousness as well as its limitations, particularly in its relation to the material world. Shakespeare's Prospero spends much of the play torn between fascination with the illusions he creates through magic and his responsibilities, whether in the political world as Duke or in the private world as father. Through Prospero, but in other characters as well, *The Tempest* questions whether art is an escape from everyday realities or a way to transform the corrupt and unjust world we live in. Although Prospero uses his art successfully to arrange his daughter's marriage and evoke repentance from Alonso, Antonio's silence in the play's final moments suggests that the magus's reformatory project has failed at least once and, arguably, also with Caliban. 'That art cannot ... transform men grieves Prospero greatly,'

155

observes Auden. 'His anger at Caliban stems from his consciousness of this failure' (Auden, p. xxi). For many readers and viewers Caliban's impassioned resistance to Prospero's power calls into question the magician's role as moral arbiter. And in his most famous soliloquy, Prospero seems to question his art's viability: 'Our revels now are ended,' he proclaims. His actors and the 'great globe itself' will 'dissolve and leave not a rack behind' (4.1.148–56). If art, like human life, is the stuff that dreams are made on, why pursue it? *The Tempest*, in other words, raises a host of questions about art and its relation to 'reality', but provides no clear answers. But while Shakespeare's *Tempest* remains elusive about the role of art, over the centuries poets, playwrights and novelists have not been reluctant to provide their own answers.

Prospero's belief in the artist's role as moral teacher was shared by many nineteenth-century writers. Like the Victorian critics Anna Jameson and A. C. Bradley, they sought to round out Shakespeare's elusive characters by supplying biographical details omitted from the dramatist's original script. Their attitudes were shaped, in part, by Europe's colonial rule over subjugated peoples around the world, particularly in Africa and India. Sharing the 'white man's burden', they often identified with Prospero's drive to educate his subalterns, especially Caliban. A prominent example is Daniel Wilson, whose *Caliban: The Missing Link* (1873) identified Caliban as an evolutionary intermediary who, under Prospero's tutelage, had the potential to crawl up the developmental ladder toward true humanity.[4] The French philosopher Ernest Renan also used Caliban as a vehicle for philosophical reflection in his dramatic sequel, *Caliban: Suite de La Tempéte* (1878), which depicted the former slave spearheading a Milanese revolution against Prospero, but later repenting and attempting to save his old master.[5] In Caliban these writers saw a species of sub-humanity that with proper cultivation could evolve into civilized humanity.

   The nineteenth century's most extensive poetic appropriation of Caliban is Robert Browning's 'Caliban upon Setebos', a dramatic monologue which appeared in *Dramatic Personae* (1864). While Prospero and Miranda sleep, Caliban stares at the sea and ponders the mysteries of his universe and the nature of his god, Setebos. In a series of analogies, Caliban adopts the anthropomorphic view that Setebos is a larger, more powerful version of himself. Playing in the sea marge, Caliban envisions Setebos as an artist who creates the natural world in the same way he creates a bird out of clay. Like Caliban, the god is not benign. If he feels like snapping off a leg, he does so, and whether or not he repairs the damage depends on his mood. Setebos creates the world on a whim and acts inexplicably. No one can knows how to please him. Instead, speculates Caliban, one lives in fear, because 'He doth

His worst in this our life, / Giving just respite lest we die thro' pain, / Saving last pain for worst, – with which, an end.'[6]

Caliban's theological speculations undermine any sense of a rational universe governed by divine providence. Indeed, God is only comprehensible if we see him in terms of ourselves. We can never discover the absolute truth about the Creator – or ourselves, for that matter – because we can only see him from our individual viewpoint. Browning's religious scepticism is perhaps not surprising in the age of Darwin, when poets like Matthew Arnold felt an 'eternal note of sadness'. Browning's theological musings were a poignant contrast to Wilson's and Renan's optimistic assumption that even if man had emerged out of the primordial slime, his trajectory was to be ever upward.

American playwright Percy MacKaye shared Renan's and Wilson's belief in Caliban's educability, and like them, he used Caliban as an ideological platform. Born in 1875, MacKaye began his career as a teacher in New York, but starting in 1904 he devoted himself to democratising the American theatre by writing plays and pageants intended to bring together spectators from all ethnic groups and classes to share a collective vision of civic responsibility. In 1916 the city of New York commissioned him to create a popular masque for the celebration of the tercentenary of Shakespeare's death. His *Caliban by the Yellow Sands* was first performed at Lewisohn Stadium on 23 May, and during subsequent weeks was enjoyed by as many as 135,000 people. In addition to the thirty professional actors required for the speaking roles, MacKaye's pageant included pantomime roles for 2,500 participants from immigrant committees throughout the city.

The masque's goal, MacKaye explained, was 'to present Prospero's art as the art of the theater culminating in Shakespeare and to lead Caliban step by step from his original path of brute force and ignorance to the realm of love, reason, and self discipline'.[7] Caliban represented primitive man. Beset by lust and aggression, he struggles to become civilised into the European values represented by Prospero and Miranda. Thus Prospero's art is conflated with Shakespeare's stagecraft, which is also conflated with MacKaye's creative process. In repeated episodes, MacKaye's Prospero tries to turn Caliban away from his pagan god Setebos and its associations with Lust, War and Death. MacKaye's method is reminiscent perhaps of early twentieth-century schoolmasters' use of Shakespearean scenes to trace the rise of western civilisation: Egypt (*Antony and Cleopatra*), Greece (*Troilus and Cressida*), Rome (*Julius Caesar*), the 'dark ages' (*Hamlet*), and the Renaissance (*Henry VIII*, *Romeo and Juliet* and *As You Like It*). The leitmotif is a lesson in Anglo-Saxonism. To MacKaye, Shakespeare's England represented the apogee of civilisation; he hoped that, by participating in his community masque, New York's various ethnic groups (Egyptian, Greek, Italian, German, French, Spanish and Italian) would share in the blessings of western culture and art and thereby assimilate into Anglo-American culture.[9]

Browning and MacKaye illustrate two perspectives on the role of art in human experience. Caliban's poetic monologue encourages Browning's readers to ponder the important religious and philosophical questions of his day; the poem is a catalyst for thought if not for action. MacKaye's pageant, in contrast, is overtly didactic, proffering answers rather than questions. By participating in his mammoth masque, audiences and actors alike would subscribe – MacKaye hoped – to his vision of western history and his faith in Anglo-Saxon ideals. By fostering a homogeneous community, the art of Shakespeare and his own appropriation of that art could transform American culture.

The United States entered the First World War the year after MacKaye's masque. Not surprisingly, in the carnage's aftermath and, later, during the rise of fascism in Europe, the nineteenth-century conviction that humanity was on an upward moral trajectory lost purchase in England and America. *The Tempest* again served as a catalyst for poetic reflection in W. H. Auden's *The Sea and the Mirror*, written between August 1942 and February 1944 while the poet was teaching at Swarthmore College in Pennsylvania. Against the dark backdrop of a second world war, Auden explores the complicated interrelation between art, represented in the Shakespearean trope of the mirror, and nature, signified by the sea. Written as a poetic postscript to *The Tempest, The Sea and the Mirror* presents a series of interior monologues spoken by Shakespeare's characters as they contemplate their future now that the play has ended.

Not long after Auden composed *The Sea and the Mirror*, another twentieth-century poet turned to Shakespeare's text for inspiration. Hilda Doolittle (commonly called H. D.) was raised in Pennsylvania, became friends with Ezra Pound, and later immigrated to England, where she was widely recognised as a founding figure in the literary movement known as 'imagism'. H. D. composed *By Avon River* at the end of the Second World War.[9] The poem's first section, 'Good Frend', records the poet's visit to Stratford in April of 1945; the second section, 'The Guest', was written during 1946 after a mental breakdown. H. D.'s illness was perhaps exacerbated by the stress of living in London during heavy bombing. Like Auden, she wondered whether humankind was on the brink of total destruction. And, like Auden, she saw characters from *The Tempest* – in her case the voiceless figure of Claribel – as catalysts for speculation about her vocation as an artist.

In style, structure, and form, *The Sea and the Mirror* and *By Avon River* are easily characterised as 'modernist'. Both poems demonstrate a shift from nineteenth-century character criticism to a focus on language and human psychology; both eschew nineteenth-century optimism, resonating instead with disillusionment and even despair; and, like many modernist paintings, both are divided into sections that display alternate modes of being, different sides of the twentieth-century fragmented self.

Auden's poem is a triptych. After a short preface by the Stage Manager, Prospero's dialogue with Ariel (the first panel) introduces the poem's concern with the limitations and value of the aesthetic. Prospero envisions himself in retirement, living in the face of death; he concludes that, art and language notwithstanding, 'the way of truth' is 'a way of silence'. The second panel of Auden's triptych is represented by '*The Supporting Cast, Sotto Voce*'. Each character speaks a monologue in a different lyric form, from simple ballad to sestina and villanelle, and in that form the character comments on the events of Shakespeare's play, their meaning and the future. All but Antonio see the transition from play to afterlife as a new beginning, suggesting a renewed sense of community and interconnection. Antonio, the self-centred egoist, instead chooses 'to stand outside' Prospero's charmed circle. Like a lurking shadow, Antonio echoes the negative refrain, 'I am myself alone', between the poems that follow.

Panel 3, 'Caliban to the Audience', is a lengthy prose monologue; Caliban's stream-of-conscious prose, written in the convoluted style of the later Henry James, probes the interrelationship of the 'poetic' and the 'real'. Caliban speaks for an audience afraid of poetry's power to distort our sense of reality. As Prospero gazes at Ariel (the imaginative faculty) in the mirror, the spirit's image suddenly morphs into that of the monster Caliban, 'the dark thing you could never abide to be with' (Auden, p. 41). One by one, the artist's ideals and illusions are stripped away, until he realises that art is powerless in the face of humanity's penchant for destruction. 'What else,' ponders Caliban, 'is the artistic gift … if not to make you unforgettably conscious of the ungarnished offended gap between what you so questionably are and what you are commanded without any question to become …' (Auden, p. 50). Although art may allow us to see through a glass only darkly, at least it offers a mode of vision. The poem's postscript expresses the ultimate harmony of mind and body, vision and reality in a 'restored relation' – the mutual embrace of Caliban and Ariel, who become 'one evaporating sigh', the I of human consciousness (Auden, pp. 53, 56).

By Avon River embodies the divided self in a diptych. The first section, 'Good Frend', consists of an increasingly intense series of lyric poems that record the poet's thoughts as she visits Shakespeare's grave in Stratford-upon-Avon. The dramatist becomes a vehicle for the poet to reimagine her place within a male literary tradition. After H. D. considers Shakespeare's most famous heroines, the speaker identifies with Claribel, Alonso's voiceless daughter, who, torn between 'loathness and obedience' (2.1.125),[10] was married to the African King of Tunis. Who was Claribel and what, the poet wonders, was she to Shakespeare?

Having identified with Claribel, H.D. traces her quest for a voice and a vocation. First she meets a nun, a 'Poor Clare' who offers the consolation of organised religion. Then a prelate directs her to the classical traditions of rhetoric and philosophy, but these, too, are unsatisfactory. The answer finally comes as a mystery, coded in the songs of medieval troubadours, the *ros maris* that symbolises divine love. As H.D.'s biographer, Susan Friedman, notes, 'The poet's original identification with the speechless woman [Claribel] has been transformed to an identification with artistic and religious power.'[11]

H.D. moves from the mystic to the scholarly in 'The Guest', the second section of *By Avon River*. This prose remembrance of Shakespeare situates the dramatist inside the discursive framework of English Renaissance lyric poetry from Wyatt to Davenant. The scholar's catalogue moves from poet to poet, disregarding chronology, interrupting the researcher's narrative with the voice of the aged Shakespeare, tired after a prolonged drinking bout with Ben Jonson and Michael Drayton. Soon to die, the dramatist thinks over his life, his art and his relationship to his daughter Judith. Twin to her lost brother Hamnet, she comes to represent Shakespeare's own 'twin' or androgynous nature. As Kate Chedgzoy suggests, H.D. shows 'that the female principle has always been at the heart of his writing'.[12] 'The presence of woman within Shakespeare,' notes Friedman, 'counters the absence of women in the Elizabethan anthology. Judith's power in turn foreshadows the development of a strong female literary tradition in later generations',[13] a tradition that gives H.D., who began identified with the voiceless Claribel, permission to speak and modes in which to express herself.

The tripartite structure of *The Sea and the Mirror* and H.D.'s diptych embody the modern conception of human consciousness as divided, its parts in dialogue with one another. In Auden, Prospero speaks to the Ariel and Caliban within himself in an inner dialectic. In the final analysis, *The Sea and the Mirror* demonstrates, in Susan Snyder's words, that 'Art still cannot go beyond the wall [created by human mortality]; but the art of disjunctions and gaps, of Ariel and Caliban irreconcilable but bound together, can impress on us forcibly that there *is* a wall and another side'.[14] For H.D., the researcher, the poet, and the mystic are on the same quest, the search for the space where the dream, the dreamer and the song can become one. *By Avon River* and *The Sea and the Mirror* frame that quest in the artist's interior life, a consciousness that in the age of Freud is fraught with contradictions. But strangely enough, both texts find a *modus vivendi*, if not a resolution, in a quasi- religious vision that transcends the binaries of art and nature.

With the devolution of Europe's colonial empires that followed the Second World War, writers once again turned to *The Tempest*. Cultural materialist and new historicist critics, in particular, mined the Caliban–Ariel–Prospero triangle because it seemed prescient of Europe's future colonial history. To post-colonial writers as well Prospero was the ultimate coloniser. He took over an island inhabited by two indigenous creatures, Caliban, the son of the Algerian witch Sycorax, and Ariel, an airy spirit native to the island. Ariel serves under contract as an indentured servant with the promise of freedom in twelve years time. Caliban's servitude, on the other hand, is perpetual, a punishment for his attempted rape of Prospero's daughter.

The Prospero–Caliban and Prospero–Ariel master–slave relationships coalesce a variety of post-colonial issues, including racial discrimination, cultural imperialism and economic oppression. Tied to all is the issue of language. Miranda contends that when she first arrived on the island, Caliban did not 'Know thine own meaning, but wouldst gabble like / A thing most brutish' until she 'endowed thy purposes / With words that made them known'. Caliban responds:

> You taught me language, and my profit on't
> Is I know how to curse. The red plague rid you
> For learning me your language.   (1.2.356–65)

Miranda assumes, rather ethnocentrically, that Caliban's native speech patterns were 'brutish', mere gabble without meaning. Yet Caliban presumably grew up speaking the language of Sycorax. After Miranda's lessons, Caliban is in a sense a hybrid, a Creole who speaks the imperialists' European language with his own inflections and emphases.

Caliban's rhythmic speech patterns – evocative descriptions of the island and a calypso song, 'Ca-ca-caliban' – perhaps difficult for the First Folio's compositors to set and certainly a problem for late twentieth-century editors – may in fact be the earliest version of what Barbadian poet Edward Kamau Brathwaite describes as nation language:

> English it may be in terms of some of its lexical features. But
> in its contours, its rhythm and timbre, its sound explosions,
> it is not English … Nation language … may be in English: but
> often it is in an English which is like a howl, or a shout or a
> machine-gun or the wind or a wave. It is also like the blues.
> And sometimes it is English and African together.[15]

For Brathwaite, nation language is a mode of expression; its intonations resonate with human suffering under slavery and colonial rule. But it is also a mode of resistance that makes 'English sing with the "xperience" of Caribbean people' (Savory, p. 209).

The experience of black Africans under colonialism was just what Aimé Césaire hoped to convey in his dramatic rewriting of *The Tempest, Une Tempête*. Born in 1913 on the Caribbean island of Martinique, Césaire studied in Paris, where he joined fellow students Léopold Sédar Senghor (future president of Senegal) and Léon Damas in creating a literary review, *L'Ètudiant Noir* (the Black Student). In this youthful effort, the editors began a movement that is now known as 'Negritude', an intellectual and political response to colonialism calling for Blacks around the world to reject the domination of the West and take pride in their African heritage. To Césaire, as to Brathwaite, the black experience should be the black poet's primary subject.

During the 1940s Césaire joined the French Communist Party. He was elected mayor of Fort-de-France and served as a deputy for Martinique to the French National Assembly. After the Soviet Union's 1956 invasion of Hungary, he became disillusioned with communism and founded the Parti Progressiste Martiniquais. His poems and plays reflect an intense political and social commitment to the peoples who had been colonised by European powers, a vision that informs his adaptation of *The Tempest*.

Une Tempête was written in 1968, a year of student revolution in France and race riots in the United States. Not surprisingly, in a calculated reversal of traditional power relations, Césaire's text was to be performed by black actors who take ownership over Shakespeare's plot and characters. In the play's opening scene, the actors select their roles; those who choose the European parts of Prospero, Miranda, Alonso, Antonio and Gonzalo don white masks. Richard Miller, who translated Césaire's French script into English, also suggests that the actors assign accents – indicators of social class – to the various characters.[16] The shipwreck that opens the play underscores the class hierarchy when the Boatswain tells the Europeans to get back to their 'first-class cabins'.

In a major change from Shakespeare's text, Césaire's Prospero explains to Miranda that he had planned to colonise the land on which they are marooned long before his brother's *coup d'état*. Learning of Prospero's imperial ambitions, Alonso and Antonio decide to turn Prospero over to the Inquisition so they can steal his Empire from him. Prospero's prescience that they will be sailing close to his island is political rather than magical, for he knows that, having taken Milan, they would soon try to colonise the lands he had already scouted.

The Prospero–Ariel–Caliban triangle dominates Césaire's play, with Ariel an 'intellectual', the mulatto indentured servant who patiently labours in hope of freedom later, and Caliban the rebellious black slave who wants freedom now. While Ariel has absorbed some of Prospero's language and values, Caliban repeatedly hearkens to his African heritage. He first enters muttering 'Uhuru', an African word for freedom, to which Prospero responds, 'Mumbling your native language again!' (Césaire, p. 11). Soon after this confrontation, Caliban rejects his name and asks to be called 'X', because his African name had been stolen from him. Caliban's 'X' is also reminiscent of Malcolm X and the more radical side of the American civil rights movement; Ariel, in turn, like Martin Luther King, doesn't believe in violence, but instead dreams of a world where people live like brothers.

Césaire follows the same plot line as Shakespeare's *Tempest* but always with a difference. For example, Prospero's masque of Juno, Ceres and Iris is included in Césaire's 3.3, but, after speaking a couple of Shakespeare's lines, the goddesses are chased away by Eshu, the African trickster god, whose sexually explicit lyrics shock the chaste goddesses' sensibilities. Eshu's African animism trumps the stylised containment of the West's classical myths.

In retelling Prospero's story from a black perspective, Césaire connects Europe's colonial project with the despoliation of Nature. Indeed, *Une Tempête* can be seen as a precursor to twenty-first century 'green' criticism because the text excoriates the colonialist's greedy abuse of the land. Ariel loves trees and even wishes to be one, while Caliban respects the earth and the natural forces that inhabit it: 'I know that it is alive' (Césaire, p. 12). He later charges Prospero with being Anti-Nature and calls on Shango, 'that howling impatient thing that suddenly appears in a clap of thunder like some God and hits you in the face' (Césaire, p. 53), to reinforce his point.

Césaire ends his play with Ferdinand's and Miranda's betrothal, the Europeans reconciled and everyone ready to sail back to Europe. Then, in an abrupt change from Shakespeare, Césaire's Prospero suddenly decides he can't leave the island. As Caliban charges, he is 'just an old addict', a colonialist who can't live unless he can feel superior to the colonised. The final scene shows the decaying Prospero, surrounded by possums, fearful that nature will take back his islands; the scene concludes with Caliban's words 'FREEDOM HI-DAY, FREEDOM HI-DAY!' (Césaire, p. 68). Through Shakespeare's plot and characters, and especially in Caliban, Césaire highlights the drive for black independence and recognition of an African heritage quite different from western values.

Like Césaire before him, Kamau Brathwaite uses Caliban as a symbol of African resistance. His 1960s poem 'Caliban' has been widely discussed as a post-colonial appropriation of *The Tempest* because its limbo beat expresses the African slave's downward trajectory during the Middle Passage and his upward rise in resistance to colonial oppression. In *Letter Sycorax*, Brathwaite focuses more clearly on the language issue, particularly the black poet's challenge in using the colonist's language – English – to express his own identity. Brathwaite fuses the oral, African tradition, the signifiers of which are based on the performance of sound and intonation, with a European text-based tradition, a challenge especially difficult for a poet whose work is most widely circulated through books. Brathwaite's method, particularly in poems crafted during the 1990s, is to reproduce the words just as he composes them on the screen of a computer, using spacing, changes in print font and punctuation to convey the stress and emphasis of the Caribbean oral tradition. Brathwaite's poems make us *see* the voice we cannot hear.

Letter Sycorax is an epistle to Caliban's mother, Sycorax; Caliban gleefully reports his discovery of a wonderful machine[17] that has a keyboard like the old Remington his mother kept on top of the wardrobe. The only difference is that, with this machine, mistakes are easily corrected; Caliban rejoices at the ease of composition and revision afforded by a word processor. While the white man's technology, like Prospero's magic, has historically been used to oppress native peoples, in *Letter Sycorax* that technology, in the form of a computer, becomes a source of power and resistance. The black letters that appear seemingly miraculously on a white screen become a synecdoche for the expression of black identity in a dominantly white world. Moreover, Brathwaite's reimagining of Shakespeare to include Sycorax, the ancestral female principle – the muse in the computer – allows Caliban to be reunited with an African tradition that is non-linear, intuitive and matriarchal. In the computer, the poet Brathwaite finds the space to convey the feelings and experience of Caribbean people, transforming Prospero's language into a new and unique mode of expression.

While post-colonial writers found a colonial paradigm in *The Tempest*, late twentieth-century women writers, following in H. D.'s footsteps, found in its plot and characters vehicles for a feminist agenda, reshaping the plot from a woman's point of view. Through his magical powers, Prospero enjoyed the ultimate patriarchal control over his daughter Miranda; her marriage to Ferdinand was essential to his 'project'. For Canadian novelist Margaret Laurence, Miranda, not Caliban, was the key figure, and finding her own voice, not Prospero's, was the issue. Laurence's *The Diviners* (1974) tracks the biography of a Miranda figure, Morag Gunn (alter ego for Laurence herself), whose struggle to find her artistic vocation mirrors Canada's cultural development. Throughout the novel, Laurence uses two metaphors to describe the artistic process: divining and scavenging. Divining depends upon nature, and Morag's friend 'Royland' (king of the land), a man skilled in using a divining rod, can discover springs of water trapped below the earth. Scavenging is a more active process. Morag's adopted father, Christie Logan, makes his living as a collector of junk and garbage, and, as she grows up, Morag sifts through the detritus she finds at the town dump. Just as Christie Logan uses other people's leavings to furnish his squalid house, Morag takes the bits and pieces she finds in human culture as building blocks for her art.

As a young student of English literature, Morag finds other bits and pieces to add to her art. Scraping enough money together to attend the University of Toronto, she meets and marries one of its English professors, Brooke Skelton, who serves as the novel's Prospero figure. Together they explore the English canon and Morag begins working on her first novel, but after eight years of marriage, Morag rejects Brooke's paternal authority. 'By positing an independent life for Morag, the woman-writer', observes Chantal Zabus, 'Laurence presents an allegory of the making of the Canadian artist, who has to abandon the patriarchal sterility of British letters, here represented by Skelton' (p. 113).

She moves from the staid cultivation of Brooke Skelton to a brief fling in the arms of Skinner Tonnere, a Meti, a mixed-race combination of French and Indian, Morag had known during her youth in Manawaka. An itinerant musician who takes his guitar and his songs on the road, Tonnere is not the kind of man to settle down and Morag knows it. But her interlude with him gives her what she has been craving, a child, the daughter Pique.

Laurence uses Morag's troubled relationship with Pique to frame the novel. As she awaits her daughter's visit, Morag offers snapshots, vignettes of her life from the earliest years through her marriage, her struggles as a writer, her sojourn in England and visit to her ancestral home in Scotland and her decision to live alone by the river. Morag's memories also raise fundamental questions about the artist's vocation. Throughout her journey, she struggles with the imperatives of her writing – the proverbial 500 pounds a year and a room of her own – and her longing for human connection, for love and relationships. She begins by claiming 'I've got my work to take my mind off life',[18] and throughout the novel she is frustrated by her inability to communicate with those she loves. As the novel ends, Pique is becoming an artist in her own right, writing songs like her father had before her and setting them to music. In Morag's daughter Pique, who combines her father's French and Cree origins with her mother's British heritage, the true Canadian is born. Morag, in turn, embraces her solitary life and accepts her gift, the gift of art.

The Miranda of Marina Warner's *Indigo* is also an artist, but in her novel the feminist theme is imbricated in the legacy of colonialism. Miranda is the granddaughter of Sir Anthony Everard, a direct descendant of the English founder of a colony on the Caribbean island of Liamuiga, Enfant Béate (a space strikingly similar to Warner's birthplace, St Kitts). Miranda also comes from Creole blood through her grandmother, Estelle Desjours. Described by the women of her family as 'high yellow', 'swarthy', and 'dirty' looking, she refers to herself as a 'musty' and for a time she sports an Afro hairstyle to signal her black heritage. Brought up by parents, whose turbulent quarrels create repeated psychological tempests, Miranda, like her namesake, is an obedient daughter. Throughout the novel she subordinates herself to the emotional demands of her family, anguishes about the racial inequities around her, yet remains loyal to her ne'er-do-well father.

Miranda's art is photography. During her visit to the ancestral island Enfant Béate, she ponders taking pictures of the native women, 'with their opal eyes and skin lustrous as horse chestnuts, which would be … neither Noble Savage nor Heroic Victim, but would connect with their history all the same'. She remembers that her friends from art school believed that photography's 'clean surgical objectivity could excise the corrupt legacy of racism, imperialism, orientalism and the other -isms that turned all Western consciousness into damaged goods'.[19] But Miranda hesitates. She realises that any photograph she takes will still have her stamp upon it, that artists can't step outside of the situations in which they're involved.

Photography introduces Miranda to George Felix, a black actor. When she sees him perform Caliban on stage, she wishes, 'Oh God, how I'd like to learn me a new language. Beyond cursing, beyond ranting' (Warner, p. 388). For her, as for Morag Gunn, there is no easy solution to the contradictions of her past; there is consolation, however, in the legacy she will leave through her child. As the novel concludes, we learn that Miranda has married George Felix, who takes the African name Shaka Ifetabe, and that their infant daughter is named Serafine, for the black native of Enfant Béate who has cared for her family for three generations. Like Morag's daughter, Pique, this baby girl embodies the hope of the future, a hope based on multi-racialism and a blending of cultural heritages.

Warner weaves her narrative web by moving between the present and the past. She begins the novel during Miranda's childhood and then moves back over 300 years to the settlement of Enfant Béate by Christopher (Kit) Everard. Here she reshapes Shakespeare's plot. In a critical essay written some time after the novel, Warner observes that in *The Tempest*, 'Among the noises of the island, the voice of Sycorax is silenced. Her story is evoked in a few scant lines that do not flesh out a full character or even tell a coherent tale.'[20]

Warner provides what is missing in Shakespeare's play by showing Sycorax, first as a woman with a husband and vocation (indigo-maker), later as a wise-woman who gathers herbs for healing and finally as a full-fledged sorceress. She adopts Dulé, the novel's Caliban, a black boy who survived the shipwreck of the slave ship that was carrying him from Africa to the West Indies. Soon Ariel, a female Arawak from the mainland, joins her household. Sycorax uses the knots and grooves in the wood of the saman tree for divining the future, 'for promise and destiny'. She does not see time as a continuous, linear trajectory as the English settlers do with their calendars and dates. As Warner observes in her essay on Sycorax and Circe, 'The contrast between the two magi of the play – the living male duke and the dead female hag – [lies] in the difference between metamorphosis and stasis, between a condition of continuing somatic, elemental and unruly mutation and a steady-stage identity.' *Indigo*'s Sycorax embodies 'pagan notions of physical identity as multiple and shapeshifting' which clash with Prospero's 'Christian idea of fixed, stable, and seemly bodily identity' (Warner, 'Foul Witch', p. 98).

In *Indigo*, Warner approaches Shakespeare's *Tempest* in light of her own hybrid heritage. Similarly, to contemporary African-American writers, as Julie Sanders argues, 'Shakespeare can represent both a figure of cultural imperialism, to be resisted and contested, and an enabling and empowering literature'.[21] Such ambivalence is especially apparent in the work of African American novelist Gloria Naylor. When she came to my university as a guest speaker, I asked her directly if she had *The Tempest* in mind while writing *Mama Day*, and she declared that it hadn't occurred to her. Yet many critics find palpable resonances of Shakespeare's romance in her novel.[22] Naylor's reply suggests, I suspect, her commitment to making her novels Afrocentric rather than Eurocentric. While Shakespeare and other European writers are central to the cultural milieu in which she was educated and in which she writes, she nevertheless desires to separate her work from Shakespeare, the text the British taught in colonial schools and used as an instrument of empire.

Given Naylor's Afrocentric aesthetic, it is not surprising that *Mama Day* is less an appropriation of *The Tempest* than a transformation. Naylor rewrites Shakespeare's Prospero as an aged black woman, Miranda Day, known by all in her island home of Willow Springs as 'Mama Day'. Like Prospero, Mama Day uses the magical powers she has mastered through long study to raise a tempest that punishes her enemies. Unlike Prospero, she is not a biological parent; she has never married. But her nurturing care for her sister Abigail, her great niece Ophelia (nicknamed Cocoa) and all the denizens of Willow Springs make her the earth mother incarnate. She serves her community as healer and midwife. She knows all the secrets of the island – the healing properties of the bark of various trees, of herbs and of plants. From natural ingredients she makes potions, powders and pomades that soothe and heal. She appears frequently with her chickens, her nimble fingers seeking the eggs they lay. Some are used for food, but she seeks others as instruments of fertility. Mama Day is, in other words, the feminine life force itself.

Naylor provides her readers with a family tree that traces the history of the Day family from its inception. Founded by Sapphira , an African slave woman and the Norwegian plantation owner Bascombe Wade, the Day family descends matrilineally from mother to daughter to granddaughter. In Willow Springs ancient customs brought from Africa are shaped and reshaped by the generations. As Mama Day observes at the novel's beginning, 'It aint about right or wrong, truth or lies.' Whatever actually happened back in 1823 between Sapphira Wade and her lover, her legend 'don't live in the part of our memory we can use to form words'.[23]

Like Prospero, Mama Day admits the limits to her power. As she 'thinks of the things she can make grow', she remembers 'The joy she got from any kind of life. Can't be nothing be wrong in bringing on life … But she aint never, Lord, she aint never tried to get *over* nature" (Naylor, p. 262). Instead of the binary of nature and art so often observed in Shakespeare's *Tempest*, in Mama Day Naylor gives us an art that is nature, nature observed through the seasons and thoroughly understood.

The plot of *Mama Day* is too complicated to unravel here, but its invocation of past, present and future is similar in some ways to Warner's. Instead of dividing her novel into sections as Warner does, Naylor uses repeatedly alternating voices, moving from Mama Day's first-person recollections and reflections to those of her great niece Cocoa and Cocoa's husband George. Their everyday speech – written as if they were speaking right to you – reflects African American oral traditions. The novel is framed by Cocoa at the age of forty-seven; she frequently returns to Willow Springs to visit the cemetery where George is buried, and as she talks to him, he answers. Together they recall the events of their courtship and marriage, as well as the visit to Willow Springs that resulted in George's death from heart failure. Their recollections are interwoven with those of Mama Day, who at the age of 104 provides a broader historical perspective. The narrative structure is much like the quilt Abigail and Mama Day make for Cocoa's wedding. As she works the quilt, Mama Day reflects: 'The past was gone, just as gone as it could be. And only God could change the future. That leaves the rest of us with today, and we mess that up enough as it is. Leave things be.' She thinks about the family heritage woven into the quilt's texture and realises that, when the quilt is finished, 'you can't tell where one ring ends and the other begins. It's like they aint been sewn at all, they grew up out of nowhere' (Naylor, p. 138). Past, present and future are all interwoven in the family's collective consciousness.

As Sanders notes, Willow Springs is 'a world where ghosts speak and ancestors are a living presence'. Like the quilt, 'the women's lives and folkloric memories conjoin and strengthen each other' (Sanders, p. 184). And, like the quilt, time moves in circles turning back, in and under each other.

With the exception of Percy MacKaye, these literary invocations of *The Tempest* are unanimous in their decentring of Prospero. While Gloria Naylor transforms the Milanese Duke into a female African American herbalist, other writers retell *The Tempest* story from the viewpoint of another character – Caliban, Miranda or Ariel. Prospero is still important to their narratives, but their characters resist his power and craft stories counter to his. Their resistance extends to the authors' manipulation of narrative structure and their common exploration of the nature and power of art.

To begin with, Shakespeare's Prospero is obsessed with time. He repeatedly asks Ariel what time it is, insisting that their work must be done by six o'clock. For Prospero – and for Percy MacKaye – time is linear; it follows a clear progression from beginning to end. Not so for the twentieth-century writers described here. The past, these works suggest, is programmed in us, in the genetic material we receive from our forebears, in the communal memories and myths we learn in childhood, in the legacy of settlement and colonisation we have inherited and in our longings for things long gone – or things that have never been but which we imagine have been. The future is in the present, divined by a sixth sense, shaped and reshaped through consciousness. Narrative is not a movement through time; it is a diptych, a triptych, or a circle that moves back and forth, in and out, endlessly like the waves of the sea.

Prospero's pain in remembrance of past things is conveyed in 1.2. by the irregularity of his blank verse lines and his frequent interruptions to ask Miranda if she is listening. When Alonso talks of begging forgiveness in the play's final scene, the magus stops him: 'Let us not burden our remembrances with / A heaviness that's gone' (5.1.199–200). For Prospero, memories of the past are an obstacle to harmony in the future. This is not the case for most of the characters in the works discussed here. H. D.'s speaker takes comfort and inspiration from the writers of the past, Laurence's entire novel is based on Morag Gunn's reveries about the past, and Naylor structures her narrative by alternating the recollections of Cocoa, George and Mama Day. The postcolonial writers – Césaire, Brathwaite and Warner, seem at first to be exceptions, because for them, as for Prospero, the past is haunted by injustice and inequality. But for these writers, too, it is important to remember the past, and, through remembering, to understand and to change the future.

Prospero is also obsessed with his daughter's chastity. His plan for the future union of Milan and Naples depends upon her marriage to Ferdinand

and their production of legitimate offspring. Indeed, Shakespeare posits two avenues to immortality in Sonnets 18 and 12. One is through the poem itself, through art; the other is through 'breed': the young man to whom the poems are addressed can live on after death not simply through the poet's art, but also through the children he sires. The novelists discussed here are also concerned with children, and even H. D.'s *By Avon River* underscores the importance of tradition, the legacy passed from one generation of poets to another. Laurence, Warner and Naylor are more specific, emphasising the role daughters play in their mother's self-awareness and vice versa. In all three novels the mother–daughter relationship has to be worked out – by acceptance as in Laurence, by rejection as in Warner, or through tragedy as in Naylor – before the next generation can move toward the twin goals of maturity and regeneration. Seeing the individual as part of a larger pattern that moves from one generation to another through time, these novelists remake *The Tempest* as a family saga with much more at stake than Prospero's dukedom. All four writers work toward the feminist project to insist – as Kate McLuskie puts it – that 'the alternative to the patriarchal family and heterosexual love is not chaos but the possibility of new forms of social organization and affective relationships' (Sanders, p. 11).

The Tempest's opposition between Caliban, a creature of the earth 'upon whom nurture never stuck', and Prospero, the cultivated European, also raises a seeming opposition between nature and art. For Prospero, the land is to be cultivated, the native to be civilised. To Césaire, Prospero is Anti-Nature. Just as the magician uses his power to control his servants Ariel and Caliban, he exploits European technology – brave utensils – to insulate himself from the earth. Drawing on an African tradition, Césaire posits a spiritual dimension to the forests and the animals that haunt them. For Auden, the poet's challenge is, as Hamlet mused, to hold the mirror up to nature, human nature. Laurence, Warner and particularly Naylor present the natural world as a place to be observed (as by Morag, the writer), studied (as by Miranda, the photographer) and understood (as by Mama Day, the healer). The ideal relationship to nature, these rewritings suggest, is not domination and control, but awareness, accommodation, even spiritual union.

In his 'Our revels now are ended' speech, Prospero affirms the evanescence of human existence, and at the play's conclusion he gives up magic by breaking his wand and drowning his books. By contrast, W. H. Auden, H. D., Margaret Laurence, Marina Warner and Gloria Naylor embrace the spiritual as an essential ingredient in the writer's consciousness. The committed writer must never give up the magic, no matter how painful it may be. Textual records like Christopher Everard's church monument or Sapphira Wade's bill of sale in *Mama Day* become obliterated, their meaning obscured. Unlike the historian bound by 'fact', the artist is a 'diviner' who embraces the spiritual as well as the physical. As diverse as their works are, Browning, Auden, H. D., Laurence, Warner and Naylor appropriate Shakespeare's characters to posit a different kind of knowledge, born of an intuitive understanding of people, the natural world and a spiritual world we can't touch but often feel.

Prospero's art has a powerful effect in Shakespeare's play, and, even though he drowns his books and breaks his staff, the spells he cast remain in the audience's imagination, captured for all time through the dramatist's language. Perhaps that is the ultimate answer to questions about the efficacy of art. For the poets, playwrights and novelists described here, the literary work matters insofar as it works on the mind and heart of its intended audience. Whether the artist's purpose is simply to explore the avenues of human consciousness (as in Browning, Auden and H. D.), to further a political agenda (as in MacKaye, Césaire and Brathwaite), or some combination of both (as in the novels of Laurence, Warner and Naylor), the works themselves offer us something unique, rich and strange, like *The Tempest* that inspired them.[24]

NOTES

1. William Davenant and John Dryden, *The Tempest, or, The Enchanted Island* (London, 1670).
2. Quoted from Arthur Kirsch's introduction to Auden's *The Sea and the Mirror* (Princeton: Princeton University Press, 2003), p. xi.
3. See Chantai Zabus, *Tempests After Shakespeare* (New York: Palgrave, 2002) for an overview of the varied ways Shakespeare's *Tempest* has been appropriated, especially in the late twentieth century.
4. Daniel Wilson, *Caliban: The Missing Link* (London: Macmillan, 1873).
5. See Ernest Renan, *Caliban: A Philosophical Drama Continuing 'The Tempest' of William Shakespeare*, trans. Eleanor Grant Vickery (New York: Shakespeare Press, 1896).
6. 'Caliban upon Setebos' is reprinted in its entirety as an appendix to *The Tempest*, ed. Virginia Mason Vaughan and Alden T. Vaughan (London: Thomson, 1999), pp. 316–25.
7. Jane P. Franck, '*Caliban* at Lewisohn Stadium, 1916', in Anne Paolucci (ed.), *Shakespeare Encomium* (New York: The City College, 1964), pp. 154–68, at p. 159.
8. Percy MacKaye, *Caliban by the Yellow Sands* (New York: Doubleday, 1916).
9. H[ilda] D[oolittle], *By Avon River* (New York: Macmillan, 1949).
10. Quotes from *The Tempest* are from the New Cambridge Edition, ed. David Lindley (Cambridge: Cambridge University Press, 2002).
11. Susan Stanford Friedman, 'Remembering Shakespeare Differently in H. D.'s *By Avon River*', in Marianne Novy (ed.), *Women's Revisions of Shakespeare* (Urbana: University of Illinois Press, 1990), pp. 143–64, at p. 154.

12. Kate Chedgzoy, *Shakespeare's Queer Children: Sexual Politics and Contemporary Culture* (Manchester: Manchester University Press, 1995), p. 154.

13. Friedman, 'Remembering', p. 157.

14. Susan Snyder, 'Auden, Shakespeare and the Defence of Poetry', *Shakespeare Survey* 36 (1983), pp. 29–37, at p. 37.

15. Quoted from Elaine Savory, 'Returning to Sycorax / Prospero's Response: Kamau Brathwaite's Word Journey', in Stewart Brown (ed.), *The Art of Kamau Brathwaite* (Brigend: Seren, 1995), pp. 208–30, at p. 215.

16. Aimé Césaire, *A Tempest*, trans. Richard Miller (New York: Ubu Theater, 1992), Translator's Note.

17. Edward Kamau Brathwaite, *Middle Passages* (New York: New Directions, 1993), pp. 75–88.

18. Margaret Laurence, *The Diviners* (Chicago: University of Chicago Press, 1974), p. 4.

19. Marina Warner, *Indigo* (London: Vintage, 1993), p. 320.

20. Marina Warner, '"The Foul Witch" and Her "Freckled Whelp": Circean Mutations in the New World', in Peter Hulme and William H. Sherman (eds.), *The Tempest and its Travels* (London: Reaktion, 2007), pp. 97–113, at p. 97.

21. Julie Sanders, *Novel Shakespeares: Twentieth-Century Novelists and Appropriations* (Manchester: Manchester University Press, 2001), p. 176.

22. For example, see ibid., pp. 170–90, and Peter Erickson, *Rewriting Shakespeare, Rewriting Ourselves* (Berkeley: University of California Press, 1991), pp. 124–45.

23. Gloria Naylor, *Mama Day* (New York: Vintage, 1988), pp. 3–4.

24. Portions of this essay were delivered at the 2000 meeting of the Deutsche Shakespeare-Gesellschaft, at the University of Munich in 2005, and at the University of Bologna in 2007. Thanks are due to my hosts, Professors Dieter Mehl, Tobias Döring and Keir Elam.

9

EUGENE GIDDENS

Pericles: the afterlife

In Shakespeare's day, *Pericles* was one of his most popular works. It was first staged by the King's Men at the Globe Theatre sometime in late 1607 or 1608, and contemporary dramatists referred to it as a model of popularity. Robert Taylor's Prologue to his *c*.1613–14 *The Hog Hath Lost His Pearl* hopes that: 'And if [the play] prove so happy as to please, / We'll say 'tis fortunate, like *Pericles*'.[1] Ben Jonson's 1631 poem 'On *The New Inn*' complains of the lasting audience interest in Shakespeare's 'mouldy tale', some twenty years after it was first staged.[2] A licence to revive the play was granted in that same year, suggesting that Jonson's envy had some basis in fact. In 1640, James Shirley alludes to *Pericles* in his *Arcadia*, in which one of his characters exclaims: 'Tire me? I am no woman. Keep your tires to yourself. Nor am I Pericles Prince of Tyre.'[3] The pun suggests that Shakespeare's play was still current towards the close of the theatres in 1642. In the Interregnum, Samuel Sheppard's poem *The Times Displayed in Six Sestiads* (1646) singles out *Pericles* in praise of Shakespeare:

> See him whose tragic scenes Euripides
> Doth equal, and with Sophocles we may
> Compare great Shakespeare. Aristophanes
> Never like him, his fancy could display.
> Witness his Prince of Tyre, his *Pericles*.[4]

Pericles also appears to have been the first Shakespeare play to be staged during the Restoration, when theatres reopened in 1659, and it was revived again in 1661.

The available evidence suggests that the play was just as well received by the contemporary reading public. It was published in quarto twice in 1609, and again in 1611, 1619, 1630 and 1635. Few plays of the period received so much print circulation. Amongst Shakespeare's plays, only a handful of his histories sold so well. With little direct evidence of audience or reader response, it is difficult to say what made *Pericles* so popular. It is an early instance of the romance genre, in which tragic events are fantastically resolved, and that genre proved very popular in the 1610s. Yet Shakespeare's other late plays are also exemplars of romance and do not appear to have been as admired by his contemporaries.

Pericles is the only late play to be published during Shakespeare's lifetime. *The Two Noble Kinsmen*'s first quarto was not published until 1634, and all of the other late plays first appear in the folio *Works* of 1623. *Pericles* was unfortunate, however, in being excluded from that important collection, which has led to much speculation about its place in Shakespeare's canon. The folio *Works* has long and rightly been considered the most important Shakespearean text. The volume was put together by John Heminges and Henry Condell, actors who had been associated with Shakespeare as friends and theatrical partners, so their judgement on the content of his canon was an informed one. We are still uncertain as to why *Pericles* was excluded from the collection. In the eighteenth century it was thought that the play might be Shakespeare's earliest, and as such too juvenile to include alongside his mature works. Dryden had put forward this view in his prologue to Charles Davenant's opera, *Circe*:

> Shakespeare's own muse her *Pericles* first bore;
> The Prince of Tyre was elder than the Moor:
> 'Tis miracle to see a first good play;
> All hawthorns do not bloom on Christmas Day.[5]

A more credible explanation for exclusion is that the play was a collaborative effort – today most scholars agree that George Wilkins, the author of a prose narrative about Pericles in 1608, was co-author. Yet this explanation is complicated by the publication history of two other late plays. The similarly collaborative *Two Noble Kinsmen*, written with John Fletcher, was absent from the Folio, but *Henry VIII*, which Shakespeare also wrote with Fletcher, was included. Therefore, no single explanation can unambiguously solve the riddle of *Pericles*' absence. Whatever its cause, this absence has had a detrimental influence on the later dissemination of the text in print and on stage.

The lack of a folio version of *Pericles* has had a further negative impact on the reception of the play: the 1609 quarto is textually corrupt, making it one of the so-called 'bad' quartos of Shakespeare, which include *Romeo and Juliet* and *Hamlet*. Those more famous plays have subsequent corrected editions in both quarto and folio, so the 'bad' quartos have had less impact on their reception histories. *Pericles* is the only one of Shakespeare's plays to survive as a bad quarto alone. The play was not included in the Second Folio (1632) or the Third (1663), though it was reprinted in the second issue of the Third Folio, which included seven additional plays, most of them not now believed to be by Shakespeare. *Pericles* gained a firmer place in the canon following its appearance in the Fourth Folio of 1685, upon which most of the eighteenth-century editions were based. Although today the play's place in the canon is assured, its corrupt text makes it difficult for students and theatrical practitioners to work with.

Textual and theatrical interest in *Pericles* declined sharply in the eighteenth century. The high-points for the play were Edmund Malone's 1780 and 1790 editions, which were the first to go back to the 1609 quarto as the basis for the texts. His editions offered several textual emendations that are still accepted today. The only eighteenth-century production on record is an adaptation called *Marina*, performed at Covent Garden in August 1738. George Lillo rewrote the play to focus on the final two acts, which then, as now, were believed to be written by Shakespeare. Lillo's adaptation muted the threat to Marina in the bawdy house, in part by making that space less sexually overt. Importantly, she does not rescue herself but is saved by representatives of Lysimachus. The gendered sensibilities of this adaptation (with a relatively helpless heroine) point to problems with the sexual politics of the play that were to shape its negative reception in later periods.

In 1816 William Hazlitt said that *Pericles, Prince of Tyre* 'is not much to our taste … this is not like Shakespear'.[6] Nineteenth-century 'taste' was unlikely to accommodate the sexual elements of the plot, including incest, attempted rape and a whore house. Intriguingly, however, the play was retold in Charles and Mary Lamb's *Tales from Shakespeare* of 1807, a volume that selected stories for children from just over half of Shakespeare's plays. Perhaps the peripatetic plot was seen to fit the emergent genre of children's literature. The play's sexual frankness was excised, so that Antiochus had performed 'a shocking deed … in secret' and Marina was sold into slavery but not prostitution.[7]

The play had been absent from the stage for over 100 years until 1854, when it was put on by Samuel Phelps at Sadler's Wells. Phelps, like the Lambs, carefully removed references to incest in the opening scene, which led to some confusion over the exact nature of Antiochus' 'sin' – *The Athenaeum* approved of the cut, but thought that it was 'at the risk of unintelligibility'.[8] The reviewer for *The Times* noted that the scenes of prostitution had also been severely expurgated, because 'the most elaborated scenes, those which take place at Mitylene, are too gross for representation, save in a most attenuated form'. The same reviewer found 'delight in a succession of brilliant decorations', characterising the production as 'a spectacle' and 'a marvel'. Pericles' ship, for instance, 'rocks in real earnest'.[9] Spectacle here replaced some of the dramatic tension lost in censorship.

The play was ushered into the twentieth century by its first performance at Stratford-upon-Avon, in 1900. This production, like Phelps's, was heavily cut. As Frank R. Benson, the director of the Shakespeare Memorial Theatre, put it, 'I should not mind my little girl of 10 coming to see it'.[10] The first unexpurgated version of Shakespeare's text was Robert Atkins's production at the Old Vic in 1921, as part of a series of the complete works of Shakespeare. Atkins's fuller text and minimalist staging seems to have provided a helpful environment for the play, as the most successful subsequent productions have also simplified scenery and been frank about sexual content. This lesson, however, was learned slowly. Nugent Monck's 1947 production at the Shakespeare Memorial Theatre in Stratford-upon-Avon cut the entire first act, for instance, to avoid the controversy of incest. The sexual content of the play has continued to be muted in some performances,[11] but the most well-received productions have negotiated the difficult topics of incest, prostitution and rape directly. Tony Richardson's 1958 production at Stratford, for instance, set the entire play upon a galley, restored the first act and allowed the Bawd to steal the show in the brothel scenes.

The 1969 production at Stratford, directed by Terry Hands, also proved enormously successful. Hands went further than Richardson's scenic simplification by staging the play against a very bare setting. He was also innovative in keeping Gower onstage for the entire production, and in doubling the parts of Thaisa and Marina, played by Susan Fleetwood. Eroticism was embraced – a wooden Priapus was part of the market at Mytilene, for instance, and Marina was impaled upon it. This comic turn, coupled with the doubling of Thaisa and Marina, led to some audience discomfort. Jeremy Kingston in *Punch* noted that 'the play opens by condemning incest and closes with something that, allegory notwithstanding, toys with the joys of it'.[12]

By 1976 F. David Hoeniger could write: 'I think I am not alone in being struck by how well audiences accept the first two acts of *Pericles*'.[13] The increasing acceptance of sexuality on stage has freed directors to face the narrative of *Pericles* directly, which has in turn allowed the play to flourish. Toby Robertson's 1973–4 production, first at the Edinburgh Festival and then at London's Roundhouse Theatre, for instance, staged the play inside a homosexual brothel. Even the conservative 1984 BBC version has a heavily sexualised Bawd, but the sexual threat to Marina, played by Amanda Redman, is kept fairly light-hearted, without a realistic sense of danger. The Royal Shakespeare Company production of 2003 (in association with Cardboard Citizens), represented the bordello in the context of the illegal sex trade. As Paul Taylor wrote for the *Independent*, Marina's conversions of the customers therefore seem to lack credulity: 'She'd struggle to pull that trick off at the sleazy modern establishment we are shown here.'[14] On the other hand, Hannah Betts in *The Times* complained about the humour of this scene in the Globe production of 2005: 'so unremittingly does the production fall back upon a principle of larking about that, when presented with the prospect of a virgin being about to be raped by a blunt instrument, the audience falls about laughing – not edgy, uncomfortable laughter, but great guffaws of hilarity as the child-like victim cowers centre stage'.[15] Such humour contrasts strongly with other productions, like the 1989 Royal Shakespeare Company staging, where Boult's treatment of Marina was shockingly aggressive.

The difficulties surrounding Marina's chastity and, in particular, her conversion of Lysimachus, make her role a taxing one. Marina requires a powerful force of character to maintain audience sympathy in the face of the Bawd and Boult's aggressive low humour. Yet even recent scholars have had difficulty in seeing how such a strong character can also be sexually timid. In the Royal National Theatre production of 1994, Susan Lynch played Marina 'as a gruff, Ulster-accented waif that some critics saw as interestingly against type while others thought it made nonsense of Shakespeare's intentions, especially in the brothel scene'.[16] The implication is that Marina must be meek to be sexually unavailable. Even sensitive productions can be uneasy about Marina's status. Mary Zimmerman's 2004 staging at the Shakespeare Theatre, Washington, DC, changed her age from fourteen to sixteen throughout. One reviewer noted unfavourably that 'Marguerite Stimpson played her as shrill, overly loud, and determinedly adolescent ... She wore childish braids ... and a severe, high-necked, long-sleeved black jacket, even in the brothel' and lacked 'either mystery or eroticism'.[17] Clearly a fourteen-year-old of such strength and innocence does not fully comply with contemporary sexual expectations. E. M. W. Tillyard's conclusion about the character seems to get to the crux of the issue: 'We cannot indeed be at ease simultaneously with Marina and the other inmates of the brothel'.[18] Critics rightly feel uncomfortable about siding with slave owners and rapists, yet Boult and Bawd often steal the show. The sheer variety of possible representations of Marina's difficulties have, in part, contributed to the play's popularity in the twenty-first century. The eighteenth-century sensibility that renamed the play *Marina* predicted what would give the play its recent success.

Another reason for *Pericles*' success might be that it seems to thrive on a minimal stage that embraces its late-play qualities: music, dance and ritual. This approach was particularly successful in Ninagawa Yukio's production of 2003 at the National Theatre, London. Ninagawa deployed *ningyō-buri*, live actors as puppets, throughout the production. The beauty of Shakespeare's verse was not an issue for this Japanese-language version, while the electronically scrolling English translation to the sides of the stage seemed to make the distinction between text and performance even more apparent. Recent turns to the bare stage, hand props and more direct communication with the audience – the things that suit the play so well – are in fact returning it to a stage more in keeping with its origins. Here the history of Gower's increased presence on the stage is telling. Early productions removed him entirely, while several recent directors have emphasised the role.

However, as Suzanne Gossett warns, recent theatrical trends can also have a negative impact upon the play. For instance, an interest in episodic scenes as opposed to continuity can cause difficulties with the play's ending, where the emotional impact of the reunion is dependent upon earlier events.[19] This reunion scene has long been held as one of the best moments in the play. Tillyard, whilst otherwise denigrating *Pericles*, called the final scene 'very fine', against the 'not ultimately effective' brothel scenes.[20] It is nonetheless surprising how often reviewers and audiences are struck by the scenes of sexual deviance and left under-awed by the doubled reunion at the close.

Pericles, unlike the other late plays, was written for the Globe Theatre. Tragicomedy is generally considered a genre of the smaller indoor theatres, like the Blackfriars, which became available for King's Men performances later in 1608. The indoor theatres encouraged a greater use of music, dancing, far-fetched action and episodic plots – all traits that the Globe's *Pericles*, for reasons that critics have not yet fully explained, shares with *The Winter's Tale* and *Cymbeline*. It is easy to imagine *Pericles* as an intimate play at first reading, but it is often full of lords and attendants, making much of the action far more public than it first appears. The opening scene, for instance, with Antiochus, his daughter and Pericles, is all the more politically perilous for being staged at court, probably in front of several onlookers, with a very significant row of dismembered heads. Similarly, the presence of female partners for the dancing knights in 2.5, adds an extra, gendered dimension to Pericles' performance. These public scenes remind us that the play is as much a political as a family romance. They also highlight potential reasons why it has been better received on the stage than by the reading public for the past 300 years, or how, as Robert Smallwood puts it: 'The textual and scholarly problems surrounding *Pericles* have, in my experience, an extraordinary habit of disappearing when one sees the play in the theatre.'[21]

The rise in stage productions has not been fully matched by critical interest in the play. *Pericles* has been discussed less frequently than *The Tempest*, *The Winter's Tale* or *Cymbeline*. Tillyard barely mentions it in his seminal work on the 'last plays' (although his succinct comments are especially thought-provoking). The play has been condemned for its subject matter, as is seen in the theatrical history above, for its loose structure, 'a mere chronological sequence of disconnected adventures',[22] and for its poor versification, 'it quite lacks the fullness and complexity that mark most of the verse of the three last plays'.[23] Most scholarly work on the play has been concerned with textual corruption, authorship and, more rarely, sources, but seldom does it apply the kinds of historicised or cultural criticism we tend to find in Shakespeare scholarship generally. J. M. S. Tompkins's simple question 'Why Pericles?' sums up the tone of early scholarly views, whereby critics ponder over why Shakespeare elected to write the play at all.

Critical editions probably provide the most telling comments on the concerns of recent scholarship. The authorship debate became particularly heated after the publication of the *New Cambridge Shakespeare* edition of Doreen DelVecchio and Antony Hammond in 1998.[24] DelVecchio and Hammond argued that the play was wholly by Shakespeare. Even more contentiously their editorial policy sought to preserve the text of the quarto, so that their practice included 'emending only when forced to admit defeat'.[25] They retained the quarto's 'air-remaining lamps' from Pericles' famous speech at 3.1.62, for instance, glossing this phrase as 'stars that always hang in the firmament'. (Previous editors, following Malone, have usually emended to 'aye-remaining lamps'.) *Pericles* has been subject to an unusual degree of emendation, so the New Cambridge Shakespeare edition was quite radical in its aims and execution, but often at the risk of making the text nonsensical.

At the other extreme are editors who rely on George Wilkins's *Painful Adventures*, a text closely akin to *Pericles*, to smooth out confusing moments in the quarto. George Wilkins, a minor dramatist who is known primarily for his 1607 play *The Miseries of Enforced Marriage*, published in 1608 a prose narrative, *The Painful Adventures of Pericles Prince of Tyre*. The explicit connection made between Wilkins's narrative and the play suggests that he had an authorial stake in the drama, but the need to publish his prose version immediately before the 1609 quarto suggests a contested stake. There is a long history of interpolating material from *Painful Adventures* into the text of *Pericles*, with additions thought by many directors to be necessary in performance. Even the textually conservative BBC Shakespeare series added lines from Wilkins for its 1984 television adaptation. The Oxford Shakespeare *Complete Works*, edited by Stanley Wells and Gary Taylor, went so far as to include a scene 'reconstructed' from Wilkins, which they call scene 8a.[26] The Oxford World's Classics individual text of *Pericles*, edited by Roger Warren, did the same, as did *The Norton Shakespeare*.[27] Both of these subsequent, popular editions derived their texts from the Oxford *Complete Works*. In reading or producing this play, more than most in Shakespeare's canon, care must be taken in deciding what textual approach is most plausible. Suzanne Gossett's edition for the Arden Shakespeare includes more information about the editorial history of the play than any other, and makes an excellent place to start.[28] Gossett's earlier '"To Foster Is Not Always to Preserve": Feminist Inflections in Editing *Pericles*' usefully shows how an editor's politics might impact upon textual readings.[29] Appendix 1 of MacDonald P. Jackson's *Defining Shakespeare* is probably the most lucid account of the overall textual situation.[30] The best resource from which to compare *Pericles* with its sources and analogues, including Wilkins, is Geoffrey Bullough's *Narrative and Dramatic Sources of Shakespeare*.[31] Bullough includes both John Gower's *Confessio Amantis* and Laurence Twine's *The Pattern of Painful Adventures*.

Recent work by Brian Vickers and MacDonald P. Jackson has settled (almost beyond a doubt) that *Pericles* is a collaboration with Wilkins. Brian Vickers's *Shakespeare Co-Author* offers a historical survey of responses to this issue. He contends that the weight of evidence heavily favours the presence of George Wilkins in Acts 1 and 2.[32] MacDonald P. Jackson's *Defining Shakespeare* gives an impressive range of authorship tests based upon intrinsic evidence. Jackson comes to the same conclusion as Vickers, and he analyses *Pericles* at greater length and with more types of stylistic evidence. The work of both of these scholars has made issues of authorship of less moment than they were in the 1990s.

Recently scholars have sought to move beyond the question 'Why Pericles?' in other ways, including concerns with history, genre, and form. Paul Dean, for instance, considers constructs of 'play' to show how the episodic scenes function as a unified whole.[33] Dean sees *Pericles* as a peripatetic play which involves a search for both truth and patience. Dean's consideration of the sources behind the play is especially useful, as he argues for the importance of pre-Reformation material within the context of the play's possible performance by a group of Catholic recusant players at Gowthwaite Hall, Yorkshire in 1609.[34] The play obviously had strong Catholic connotations that critics have not fully worked through, as a copy was also held by the English Jesuit mission in Saint-Omer, as attested by a booklist from 1619.[35]

Like Dean, most of *Pericles*'s recent defenders (and it has proven difficult to write about the play without some kind of disclaimer) have worked to show how it is thematically integral. Probably the most important work on the play's structure is Ruth Nevo's article 'The Perils of Pericles', which finds it 'so far from being fractured, to possess a degree of unity bordering on the obsessive'.[36] Nevo rehabilitates the play from accusations of a corrupt narrative by pointing to the unified psychological concerns of the protagonist. A recent engagement with issues of unity is Amelia Zurcher's 'Untimely Monuments: Stoicism, History, and the Problem of Utility in *The Winter's Tale* and *Pericles*'.[37] Zurcher effectively reject's Dean's interpretation by finding a moral vacuum: 'The plot of *Pericles* is repetitive and circular, as we might expect in a romance, but the characters do not seem to be educated by their travail, nor does the circularity provide any compensation for death' (918–19). This wide range of interpretation points to how difficult it is to make concrete pronouncements about the play.

Pericles' representation of familial crises and aberrant sexuality has led to strong interest from gender scholars. This movement corresponds to a similar focus on Marina and reunion in stage productions. T. S. Eliot's *Marina* (1936) points to this trend, as the poem is inspired by Pericles' relationship with his daughter. The disturbing mixture of sex and family has particularly exercised critics since C. L. Barber's memorable assertion that 'where regular comedy deals with freeing sexuality from the ties of family, these late romances deal with freeing family ties from the threat of sexual degradation'.[38] Deanne Williams finds inspiration from Madonna in 'Papa Don't Preach: The Power of Prolixity in *Pericles*'.[39] Williams traces the importance of rhetorical skill in the play to show how silence leads to tragedy and prolixity to salvation. Female silence is particularly dangerous, and Marina's powers of speech in the final scenes are therefore important: '*Pericles* reflects upon the misogynist ideal of female silence, questioning the cultural valorization of a woman's absolute compliance with her husband's or her father's will, and exploring the kinds of 'unspeakable' crimes that are concealed by her quiet obedience'.[40] Williams's concern with obedience had been taken up earlier by Richard Wilson in *Will Power: Essays on Shakespearean Authority*, which offers one of the most sophisticated gendered readings of the play. Using contemporary medical discourse about childbirth, he shows how paradigms of female secrecy and knowledge, when set against male 'science', paradoxically work to make female characters deliver 'the female body into compliance … [and] ready for inspection'.[41] Wilson's conclusion works well alongside a reading from the year before by Janet Adelman, who argues: 'Whatever the overt sympathy extended to Thaisa in childbirth, the play proceeds to treat her as though her maternity had made her taboo or tainted, allowing her to return only after a long period of penitential cleansing'.[42] The focus on the body and the need for purification has led more recent scholars to investigate tropes of disease in the play. Margaret Healy's '*Pericles* and the Pox' disrupts a sense of happy ending by arguing that Lysimachus, to many in the original audience, would be seen as corrupted by syphilis.[43] Kaara L. Peterson similarly focuses on the body in 'Shakespearean Revivifications: Early Modern Undead', where she finds that 'Thaisa must be cleansed of a hysterical disease that is a powerful reminder of sullying female sexual and reproductive processes, and she is "treated" in a temple appropriately designated to the worship of the pagan goddess Diana's admirable state of perpetual virginity.'[44]

These gendered readings complicate an unadulterated sense of 'wonder' or 'reunion', what Healy calls 'unalloyed aestheticism and "happy Ever-afters"',[45] that had characterised some of the earlier, more positive approaches to the play. *Pericles* has since the eighteenth century proved an enigma to critics, if not to theatrical audiences. But it seems no longer necessary to defend the play (or reasons for offering a response to it), in part because of its growing popularity on the contemporary stage. The play has undergone remarkable theatrical success, finding a permanent place in the Shakespearean repertory and being consistently well received. In London alone, the play received three major productions in 2002–3.[46]

Criticism, however, has yet to catch up with this stage popularity, and much work is still needed on this first, unusual, late play. Even longstanding critical concerns, like the collaboration with Wilkins, are due more elaborate (if conjectured) narratives of why Shakespeare worked with him and how the working relationship came about. The play's Catholic elements could be further explored, as could its relationship to Jacobean politics. (Here the very interesting work of Constance Jordan and, especially, Simon Palfrey, from 1997 has not been sufficiently built upon.[47]) More work is also needed on the play's ending, examining, for instance, the seemingly irresolvable tension between Acts 4 and 5 in performance. Because *Pericles* has heretofore hovered under-researched at the edges of the Shakespeare canon, it offers almost unrivalled opportunities for further scholarship. Given its current popularity with audiences, it is very likely that scholarship will enjoy a period of growth in the future.

NOTES

1. Robert Taylor, *The Hog Hath Lost His Pearl* (London, 1614), sig. A3v, modernised.
2. Ben Jonson, 'On *The New Inn*. Ode. To Himself', in Ian Donaldson (ed.), *Ben Jonson* (Oxford: Oxford University Press, 1985), pp. 502–3, at line 21.
3. James Shirley, *The Arcadia* (London, 1640), sig. B4v, modernised.
4. Samuel Sheppard, *The Times Displayed in Six Sestiads* (London, 1646), p. 22, modernised.
5. John Dryden, *The Poetical Works of John Dryden*, ed. George Gilfillan (Edinburgh, 1855), vol. II, p. 131.
6. William Hazlitt, 'Lectures on Dramatic Literature', *The Edinburgh Review* 26 (1816), p. 104.
7. Charles and Mary Lamb, *Tales from Shakespeare* (London: Collins, n.d.), p. 410.
8. *The Athenaeum*, 21 October 1854, pp. 1268–9, in *Shakespearean Criticism*, vol. XV, ed. Sandra L. Williamson (Detroit and London: Gale Research, 1991), pp. 132–3, at p. 133.
9. *The Times*, 16 October 1854, p. 4, in Williamson (ed.), *Shakespearean Criticism*, vol. XV, pp. 131–2.

10. Quoted in J. C. Trewin, *Benson and the Bensonians* (London: Barrie and Rockliff, 1960), p. 115, in Williams (ed.), *Shakespearean Criticism*, vol. XV, pp. 136–8, at p. 136.

11. The Nebraska Shakespeare Festival production, directed by Scott Freeman in 2005, for instance, cut all of Act 1 and replaced it with a narrative drawn from the Lambs' *Tales from Shakespeare*.

12. Jeremy Kingston, 'Pericles', *Punch*, vol. 256 (16 April 1969), pp. 578–80, in Williamson (ed.), *Shakespearean Criticism*, vol. XV, pp. 150–1, at p. 151.

13. F. David Hoeniger, 'Shakespeare's Romances since 1958: A Retrospect', *Shakespeare Survey* 29 (1976), pp. 1–10, at p. 7.

14. Paul Taylor, *The Independent*, 31 July 2003, in *Theatre Record* (16–29 July 2003), pp. 691–2, at p. 692.

15. Hannah Betts, 'Who Says that Rylance Is Golden?', *The Times* (11 June 2005), www.timesonline.co.uk, accessed 16 June 2005.

16. Melissa Gibson, 'Pericles at the Royal National Theatre [1994]', in David Skeele (ed.), *Pericles: Critical Essays* (New York: Garland, 2000), pp. 332–8, at p. 334.

17. Suzanne Gossett, '"Tell Thy Story": Mary Zimmerman's *Pericles*', *Shakespeare Quarterly* 57 (2006), pp. 183–94, at p. 193.

18. E. M. W. Tillyard, *Shakespeare's Last Plays* (London: Chatto and Windus, 1938), p. 23.

19. Suzanne Gossett, 'Political *Pericles*', in Sonia Massai (ed.), *World-wide Shakespeares: Local Appropriations in Film and Performance* (London and New York: Routledge, 2005), pp. 23–30, esp. p. 28.

20. Tillyard, *Shakespeare's Last Plays*, p. 23.

21. Robert Smallwood, 'Shakespeare at Stratford-upon-Avon, 1989 (Part II)', *Shakespeare Quarterly* 41 (1990), pp. 491–9, at p. 497.

22. J. M. S. Tompkins, 'Why Pericles?', *Review of English Studies* n.s. 3 (1952), pp. 315–24.

23. Tillyard, *Shakespeare's Last Plays*, p. 23.

24. William Shakespeare, *Pericles*, ed. Dorren DelVecchio and Anthony Hammond (Cambridge: Cambridge University Press, 1998).

25. Ibid, p. 80.

26. William Shakespeare, *The Complete Works*, ed. Stanley Wells and Gary Taylor (Oxford: Oxford University Press, 1986).

27. William Shakespeare, *Pericles, Prince of Tyre*, ed. Roger Warren, on the basis of a text prepared by Gary Taylor and M. P. Jackson (Oxford: Oxford University Press, 2003); William Shakespeare *The Norton Shakespeare*, ed. Stephen Greenblatt *et al.* (New York and London: Norton, 1997).

28. William Shakespeare, *Pericles*, ed. Suzanne Gossett (London: Thomson Learning, 2004).

29. '"To Foster Is Not Always to Preserve": Feminist Inflections in Editing *Pericles*', in Ann Thompson and Garden McMullan (eds.), *In Arden: Editing Shakespeare* (London: Thomson Learning, 2003), pp. 65–80.

30. MacDonald P. Jackson, *Defining Shakespeare: 'Pericles' as Text Case* (Oxford: Oxford University Press, 2003).

31. Geoffrey Bullough, *Narrative and Dramatic Sources of Shakespeare*, vol. VI (London: Routledge, 1966).

32. Brian Vickers, *Shakespeare Co-Author* (Oxford: Oxford University Press, 2002).

33. Paul Dean, 'Pericles' Pilgrimage', *Essays in Criticism* 50 (2000), pp. 125–44. Dean here builds upon the insights of Anne Righter's *Shakespeare and the Idea of the Play* (London: Chatto and Windus, 1962).

34. See C. J. Sisson, 'Shakespearean Quartos as Prompt-Copies, with some Account of Cholmeley's Players and a New Shakespeare Allusion', *Review of English Studies* 18 (1942), pp. 129–43, at p. 138.

35. See W. Schrickx, '*Pericles* in a Book-List of 1619 from the English Jesuit Mission and Some of the Play's Special Problems', *Shakespeare Survey* 29 (1976), pp. 21–32. *Pericles* is, importantly, the 'only work of imaginative literature in a long list of devotional and controversial works' (p. 22).

36. Ruth Nevo, in Kiernan Ryan (ed.), 'The Perils of Pericles', in *Shakespeare: The Late Plays* (London and New York: Longman, 1999), pp. 61–87, at p. 62.

37. Amelia Zurcher, 'Untimely Monuments: Stoicism, History, and the Problem of Utility in *The Winter's Tale* and *Pericles*', *Journal of English Literary History* 70 (2003), pp. 903–27.

38. C. L. Barber, '"Thou that Beget'st Him that Did Thee Beget": Transformation in *Pericles* and *The Winter's Tale*', *Shakespeare Survey* 22 (1969), pp. 59–67, at p. 61.

39. Deanne Williams, 'Papa Don't Preach: The Power of Prolixity in *Pericles*', *University of Toronto Quarterly* 71 (2002), pp. 595–622.

40. Ibid, p. 597.

41. Richard Wilson, *Will Power: Essays on Shakespearean Authority* (New York: Harvester Wheatsheaf, 1993), p. 181.

42. Janet Adelman, *Suffocating Mothers: Fantasies of Maternal Origin in Shakespeare's Plays, 'Hamlet' to 'The Tempest'* (New York: Routledge, 1992), p. 199.

43. Margaret Healy, '*Pericles* and the Pox', in Jennifer Richards and James Knowles (eds.), *Shakespeare's Late Plays: New Readings* (Edinburgh: Edinburgh University Press, 1999), pp. 92–107.

44. Kaara L. Peterson, 'Shakespearean Revivifications: Early Modern Undead', *Shakespeare Studies* 32 (2004), pp. 240–66, at p. 254.

45. Healy, '*Pericles* and the Pox', p. 106.

46. RSC Roundhouse production of 2002; Royal National Theatre of 2003; and Lyric Hammersmith of 2003.

47. Constance Jordan, *Shakespeare's Monarchies: Ruler and Subject in the Romances* (Ithaca: Cornell University Press, 1997), Chapter 2; and Simon Palfrey, *Late Shakespeare: A New World of Words* (Oxford: Clarendon Press, 1997), Chapter 2 and pp. 204–13.

IO

SUZANNE GOSSETT

The Two Noble Kinsmen and King Henry VIII: the last last plays

It is frequently assumed that *The Tempest* is Shakespeare's last play: there is something satisfyingly coherent to the notion of the bard, meditating on age and imminent retirement, using Prospero as a projection to bid farewell to 'the cloud-capped towers, the gorgeous palaces, the solemn temples, the great globe itself' (*The Tempest*, 4.1.152–3) and riding off to Stratford and the shadows, only to drink himself to death, merrily, with Ben Jonson not many years later. This fairy-tale fantasy of the conclusion of Shakespeare's artistic career is found in many writings about the 'late' or 'last' plays, and is interwined with the assumption that Shakespeare, at the end of his career and in his full powers, did not bother to collaborate with lesser writers.

Unfortunately, neither of these constructions is true. Following *The Tempest* Shakespeare, who had occasionally worked with collaborators previously, most recently with George Wilkins on *Pericles*, apparently turned to a rising star of the Jacobean theatre, John Fletcher – although, as we shall see, Fletcher may have turned to him. The collaboration resulted in three plays: *Cardenio*, now lost; *King Henry VIII, or All is True*; and *The Two Noble Kinsmen*, written under varying circumstances and perhaps emerging from different methods of joint writing. Then, it seems, there was nothing more from Shakespeare's pen.

The belated nature of these plays; the difficulty of fitting them into proposed trajectories of Shakespeare's career and psychology; arguments about their authorship; peculiarities of their publication history; and complexities of their style and genre have all affected their critical reception and production history. In addition, attitudes towards the two surviving plays have been affected by varying attitudes towards Fletcher, even while some critics have tried to write him out of the picture. Despite immense popularity in his own period, in the nineteenth and twentieth centuries Fletcher was treated as no more than an 'entertainer', writing to pattern, morally either lightweight or worse, 'a general target for disapproval'.[1] This disapproval was closely tied to a political reading that claimed the Beaumont and Fletcher plays implicitly advocated servile, *jure divino*, ultra-royalism, terms used by Coleridge and cited by critics for two subsequent centuries. But in the second half of the twentieth century such views ebbed. Clifford Leech pointed out that it is 'characteristic of Fletcher to stand aloof, to refrain from a whole-hearted committal of himself to one view or to its opposite' (p. 13). More radically, Philip Finkelpearl and Gordon McMullan argued that the political aims of Fletcher and his early collaborator Francis Beaumont 'were almost precisely the opposite of those usually assigned to them',[2] and that Fletcher, in collaboration and alone, wrote complex, ironic drama, characterized by a tone of unease.[3] Both critics identify Fletcher with the anti-royalist 'country' party: for Finkelpearl Beaumont and Fletcher's three best-known collaborations 'constitute a trilogy about the public and private consequences of princely intemperance' (p. 146); for McMullan, Fletcher's plays written after Beaumont's retirement and death are 'the product of negotiation between the ethos of the aristocratic, Protestant country household and of life in London and at court' (p. 35). Fletcher also sympathetically explores 'the political roles available to women' (McMullan, p. 182).

However, even a more positive view of Fletcher has not always been enough to elevate estimates of *The Two Noble Kinsmen* and *Henry VIII*. Instead, their critical reception and production history have been unusually interconnected; both have been tied to authorship controversies – the more the plays were viewed as Shakespearean, the more they were appreciated and produced – and affected by social attitudes. Sometimes, as in the nineteenth century with *Henry VIII*, successful stagings have led to critical reevaluation; sometimes, as in the later twentieth century for *The Two Noble Kinsmen*, new cultural positions have led to fresh critical appreciation and new productions.

An end and a beginning

The early production and publication history of the three Shakespeare-Fletcher collaborations accounts for much of their subsequent treatment. We encounter at once a series of anomalies. A play on the subject of Cardenio, derived from Cervantes's *Don Quixote*, which was first published in English translation in 1612, was given at Court in May and again in July of 1613.[4] In September 1653 Humphrey Moseley entered 'The History of Cardenio, by Mr Fletcher & Shakespeare' in the Stationers' Register, but it was apparently never printed. If *Cardenio* survives at all, it does so in an adaptation by the eighteenth-century Shakespeare scholar Lewis Theobald, who claimed he owned three copies, all of them subsequently lost or destroyed. We can only speculate whether Shakespeare actually collaborated on this lost play and, if so, under what circumstances. Furthermore, we do not know why the play was not published *either* in the 1623 Shakespeare First Folio or, if it was primarily by Fletcher, in the 1647 First Folio of the plays of Beaumont and Fletcher, in which the Stationer, none other than Humphrey Moseley, assured the Readers that 'as here's nothing but what is genuine and Theirs, so you will finde here are no *Omissions*'. Neither did the play appear in the comprehensive 1679 folio of *Fifty Comedies and Tragedies* by 'Francis Beaumont and John Fletcher' – actually, by Fletcher and his many collaborators – where seventeen additional plays were printed from previous quartos. Orphaned by all three collections, it is less peculiar that *Cardenio* did not survive, despite Theobald's assertions.

Henry VIII and *The Two Noble Kinsmen* more clearly form an end and a new beginning. With the former Shakespeare completes his history cycles, bringing time up to the Jacobean present in Cranmer's prophecy of Elizabeth's 'heir / As great in admiration as herself … Who from the sacred ashes of her honour / Shall star-like rise, as great in fame as she was, / And so stand fixed' (5.4.41-7).[5] Fittingly, the play rounds out the section of histories in the First Folio 'Catalogue', and its inclusion may reflect a view, held by Heminges and Condell or by the publishers, that the play makes a satisfactory conclusion to this section, even if that meant suppressing objections to collaborative work. *King Henry VIII* is, consequently, the latest play to be printed as by Shakespeare alone by those who had actually known him, with lasting consequences for evaluation of its authorship.[6]

The production circumstances of *Henry VIII* also formed an unanticipated finale: at the performance of 29 June 1613 the Globe Theatre burned down. A letter from the following week describes the disaster and helps to date the play – 'ye howse was very full and as the play was almost ended the house was fired wth shooting off a Chamber wch was stopt wth towe wch was blown vp into the thetch of the house and so burnt downe to the ground'. Using the play's alternative title, the writer mentions that this was 'a new play called all is triewe wch had beene acted not passing 2 or 3 times before' (*TxC*, pp. 29, 133).

These events may have had something to do with Shakespeare's withdrawal to Stratford, perhaps already planned and now implemented. The King's Men still had the Blackfriars, so they were not out of business during the time that the Globe was being rebuilt, and shortly before, in March 1613, Shakespeare had invested in a 'dwelling house' over one of the gatehouses of the old Blackfriars priory. Yet the reference to 'our losses' in the Prologue to *The Two Noble Kinsmen* reminds us that theatre was above all a commercial operation, and the closing of the large summer venue cannot have been beneficial to the company. Stephen Greenblatt suggests that it is likely Shakespeare sold his shares in both the King's Men and the Globe after the fire, rather than invest in the rebuilding.[7] Meanwhile, in the same year, 1613, Fletcher had his own loss, in this case of his earliest collaborator, Francis Beaumont, a man with whom he had shared, according to Aubrey, not only composition but house, bed, cloak and 'wench'. Beaumont's latest independent work for the theatre is *The Masque of the Inner Temple and Gray's Inn* for the wedding of the Princess Elizabeth and Frederick, the Elector Palatine, in February 1613; he married and withdrew to the country that same year. In this period Fletcher, then, was trying out other collaborators, apparently Field and Massinger as well as Shakespeare.

The Two Noble Kinsmen also recalls the past but forms a more significant new initiative. The play opens with the deferred marriage of Theseus and Hippolyta, the same marriage that was impending at the beginning of *A Midsummer Night's Dream* almost two decades earlier, and it incorporates elements of Beaumont's recent *Masque* in the scenes of the morris dance performed for Theseus and Hippolyta. The subplot, which centers on the Jailer's Daughter, a heroine who is so closely identified with her father that she does not have her own name and who comes close to an Ophelia-like drowning, is full of Shakespearean echoes. Yet theatrically the play initiated new paths: Lois Potter suggests that it 'must have been one of the few King's Men plays to be written specifically for Blackfriars',[8] and while it may have been used to reopen the Globe, it confirmed the dominant position the smaller theatre would have thereafter. It also indicated the kind of comic and tragicomic drama Fletcher would write, alone and with others, as Shakespeare's replacement as the attached dramatist of the King's Men. He apparently had little taste for history plays, writing only *Bonduca* (1609–14) alone. There, characteristically, the focus is on women and the setting is not recent English history but an ancient world more like that of *King Lear* than *Henry VIII*.

The Two Noble Kinsmen was also the first play published with the names of Shakespeare and another author on the title page, that is, advertising the collaboration. In 1623, when *The Two Noble Kinsmen* was not published in the Shakespeare folio, Fletcher was not only alive but the King's Men's dramatist. Did he object, thinking of the play as his, and carry the day even if technically the company owned the rights to their plays? Or did Heminges and Condell avoid including the more recent collaborations they knew about (making an exception for *Henry VIII*), and so exclude *Cardenio*, *Pericles* and *The Two Noble Kinsmen*? The popularity of the 'Beaumont and Fletcher' plays eventually seems to have been read back into *The Two Noble Kinsmen*: The 1634 quarto title-page couples 'the memorable Worthies of their time; Mr John Fletcher, and Mr William Shakspeare' as 'Gent.' in precisely the same way that the names of Francis Beaumont and John Fletcher had been bracketed and identified as 'Gent.' on the title-page of Thomas Walkley's 1622 quarto of *Philaster*.

Restoration, eighteenth and nineteenth century

By the time of the 1679 *Fifty Comedies and Tragedies Written by Francis Beaumont and John Fletcher*, the two surviving collaborations were firmly distinguished. *Henry VIII* was a 'Shakespeare' play, *The Two Noble Kinsmen* was a 'Beaumont and Fletcher' play. And their production history varied accordingly. Yet even when 'Beaumont and Fletcher' was a dominant force on the stage, *The Two Noble Kinsmen* was treated as problematic and adapted to fit current tastes. The adaptations until the end of the eighteenth century, the first called *The Rivals* (1664) and ascribed to Sir William Davenant, a second called *Palamon and Arcite* (1779) by Richard Cumberland, and a third by Francis Godolphin Waldron called *Love and Madness; or, the Two Noble Kinsmen* (1795), all reveal their discomfort with the play's mixed genre by simplifying the play in one direction or another: the first toward comedy, the second making it 'more unequivocally tragic', the last, with the addition of songs, creating 'virtually a comic opera' (Potter, 75–7). Both the more comic versions cut the first act. Then *The Two Noble Kinsmen* dropped out of the repertory until a production by the Old Vic in 1928.

The history of *Henry VIII* was quite different. Although always treated as a 'lesser' Shakespeare play, it has had sustained success on the stage. From the Restoration on this was achieved largely through elaborate spectacle and pageantry, beginning with Davenant's revival starring Thomas Betterton in the 1660s and fully exemplified in the Drury Lane production of 1761, which incorporated a 'coronation scene' to mark the coronation of George III. A production of 1727 had similarly celebrated the coronation of George II.[9] While the tendency to grandeur lasted until the First World War – McMullan notes that 'the two most spectacular productions of all were those of Henry Irving in 1892 and Herbert Beerbohm Tree in 1910' (*Henry VIII*, 32) – a significant change began with the production of John Philip Kemble in 1788, starring his sister Sarah Siddons as Katherine. Thereafter the play was treated as a star vehicle, focused on one of its three chief roles, Katherine, Henry and Wolsey, and it was often cut to foreground their scenes.

Yet, even while the production histories diverged, the nineteenth century laid the foundation for considering these two plays together, in the first suggestions that they were both collaborations and by the same hands. A mid-century article in the *Gentleman's Magazine* by James Spedding was provocatively titled 'Who wrote Shakespere's [sic] *Henry VIII*?'; the suggestion that the second author was Fletcher apparently came to Spedding from the poet Alfred Lord Tennyson. Spedding gave Shakespeare 1.1, 1.2, 2.3, 2.4, the first part of 3.2 and 5.1 and Fletcher all the rest, including the Prologue and Epilogue. Subsequent attempts to 'disintegrate' the play, including those by Cyrus Hoy in the 1950s and Jonathan Hope in the 1990s, have fundamentally agreed with these assignments, although Hoy preferred to see 2.1, 2.2, the second half of 3.2, 4.1 and 4.2 as Shakespeare scenes touched up by Shakespeare, and Hope reconfirmed Spedding's original division.[10] Meanwhile, the Reverend Alexander Dyce, who had included *The Two Noble Kinsmen* in his 1846 edition of *The Works of Beaumont and Fletcher*, in 1866–7 included the play in his second edition of *The Works of William Shakespeare*, the first time it had appeared in such a context.

The modern authorship debate

Discussion of *The Two Noble Kinsmen* and *Henry VIII* has raised specific questions of attribution as well as theoretical issues about literary and dramatic collaboration. Both plays have been subject to all the methods of analysis used by modern scholars to detect the presence of more than one author and then to identify the collaborators. Fletcher's fondness for the eleven-syllable line (leading to a 'weak' or 'feminine' ending) and for *ye* rather than *you*; his frequent contractions; his more 'modern' use of *has* and *does* rather than of *hath* and *doth*, dominant in the work of Shakespeare, who was fifteen years Fletcher's senior, have all been cited as pointers to his hand. These tests are spelled out in detail in the *Textual Companion* to the *Oxford Shakespeare*, and a full history of the debate is given by Brian Vickers, who confirms Spedding's division of *Henry VIII*. A few uncertainties remain about *The Two Noble Kinsmen*, but the division is usually agreed to be Shakespeare Act 1 (possibly with the very brief 1.5 by Fletcher), 2.1, 3.1–2, 4.3, and 5.1, 3, and 4, with Fletcher writing the rest.[11] Significantly, these attributions reveal that both authors were involved in all parts of the two plays, refuting the impressionistic desire, frequent especially before the mid-twentieth century, to attribute whatever the critic does not like (for example, the sexuality of the subplot scenes of the Jailer's Daughter in *The Two Noble Kinsmen* or Anne's bawdy conversation with the Old Lady in *Henry VIII*) to Fletcher and whatever the critic does admire, for example Katherine's deathbed vision, to Shakespeare.

Attribution studies do not tell us *how* the two men collaborated on the play. Some critics imagine Shakespeare taking on his young colleague to show him the way; others, like G. E. Bentley, presume that Fletcher, who had had experience writing for the boys at the Blackfriars, was in a position to lead as the King's Men transitioned to their new space.[12] Even if

Shakespeare had already returned to Stratford when *The Two Noble Kinsmen* was undertaken and, as Potter suggests, a division by scenes was worked out because the two men 'did not expect to have much opportunity to talk about the work in progress' (p. 25) – which could explain some of the inconsistencies in its details – for *Henry VIII* Shakespeare was presumably in London.

Further complicating the question, the collaborations are both indebted to earlier work by both dramatists, while Fletcher's previous plays were indebted to Shakespeare's. For example, *The Two Noble Kinsmen*, which begins with the marriage of Theseus and Hippolyta and whose heroes, Palamon and Arcite, are 'dearer in love than blood' (1.2.1), echoes both *A Midsummer Night's Dream* and *Two Gentlemen of Verona*.[13] The lovelorn Jailer's Daughter, who goes mad for love and tries to drown herself, recalls not only Ophelia but also the heroine of Beaumont and Fletcher's *The Coxcomb* of 1608–10. Viola, like Jessica of *The Merchant of Venice*, runs away to meet her lover with a casket of jewels, but instead is attacked by a group of drunks rather like the countrymen who incorporate the Jailer's Daughter into their morris dance. The main plot of *The Coxcomb* also concerns two friends who 'will be – you would little thinke it; as famous for our friendship – if God please, as ever *Damen* was and *Pytheas*, or *Pylades* and *Orestes*, or any two that ever were' (2.1.152–6). The play even anticipates the Jailer endangered because his prisoners escape.

Similarly, in the fourth act of *Henry VIII*, entirely by Fletcher, the Gentleman's complaints about being 'stifled / With the mere rankness' of the crowd at the coronation of Anne Boleyn and the 'great-bellied women' who 'would shake the press / And make 'em reel before 'em' (4.1.58–79) recall difficulties in controlling the audience for the wedding masque in *The Maid's Tragedy*. In Katherine's final scene (4.2) competing evaluations of Cardinal Wolsey provide a balanced argument *in utramque partem* (from both sides of the question), like the Senecan *controversiae* that were favourite sources for Fletcher's plots,[14] while Katherine's vision of '*six personages, clad in white robes*' who dance and hold garlands over her head is clearly indebted to those in *Cymbeline* and *The Tempest*.

Responsibility for the plays' final form extends beyond the collaborators to other kinds of indirect intervention: the need of the company to balance its repertory, the impact of the move to the Blackfriars, and the resonance of recent events would all have affected the dramatists. Particularly significant was the death of the heir apparent, Prince Henry, in the autumn of 1612, while Frederick awaited his marriage to Princess Elizabeth. The marriage took place on Valentine's Day, 1613, but a portrait of Elizabeth shows her still wearing knots of black ribbon in memory of her brother (Potter, p. 36).

The events of this period may account for the strange tone, the mingling of death and marriage, at the end of *The Two Noble Kinsmen*.

The problem of tone and genre

Much of the contested response to *The Two Noble Kinsmen* and *Henry VIII* has derived from their failure to meet generic expectations. As a history play *Henry VIII* is diffuse, focused as much on Katherine and Wolsey as on the title character; it fights over no long wars;[15] and it has a 'happy' ending, the birth of Elizabeth, whose bitter sequel all audience members knew. As a tragicomedy or romance *The Two Noble Kinsmen* not only does not 'want deaths', as the definition Fletcher borrowed from Guarini enjoined, it does not confine the deaths it does include, as in *The Winter's Tale*, to a small child and a fairly minor character. Instead, in a reversal of the first scene, where the wedding procession is interrupted by '*three Queens in black, with veils stained*', the final scene ends with the onstage death of Arcite and the exit of Palamon and Emilia to another wedding, one that the bride never wanted and that Palamon laments: 'That naught could buy / Dear love, but loss of dear love!' (5.6.111–12). The tonal complications help explain both the critical reaction to these plays and the way directors have tried to push them into shape, usually a shape more generically conventional.[16]

The tradition of emphasising the pageantry of *Henry VIII* begins with Davenant – if not with the King's Men's ill-fated decision to shoot off cannons to welcome the masquers in 1.4 – and remained subservient to his 'spectacular aesthetic' (McMullan, *Henry VIII*, 24) throughout the centuries that followed. The growing use of the play as a vehicle for star performers and elaborate processions meant, inevitably, cuts and restructurings. Often the play ended after the coronation of Anne (4.1) and the death of Katherine (4.2), entirely eliminating the fifth-act scenes of political manoeuvering, as well as Cranmer's prophecy at the christening of Elizabeth.[17] As late as 1910 Herbert Tree, who reversed 4.1 and 4.2 to end with the coronation of a new queen rather than the death of the previous one, justified his excisions: 'It has been thought desirable to omit almost in their entirety those portions of the play which deal with the Reformation, being as they are practically devoid of dramatic interest and calculated … to weary an audience' (cited McMullan, *Henry VIII*, 36). Such cuts pushed the play further towards what Helen Cooper calls 'the calumny romance', the trope of the falsely accused woman. As the historical Katherine, unlike Griselda or Hermione, 'cannot look to a happy ending in this world', she is compensated by 'a vision of such a heavenly afterlife'.[18]

Restructured in this way, the play becomes a romance with a tragicomic ending. The martyrdoms in which Buckingham, Wolsey and Katherine are swept away – the actions the prologue calls 'Sad, high, and working, full of state and woe; / Such noble scenes as draw the eye to flow' – do not distort this overarching structure, because each victim, at the moment of death, blesses the King rather than condemning him, and all see themselves as moving into a better life. The promise of heavenly reward increases with each death: Buckingham is met 'half in heaven' (2.1.88); Wolsey dies giving 'his honours to the world again, / His blessed part to heaven' (4.2.29–30); and the 'blessed troop' promises Katherine 'eternal happiness' (4.2.87–90).

These cuts do distort the play by distracting attention from the central figure. Yet even uncut the full arc of this history is tragicomic, as tragicomedy had been developed in *Cymbeline* or *The Winter's Tale*. At the Field of the Cloth of Gold Henry may be a light of men, but, talking *realpolitik*, Buckingham and Norfolk make clear that Wolsey 'can with his very bulk / Take up the rays o'th'beneficial sun' (1.1.55–6). Like Prospero and Leontes, Henry is not sufficiently attentive to his kingdom but distracted by his own obsessions: at the masque where he meets Anne Boleyn Wolsey warns him he 'is with dancing a little heated' (2.1.100), and Katherine, not Henry, is aware of the subjects' 'great grievance' for excessive taxation (1.2.20). Instead Henry is misled by venal courtiers. It is not until the end that he realises which 'men of some understanding / And wisdom' are needed for his Council and rejects flatterers for Cranmer's 'truth and ... integrity' (5.2.163–9, 5.1.114) Thus, despite the number of deaths required to achieve it, the end proves the Prologue wrong: there is no final weeping. Henry gains political control of his kingdom and, like Pericles, Cymbeline and Leontes, finds the child who will restore him and his realm. The revival from death of the wives in *Pericles* and *The Winter's Tale* is transferred to the 'maiden phoenix' from whose 'sacred ashes ... Shall star-like rise [one], as great in fame as she was' (5.4.40–6). History is read teleologically, with the earlier deaths occluded, into a bright future. Henry's compliment to the Archbishop, 'Thou hast made me now a man' (5.4.64), resonates as climax and conclusion.

The maintenance of a tragicomic tone has proven harder in the case of *The Two Noble Kinsmen*, where the apparently paradoxical challenge thrown down by the Prologue to *Henry VIII*, 'see / How soon this mightiness meets misery: / And if you can be merry then, I'll say / A man may weep upon his wedding day' is enacted in the plot. The play is exceedingly dark throughout: Cooper notes that the authors intensify the problematic elements in Chaucer's 'Knight's Tale', from which they derived their plot (374). The first act introduces disturbance on political, personal and sexual levels. Three mourning, homeless queens interrupt a wedding. They remind the 'Amazonian' Queen Hippolyta of her disruption of gender norms and of the cost of restoring them: she was 'near to make the male / To thy sex captive, but that this, thy lord ... shrunk thee into the bound thou wast o'erflowing'. Rather than the nuptial bed, the queens demand that the wedding party consider '[w]hat beds our slain kings have'. Resisting their plea, Theseus coolly refers to his marriage as a 'service ... Greater than any war' (1.1.78–171); he may be glad to go fight if, as Jeanne Addison Roberts claims, the presence of an Amazon is 'an infallible clue' to male anxiety.[19] Meanwhile, at Thebes the two noble kinsmen Arcite and Palamon bemoan a city 'where every evil / Hath a good colour, where every seeming good's / A certain evil' (1.2.38–40). Their uncle Creon, the ruler, is a tyrant, and young men like themselves are in danger of becoming 'monsters' if they copy the local manners.

In Theseus' absence a conversation between Hippolyta and Emilia casts further shadows on the impending marriage, as it is Theseus and his friend Pirithous whose 'knot of love' the sisters decide 'May be outworn, never undone'. Emilia compares her own love for the dead Flavina:

> And she I sigh and spoke of were things innocent,
> Loved for we did, and like the elements,
> That know not what, nor why, yet do effect
> Rare issues by their operance; our souls
> Did so to one another. What she liked
> Was then of me approved; what not, condemned –
> No more arraignment.

Emilia's 'rehearsal ... has this end: / That the true love 'tween maid and maid may be / More than in sex dividual', and she does not deny Hippolyta's conclusion: 'you never shall, like the maid Flavina, / Love any that's called man' (1.3.59–85). The act ends with repeated images of death, as hearses appear bearing the moribund kinsmen and again in a procession of *the three Queens with the hearses of their lords in a funeral solemnity* (1.5. SD). The aphoristic final lines intone, 'This world's a city full of straying streets, / And death's the market-place where each one meets' (1.5.15–16).

Except that the kinsmen survive, the first act is dark enough to introduce tragedy, and even then the kinsmen expect to be prisoners forever (2.2.3–4). The difficult language fits Theodore Spencer's attack on Shakespeare's parts of the play as static and stiff,[20] and Lois Potter comments that 'in many productions, Act 1 [has] difficulty holding the audience' (87). One such production was that directed by Darko Tresnjak at the New York Shakespeare Festival in 2003, about which the *New York Times* critic complained that the major flaw was 'too much emphasis on the sinister ... Mr Tresnjak begins the play with a forceful dramatic thrum, which makes the onset of the play's comic elements, in the jail cell scene between Palamon and Arcite, abrupt and wrenching.'[21] Remounting the play, first in San Diego in

2004 and then in Chicago in 2006, Tresnjak found a radical solution. Like some of the Restoration adaptors, he removed the first act of *The Two Noble Kinsmen*, but he replaced it with *A Midsummer Night's Dream* 1.1.1–19, the wedding preparations of Theseus and Hippolyta, followed immediately by the entrance of the Jailer and Wooer. The cousins, two muscular young men scantily dressed, were then seen cavorting in their triangular prison cell, symbolic of the triangles around which the play is constructed. Emphasis thus fell on the competition between the kinsmen, and even more so on the story of the Jailer's Daughter, who became the major figure. The performance was comic and current, and like much recent criticism emphasised elements of the play that had been neglected or even suppressed earlier.

Henry VIII and The Two Noble Kinsmen today

Current interest in these two plays has sources in critical and cultural concerns different from those previously affecting their appeal. First, the plays are now understood to be late and last for Shakespeare, but relatively early for Fletcher, with connections to this important author's later work. Next, the very aspects of the two plays that traditionally disturbed critics and directors – religion and politics in *Henry VIII*, sexuality and madness in *The Two Noble Kinsmen* – are precisely what has brought them new life on the stage and new critical attention.

Modern political productions of *Henry VIII* can be traced to Tyrone Guthrie's four mountings of the play, beginning in Stratford-upon-Avon in 1949. Guthrie 'made all the political scenes ... absolutely electric'.[22] The politics were cynical, for instance emphasising the 'bureaucratic undermining of Katherine' (p. 312) rather than, as in G. W. Knight's interpretation, 'celebration of kingship and national values'.[23] Critics, too, have re-evaluated the play's politics: Worden notes the accurate representation of a Renaissance court, full of spies and whispers, where the nobility, characterized by 'snobbery and selfishness and petulance', struggle for dominance and access to the monarch (p. 13). The Victorians loved *Henry VIII* for its spectacle, but it is also a close study of the development of a hereditary monarch, in Ralph Berry's words 'an old brute' (p. 310). Henry, however, came to the throne at only eighteen and, although over forty at the play's beginning, like an adolescent he remains more concerned with competitive (royal) masculinity – 'The two kings, / Equal in lustre, were now best, now worst, / As presence did present them' (1.1.28–30) – than with the cost of this display to his people: 'The subjects' grief / Comes through commissions, which compels from each / The sixth part of his substance, to be levied / Without delay; and the pretence for this / Is named your wars in France' (1.2.56–60). Even worse, there are no wars, no Agincourt to justify this expense, but merely a 'largely pointless display of grandeur' (McMullan, *Henry VIII*, 1.1.6n). Henry at first is a monarch unaware of the 'piles of wealth' his chief clergyman has accumulated (3.2.107); a monarch unaware that even after Wolsey is gone his follower Gardiner has pledged 'to be commanded / For ever by your grace' (2.2.117–18); and, worst of all, a monarch without a male heir, torn by the 'conscience' which asks him whether the cause is 'the marriage with his brother's wife' or whether his desire to divorce Katherine comes because 'his conscience / Has crept too near another lady' (2.2.15–17).

An early conversation between two key noblemen foreshadows the monarch's development:

> NORFOLK.   This is the cardinal's doing: the king-cardinal,
> That blind priest, like the eldest son of fortune,
> Turns what he list. The king will know him one day.
> SUFFOLK.   Pray God he do, he'll never know himself else.   (2.2.18–21)

And indeed, by the end of the play Henry has learned to know himself, to judge other men, and not to be intimidated by the clergy, as nicely embodied in his angry slide from the polite *you* to the familiar, even contemptuous, *thou* as he addresses Gardiner in the fifth act:

> You were ever good at sudden commendations,
> Bishop of Winchester. But know, I come not
> To hear such flattery now, and in my presence
> They are too thin and bare to hide offences;
> To me you cannot reach. You play the spaniel
> And think with wagging of your tongue to win me;
> But whatso'er thou tak'st me for, I'm sure
> Thou hast a cruel nature and a bloody.   (5.2.156–63)

Furthermore, since Gardiner has attacked Cranmer (who will die a Protestant martyr at the stake) for 'new opinions ... which are heresies' (5.2.51–2), Henry's support of Cranmer, symbolised by his giving 'this good man ... this honest man' (5.2.172–3) his ring, demonstrates the King's allegiance to the true, Protestant religion and freedom from Rome. Current debates about religion and about Shakespeare's own religious views and affiliation invalidate Tree's certainty that the 'portions of the play which deal with the Reformation' are 'devoid of dramatic interest and calculated ... to weary an audience'. In fact, the rediscovery that the 'conceiver or designer' of an idiosyncratic recension of the Old and New Testament published in 1535 was none other than King Henry himself was front-page news in the *Times Literary Supplement* of 14 December 2007, which bore the headline, 'The gospel according to Henry VIII'.

Finally, whatever Henry's sexual motivation in marrying Anne, his response to Cranmer's prophecy over the royal infant who will be 'the happiness of England' – 'O lord archbishop, / Thou hast made me now a man' – confirms his maturity. The ambiguous phrase, 'Never before / This happy child did I get anything' (5.4.56–65) conveniently obliterates the daughter of Katherine who would be known as 'Bloody Mary' and the dangers that would make Elizabeth's early years less than 'happy'. The play, like the romances that preceded it, ends with the 'finding' of the right child.

In one way the reception of *Henry VIII* has been continuous from Victorian times to the present: in its focus on the two queens. The drama seems oddly current, the tale of an older, devoted spouse replaced by a fertile trophy wife many years younger. Anne's own uncertainty, the way in which she is pushed into her position and yet cannot help seeking it, nicely embodies contemporary ideas about the objectification of women and the internalised false consciousness that abets it. Anne appears only three times, the third time a silent icon at her coronation, yet she is sexualised at every appearance. At the Cardinal's masque she is paired first with Sir Thomas Sandys, who brags about his colt's tooth (1.3.48) and makes bawdy jokes; she has three one-line speeches to this 'merry gamester' before she is taken to dance by the King, to whom she says nothing while he becomes 'heated'. She may be coyly flirtatious or she may be resisting the assumptions made about her; the performance tradition tends to the first, but the uncertainty is only strengthened by her private conversation with the Old Lady (2.3), in which Anne's protestations of sympathy for her mistress are undercut by the Old Lady's double entendres about Anne's willingness to 'venture maidenhead' and to 'stretch' her 'soft cheveril conscience' to be a queen. Once Anne has been greeted by the Lord Chamberlain with money and title, the Old Lady asserts, 'I know your back will bear a duchess,' but Anne's response, 'Make yourself mirth with your particular fancy / And leave me out on't. Would I had no being / If this salute my blood a jot; it faints me / To think what follows' (2.3.25–104), reminds the audience that it will cost Anne no less than her head to lie upon her back. As a woman she is as much the plaything of larger, male forces as is Katherine.

The older queen is less ambiguously sympathetic, although her Catholicism and her deathbed speech commending her young daughter, ironically praying Mary 'will deserve well' (4.2.136), distances Katherine. Actresses have always loved the part – besides Siddons it has been played by the likes of Ellen Terry and Peggy Ashcroft – and, unlike Anne's, it is of great dramatic scope. Katherine has the political sharpness Henry at first lacks, recognising the motives of Buckingham's surveyor and aware that Wolsey has 'blown this coal betwixt my lord and me' (2.4.77). She is indignant when the cardinals speak to her in Latin – 'I am not such a truant since my coming / As not to know the language I have lived in' (3.1.42–3) – although when it suits her rhetorically she reminds Henry that she is 'a stranger, / Born out of your dominions' (2.4.13–14). Her behaviour at her trial in the Blackfriars earns from Henry the perhaps unwilling praise, 'Go thy ways, Kate; / That man i'th' world who shall report he has / A better wife, let him in nought be trusted, / For speaking false in that' (2.4.131–4). Yet the ambiguity of Henry's reaction is hidden in the last phrases of the same speech, 'She's noble born, / And like her true nobility, she has / Carried herself towards me' (2.4.138–40): the play shows this to be true but can do nothing to have Katherine 'carry' the necessary child.

Current interpretations of *The Two Noble Kinsmen* are even further from those of the nineteenth century, when it is possible that the play was not performed because its 'queer' sexuality seemed too overt. The play is one of many early modern dramatic celebrations of male friendship – Richard Edwards wrote a *Palamon and Arcite* produced for the Queen in Oxford in 1566, as well as a *Damon and Pithias* – but none is openly homoerotic. For example, *The Two Gentlemen of Verona* concerns male friendship disrupted by competition for a woman, but Valentine and Proteus seem cold compared to the cousins in *The Two Noble Kinsmen*, who console each other for their imprisonment, 'here being thus together, / We are an endless mine to one another; / We are one another's wife, ever begetting / New births of love' (2.2.78–81). The irony, that immediately after these declarations they first glimpse Emilia, only strengthens the Girardian sense that the most powerful emotion in the triangle is affection between the men.

The homoeroticism of the play is strengthened by its multiplying instances. Theseus' bond to Pirithous is described in a highly sexualized phallic metaphor: 'Their knot of love, / Tied, weaved, entangled, with so true, so long, / And with a finger of so deep a cunning, / May be outworn, never undone' (1.3.41–4). Male-male bonding is mirrored in the Amazonian Emilia's commitment to other women: besides her undying affection for Flavina, her conversation in the garden as she walks with her woman concludes with an ambiguous exchange:

> WOMAN. I could lie down, I am sure.
> EMILIA. And take one with you?
> WOMAN. That's as we bargain, madam.
> EMILIA. Well, agree then.
> *Exeunt Emilia and Woman.* (2.2.152–3)

Richard Proudfoot points out that the last 'Well' may be a misreading of a manuscript *wele*, for 'we'll' (cited Potter 2.2.153n). In recent productions (e.g. Chicago) there has been no uncertainty that Emilia and her female servant are setting up a sexual tryst nor any about Pirithous' sexual attraction to men.

Equally disturbing is the uncontrolled heterosexual desire of the Jailer's Daughter, in current productions often the character of most interest to audiences, possibly because she is English, contemporary, 'bourgeois'.[24] The Daughter, whose father the Jailer is first seen making dowry arrangements with her otherwise nameless 'Wooer', falls in love with Palamon, frees him as 'would any young wench ... That ever dreamed or vowed her maidenhead / To a young handsome man' (2.4.12–14), flees after him and goes mad. As Carol Neely shows, her behaviour mimics the familiar conventions of stage madness: singing, 'quoting' and fantasising journeys, but 'the source of her disorder is thematized in her obsessive expressions of her desire for sexual satisfaction through images of violent penetration and excessive reproduction'.[25] Ultimately she is 'cured' by sexual therapy, the Wooer pretending to be Palamon and leading her off to bed. The Daughter and Emilia are thus structurally and symbolically doubled, each at the conclusion manipulated into a heteronormative and class-appropriate marriage with 'Palamon'. Like the other daughters in Shakespeare's late romances, she is lost and refound by her father, but in her last appearance we have only the Doctor's promise to make her 'right again', and her final lines are 'you shall not hurt me ... If you do, love, I'll cry' (5.4.106–13). As Emilia asks shortly before, when it seems she is to be married to Arcite at the cost of Palamon's death, 'Is this winning?'

The great final speeches that the three major characters give at the altars of their chosen deities, Arcite to Mars, Palamon to Venus, and Emilia to Diana, are Shakespearean, structured in magnificent long periods. The difficulty of their language is balanced by the symbolic responses they elicit, which in their imagery again connect the play to the Jacobean masque, as the opening wedding procession recalled Jonson's *Hymenaei* of 1606. Mars, the 'great corrector of enormous times', sends Arcite and his men '*clanging of armour, with a short thunder, as the burst of a battle*' (5.1.60–62); Venus, the 'sovereign queen of secrets', sends Palamon music, and '*doves are seen to flutter*' (5.2.9, 61–2); at the altar of Diana Emilia, who enters 'bride-habited, / But maiden-hearted', sees the silver hind she has set on Diana's altar vanish and '*in the place ascends a rose tree, having one rose upon it ... Here is heard a sudden twang of instruments and the rose falls from the tree*' (5.3.1–32). Each man achieves his desire: Arcite, the better warrior, prays to be 'lord o'th' day' and wins the battle; Palamon, whose 'argument is love', asks for and gains 'the victory of this question', because the victorious Arcite is fatally thrown from his horse just as Palamon is persuaded that 'Venus ... is false' (5.6.45). Only Emilia, tossed between the men, 'the victor's meed, the price and garland ... of this war' (5.5.16–31), is not granted her desire but must live to 'comfort this unfriended, / This miserable prince, that cuts away / A life more worthy from him than all women' (5.5.141–3). That the prince she addresses is Arcite rather than her eventual husband is irrelevant.

The end of *The Two Noble Kinsmen* is, presumably, the last dramatic scene that Shakespeare ever wrote. Russ McDonald notes that in these last last plays the sense of affirmation found in the preceding romances is deflated. *The Two Noble Kinsmen* in particular is 'clouded with doubt, the last act marked by pain and death … [Shakespeare] seems to be changing his mind again'.[26] But these plays were far from the end of Fletcher's career, and the ways he responded to this collaboration, his reaction to *The Two Noble Kinsmen* in particular, can be found in his later work.

The most interesting example is *The Mad Lover*, which Fletcher wrote alone in 1616, only three years after *The Two Noble Kinsmen*. This play consistently reworks the earlier play's tragicomic elements as comedy. The competing cousins are replaced by two brothers, Memmon and Polidor. Memmon, the 'mad lover', like the kinsmen falls in love at first sight with the Princess Calis and offers her his heart – literally. But when the 'heart' is brought by his brother, the Princess is overwhelmed by love for Polidor. Attempts to cure Memmon of his madness include a masque of beasts, whose introduction by Orpheus recalls 'Orpheus with his lute made trees', sung for Katherine in *Henry VIII*. The masque's ape, which '*with daily hugging of a glove / Forgot to eat and died*' (4.1.81–2), is based on the 'bavian with long tail and eke long tool' from *The Two Noble Kinsmen*. Rather than include a madwoman, the masque is performed for a madman.[27]

In the fifth act Fletcher parodies most extensively. The Princess Calis goes to the temple of Venus to beg assistance (or, as one woman puts it, in a phrase suggesting the Jailer's Daughter, 'she will demand / The Goddesse pleasure, and a Man to cure her' (3.6.26–7)). Calis' entrance interrupts a tryst between the Priestess of Venus and her lover, who improvises a response to Calis' prayer to the '*Divine starre of Heaven*' until suddenly 'The Temple shakes and totters: *Musicke*. Venus *descends*' (5.3.31–40). Fletcher thus has it both ways: first he lampoons the earlier oracles, and then he has the 'real' Venus determine the ending. The oracle promises Calis '*for thou hast bin sterne and coy, / A dead love thou shalt enjoy*', and the end of the play resolves this paradox, as *The Two Noble Kinsmen* did the paradox of how Arcite could win the battle and Palamon the woman. Polidor is brought in on a hearse with a letter explaining, '*I durst not live, because I durst not wrong him*'. Like Theseus, the King awards his sister to the victor, but Memmon, overwhelmed by his brother's love – 'search through all the memories of mankind, / And find me such a friend' – determines to kill himself. Polidor rises, the general takes war as his mistress, and the younger characters are paired off, Calis like Emilia enjoying a 'dead' love, the two brothers outdoing each other by each giving up the woman rather than giving up brotherly love for a woman (5.4.246–365).

We will never know why *The Two Noble Kinsmen* was not included in the Shakespeare First Folio, or just what the play meant to Shakespeare – was he ill? Did the play arise from late creativity, or was it forced upon him by needy friends after the fire? Home in Stratford, was he, like the Jailer, seeking a husband for a troublesome unmarried daughter?[28] On the other hand a glance at *The Mad Lover* suggests why Fletcher may well have wanted *The Two Noble Kinsmen* to be recognised as his. The play received the most flattering kind of attention when it was parodied by Ben Jonson in *Bartholomew Fair* in 1613: the puppet friends Damon and Pythias fight over a woman, and Winwife chooses the name Palemon 'out of the play'. Soon Fletcher was writing his own parody, and then *The Two Noble Kinsmen* was revived in 1619–20 and again in 1625–6. It was only at this last date that it became for Fletcher, who died in the plague of 1625, 'late' and 'last'; its frequent revival today shows that there is life in it still.

NOTES

1. See Clifford Leech, *The John Fletcher Plays* (London: Chatto and Windus, 1962), p. 5.
2. Philip Finkelpearl, *Court and Country Politics in the Plays of Beaumont and Fletcher* (Princeton: Princeton University Press, 1990), p. 7.
3. Gordon McMullan, *The Politics of Unease in the Plays of John Fletcher* (Amherst: University of Massachusetts Press, 1994), p. x.
4. Chambers thought the May warrant was for plays given earlier that winter, but that is unlikely. See E. K. Chambers, *William Shakespeare* (Oxford: Clarendon Press, 1930), vol. I, p. 539; Stanley Wells and Gary Taylor, *William Shakespeare: A Textual Companion* (hereafter cited as *TxC*) (New York: Norton, 1997), pp. 132–3.
5. Citations come from John Margeson (ed.), *King Henry VIII* (Cambridge: Cambridge University Press, 1990).
6. Seven plays were added to the second issue of the Third Shakespeare Folio in 1664. Of these only *Pericles* has been generally recognised as Shakespeare's, at least in part, and modern scholarship has converged upon George Wilkins as the co-author.
7. Stephen Greenblatt, *Will in the World* (New York: Norton, 2004), p. 381.
8. Lois Potter (ed.), *The Two Noble Kinsmen* (Walton-on-Thames: Nelson, 1997), p. 59.
9. Gordon McMullan (ed.), *King Henry VIII* (London: Arden, 2000), pp. 24–6.
10. See Cyrus Hoy, 'The Shares of Fletcher and His Collaborators in the Beaumont and Fletcher Canon (VII)', *Studies in Bibliography* 15 (1962), pp. 71–89, on Fletcher's collaborations with Shakespeare; Jonathan Hope, *The Authorship of Shakespeare's Plays: A Socio-linguistic Study* (Cambridge: Cambridge University Press, 1994); and Brian Vickers, *Shakespeare Co-Author: A Historical Study of Five Collaborative Plays* (Oxford: Oxford University Press, 2002).

11. Paul Bertram's attempt to claim all of *The Two Noble Kinsmen* for Shakespeare has found no scholarly support. Critics sometimes assume that because *Henry VIII* appears in the folio it is by Shakespeare alone; see, for example, Hugh Richmond's *Shakespeare in Performance: King Henry VIII* (Manchester, 1994), where Richmond views Shakespeare as 'displaying his characteristic adaptability in assimilating the styles and devices of other artists', p. 27.

12. G. E. Bentley, 'Shakespeare and the Blackfriars Theatre', *Shakespeare Survey* 1 (1948), pp. 38–50.

13. Citations to *The Two Noble Kinsmen* come from Stanley Wells and Gary Taylor (eds.), *The Oxford Shakespeare*, 2nd edn (Oxford: Clarendon Press, 2005).

14. See Eugene M. Waith, *The Pattern of Tragicomedy in Beaumont and Fletcher* (New Haven: Yale University Press, 1952).

15. 'Shakespeare's history plays might alternatively be called war plays .... There is the peacetime play *Henry VIII*, but that ... is another exception to prove a rule', Blair Worden, 'Shakespeare and Politics,' *Shakespeare Survey* 44 (1992), pp. 1–15, at p. 7.

16. Performance histories of *Henry VIII* are found in McMullan, *Henry VIII*, and Richmond, *Shakespeare in Performance*. Richmond has a chapter entitled 'Performance as Criticism: *The Two Noble Kinsmen*', in Charles H. Frey (ed.), *Shakespeare, Fletcher, and 'The Two Noble Kinsmen'* (Columbia, MS: University of Missouri Press, 1989); see also Potter, *The Two Noble Kinsmen*.

17. In 1892 Henry Irving 'concentrated almost entirely on the first three acts' (Margeson (ed.), *King Henry VIII*, p. 52.)

18. Helen Cooper, *The English Romance in Time* (Oxford: Oxford University Press, 2004), p. 276.

19. Jeanne Addison Roberts, 'Crises of Male Self-Definition in *The Two Noble Kinsmen*', in Frey (ed.), *Shakespeare, Fletcher*, pp. 133–44, at p. 133.

20. Theodore Spencer, 'The Two Noble Kinsmen', *Modern Philology* 36 (1939), pp. 255–76, at p. 257.

21. Bruce Weber, *New York Times*, 21 October 2003.

22. Robert Hardy, quoted in Ralph Berry, '"My Learned and Well-beloved Servant Cranmer": Guthrie's *Henry VIII*', in Jay L. Halio and Hugh Richmond (eds.), *Shakespearean Illuminations: Essays in Honor of Marvin Rosenberg* (Newark: University of Delaware Press, 1998), pp. 309–16, at p. 310.

23. See Julia Briggs, 'Tears at the Wedding', in Jennifer Richards and James Knowles (eds.), *Shakespeare's Late Plays: New Readings* (Edinburgh: Edinburgh University Press, 1999), pp. 210–27, at p. 213.

24. Richard Abrams, '*The Two Noble Kinsmen* as Bourgeois Drama,' in Frey (ed.), *Shakespeare, Fletcher*, pp. 145–62.

25. Carol Thomas Neely, *Distracted Subjects: Madness and Gender in Shakespeare and Early Modern Culture* (Ithaca, NY: Cornell University Press, 2004), p. 85.

26. Russ McDonald, *Shakespeare's Late Style* (Cambridge: Cambridge University Press, 2006), p. 254.

27. Citations are to *The Mad Lover*, ed. Robert Kean Turner, in Fredson Bowers (ed.), *The Dramatic Works of Beaumont and Fletcher*, vol. V (Cambridge: Cambridge University Press, 1982).

28. See Katherine Duncan-Jones, *Ungentle Shakespeare* (London: Arden, 2001) for an unidealised picture of Shakespeare's final years.

FURTHER READING

Essay collections

Barton, Anne, *Essays, Mainly Shakespearean*. Cambridge: Cambridge University Press, 1994.

Brown, John Russell and Bernard Harris (eds.), *Later Shakespeare*. Stratford-upon-Avon Studies 8. London: Edward Arnold, 1966.

Dutton, Richard and Jean E. Howard (eds.), *A Companion to Shakespeare's Works: The Poems, Problem Comedies, Late Plays*. Volume IV. Oxford: Blackwell, 2003; repr. 2006.

Kay, Carol McGinnis and Henry E. Jacobs (eds.), *Shakespeare's Romances Reconsidered*. Lincoln: University of Nebraska Press, 1978.

Palmer, D. J. (ed.), *Shakespeare's Later Comedies: An Anthology of Modern Criticism*. Harmondsworth: Penguin, 1971.

Players of Shakespeare series, various editors. Cambridge: Cambridge University Press, 1985–.

Richards, Jennifer and James Knowles (eds.), *Shakespeare's Late Plays: New Readings*. Edinburgh: Edinburgh University Press, 1999.

Ryan, Kiernan (ed.), *Shakespeare: The Last Plays*. London: Longman, 1999.

Shakespeare Survey 11 (1958).

Shakespeare Survey 43 (1991).

Smith, Stephen W. and Travis Curtright, *Shakespeare's Last Plays: Essays in Literature and Politics*. Lanham: Lexington Books, 2002.

Thorne, Alison (ed.), *Shakespeare's Romances: New Casebook Series*. Basingstoke: Palgrave Macmillan, 2003.

Tobias, Richard C. and Zolbrod, Paul G. (eds.), *Shakespeare's Late Plays: Essays in Honor of Charles Crow*. Athens: Ohio University Press, 1974.

The last plays as a group

Adams, Robert M., *Shakespeare: The Four Romances*. New York: Norton, 1989.

Egan, Gabriel, *Green Shakespeare: From Ecopolitics to Ecocriticism*. London and New York: Routledge, 2006.

Frye, Northrop, *A Natural Perspective: The Development of Shakespearean Comedy and Romance*. New York: Columbia University Press, 1965.

Gillies, John, *Shakespeare and the Geography of Difference*. Cambridge: Cambridge University Press, 1994.

Hoeniger, F. David, 'Shakespeare's Romances since 1958: A Retrospect'. *Shakespeare Survey* 29 (1976), pp. 1–10.

Knight, G. Wilson, *The Crown of Life: Essays in Interpretation of Shakespeare's Final Plays*. Oxford: Oxford University Press, 1947.

Lyne, Raphael, *Shakespeare's Late Work*. Oxford: Oxford University Press, 2007.

Marcus, Leah, *Puzzling Shakespeare: Local Reading and Its Discontents*. Berkeley: University of California Press, 1988.

Marshall, Cynthia, *Last Things and Last Plays: Shakespearean Eschatology*. Carbondale: Southern Illinois University Press, 1991.

Nevo, Ruth, *Shakespeare's Other Language*. New York: Methuen, 1987.

Ornstein, Robert, *Shakespeare's Comedies: From Roman Farce to Romantic Mystery*. Cranbury: Associated University Presses, 1986.

Strachey, Lytton, *Books and Characters: French and English*. London: Chatto and Windus, 1928.

Tillyard, E. M. W., *Shakespeare's Last Plays*. London: Chatto and Windus, 1938.

Traversi, Derek, *Shakespeare: The Last Phase*. London: Hollis and Carter, 1954.

Yates, Frances A., *Shakespeare's Last Plays: A New Approach*. London: Routledge and Kegan Paul, 1975.

Zurcher, Amelia, 'Untimely Monuments: Stoicism, History, and the Problem of Utility in *The Winter's Tale* and *Pericles*'. *English Literary History* 70 (2003), pp. 903–27.

The theatrical context

Bentley, G. E., 'Shakespeare and the Blackfriars Theatre'. *Shakespeare Survey* 1 (1948), pp. 38–50.

Braunmuller, A. R. and Michael Hattaway (eds.), *Cambridge Companion to Renaissance Drama*. Cambridge: Cambridge University Press, 1990.

Bullough, Geoffrey (ed.), *Narrative and Dramatic Sources of Shakespeare*. 8 vols. London: Routledge and Kegan Paul, 1957–75, vols. VI, VIII.

Cox, John D. and David Scott Kastan (eds.), *A New History of Early English Drama*. New York: Columbia University Press, 1997.

Gurr, Andrew, *The Shakespearean Stage, 1574–1642*. 4th edn. Cambridge: Cambridge University Press, 2009.

The Shakespeare Company, 1594–1642. Cambridge: Cambridge University Press, 2004.

Kiefer, Frederick, *Shakespeare's Visual Theatre: Staging the Personified Characters*. Cambridge: Cambridge University Press, 2003.

Knutson, Roslyn Lander, *Playing Companies and Commerce in Shakespeare's Time*. Cambridge: Cambridge University Press, 2001.

The Repertory of Shakespeare's Company, 1594–1613. Fayetteville: University of Arkansas Press, 1991.

Leggatt, Alexander, *Jacobean Public Theatre*. London: Routledge, 1992.

Limon, Jerzy, *The Masque of Stuart Culture*. London: Associated University Presses, 1990.

Lindley, David, *Shakespeare and Music*. London: Thomson Learning, 2005.

(ed.), *Court Masques*. Oxford: Oxford University Press, 1995.

Masten, Jeffrey, *Textual Intercourse: Collaboration, Authorship and Sexualities in Renaissance Drama*. Cambridge: Cambridge University Press, 1997.

Menzer, Paul (ed.), *Inside Shakespeare: Essays on the Blackfriars Stage*. Selinsgrove: Susquehanna University Press, 2006.

Orgel, Stephen, *The Jonsonian Masque*. Cambridge, MA: Harvard University Press, 1965.

Peacock, John, *The Stage Designs of Inigo Jones*. Cambridge: Cambridge University Press, 1995.

Stern, Tiffany, *Making Shakespeare: From Page to Stage*. London and New York: Routledge, 2004.

Sturgess, Keith, *Jacobean Private Theatre*. London: Routledge and Kegan Paul, 1987.

Wiggins, Martin, *Shakespeare and the Drama of His Time*. Oxford: Oxford University Press, 2000.

The political context

Astington, John H., *English Court Theatre, 1558–1642*. Cambridge: Cambridge University Press, 1999.

Bergeron, David M., *Shakespeare's Romances and the Royal Family*. Lawrence: University Press of Kansas, 1985.

Bevington, David and Peter Holbrook (eds.), *The Politics of the Stuart Court Masque*. Cambridge: Cambridge University Press, 1998.

Butler, Martin, *The Stuart Masque and Political Culture*. Cambridge: Cambridge University Press, 2008.

Hamilton, Donna B., *Shakespeare and the Politics of Protestant England*. London: Harvester Wheatsheaf, 1992.

Jordan, Constance, *Shakespeare's Monarchies: Ruler and Subject in the Romances*. Ithaca: Cornell University Press, 1997.

Marshall, Tristan, *Theatre and Empire: Great Britain on the London Stage Under James VI and I*. Manchester: Manchester University Press, 2000.

McMullan, Gordon, *The Politics of Unease in the Plays of John Fletcher*. Amherst: University of Massachusetts Press, 1994.

Mulryne, J. R. and Margaret Shewring (eds.), *Theatre and Government under the Early Stuarts*. Cambridge: Cambridge University Press, 1993.

Orgel, Stephen, *The Illusion of Power*. Berkeley: University of California Press, 1975.

Orkin, Martin, *Local Shakespeares: Proximations and Power*. London: Routledge, 2005.

Parry, Graham, *The Golden Age Restor'd: The Culture of the Stuart Court, 1603–42*. Manchester: Manchester University Press, 1981; repr. 1985.

Rist, Thomas, *Shakespeare's Romances and the Politics of Counter-Reformation*. Renaissance Studies 3. Lewiston: Edwin Mellen Press, 1999.

Tennenhouse, Leonard, *Power on Display: The Politics of Shakespeare's Genres*. London and New York: Methuen, 1986.

Genre

Bamber, Linda, *Comic Women, Tragic Men: A Study of Gender and Genre in Shakespeare*. Stanford: Stanford University Press, 1982.

Bishop, T. G., *Shakespeare and the Theatre of Wonder*. Cambridge Studies in Renaissance Literature and Culture 9. Cambridge: Cambridge University Press, 1996.

Cobb, Christopher J., *The Staging of Romance in Later Shakespeare: Text and Theatrical Technique*. Newark: University of Delaware Press, 2007.

Cooper, Helen, *The English Romance in Time: Transforming Motifs from Geoffrey of Monmouth to the Death of Shakespeare*. Oxford: Oxford University Press, 2004.

Fawkner, H. W., *Shakespeare's Miracle Plays: 'Pericles', 'Cymbeline' and 'The Winter's Tale'*. London: Associated University Presses, 1992.

Felperin, Howard, *Shakespearean Romance*. Princeton: Princeton University Press, 1972.

Henke, Robert, *Pastoral Transformations: Italian Tragicomedy and Shakespeare's Late Plays*. London: Associated University Presses, 1997.

McMullan, Gordon, *Shakespeare and the Idea of Late Writing: Authorship in the Proximity of Death*. Cambridge: Cambridge University Press, 2007.

Mincoff, Marco, *Thing Supernatural and Causeless: Shakespearean Romance*. London: Associated University Presses, 1992.

Mowat, Barbara A., *The Dramaturgy of Shakespeare's Romances*. Athens, GA: University of Georgia Press, 1976.

Smith, Hallett, *Shakespeare's Romances: A Study of Some Ways of the Imagination*. San Marino: Huntingdon Library, 1972.

Sokolova, Boika, *Shakespeare's Romances as Interrogative Texts: Their Alienation Strategies and Ideology*. Lewiston: Edwin Mellen Press, 1992.

White, R. S., *'Let Wonder Seem Familiar': Endings in Shakespeare's Romance Vision*. London: Athlone Press, 1985.

Language

Crystal, David and Ben Crystal, *Shakespeare's Words: A Glossary and Language Companion*. London: Penguin, 2002.

Dent, R. W., *Shakespeare's Proverbial Language: An Index*. Berkeley and London: University of California Press, 1981.

Edwards, Philip, *et al.* (eds.), *Shakespeare's Styles: Essays in Honour of Kenneth Muir*. Cambridge: Cambridge University Press, 1980.

Freedman, Penelope, *Power and Passion in Shakespeare's Pronouns: Interrogating 'You' and 'Thou'*. Aldershot: Ashgate, 2007.

Hope, Jonathan, *The Authorship of Shakespeare's Plays: A Socio-linguistic Study*. Cambridge: Cambridge University Press, 1994.

Houston, John Porter, *Shakespearean Sentences: A Study in Style and Syntax*. Baton Rouge: Louisiana State University Press, 1988.

Hunt, Maurice, *Shakespeare's Romance of the Word*. London: Associated University Presses, 1990.

Kermode, Frank, *Shakespeare's Language*. Harmondsworth: Penguin, 2000.

McDonald, Russ, *Shakespeare and the Arts of Language*. Oxford: Oxford University Press, 2001.

Shakespeare's Late Style. Cambridge: Cambridge University Press, 2006.

Palfrey, Simon, *Late Shakespeare: A New World of Words*. Oxford: Oxford University Press, 1997.

Vickers, Brian, *The Artistry of Shakespeare's Prose*. London: Methuen, 1968.

Shakespeare, Co-Author: A Historical Study of Five Collaborative Plays. Oxford: Oxford University Press, 2002.

Wright, George T., *Shakespeare's Metrical Art*. Berkeley: University of California Press, 1988.

Sexuality and gender

Adelman, Janet, *Suffocating Mothers: Fantasies of Maternal Origin in Shakespeare's Plays, 'Hamlet' to 'The Tempest'*. New York: Routledge, 1992.

Bamford, Karen, *Sexual Violence on the Jacobean Stage*. New York: St Martin's Press, 2000.

Barber, C. L., '"Thou that Beget'st Him that Did Thee Beget": Transformation in *Pericles* and *The Winter's Tale'*. *Shakespeare Survey* 22 (1969), pp. 59–67.

Bieman, Elizabeth, *William Shakespeare: The Romances*. Boston: Twayne, 1990.

Erickson, Peter, *Patriarchal Studies in Shakespeare's Drama*. Berkeley and London: University of California Press, 1985.

Garber, Marjorie, *Coming of Age in Shakespeare*. London: Methuen, 1981.

Kahn, Coppélia, *Man's Estate: Masculine Identity in Shakespeare*. Berkeley: University of California Press, 1981.

Lenz, Carolyn Ruth Swift *et al.* (eds.), *The Woman's Part*. Urbana: University of Illinois Press, 1980.

McCabe, Richard, *Incest, Drama and Nature's Law, 1550–1700*. Cambridge: Cambridge University Press, 1993.

Neely, Carol, *Distracted Subjects: Madness and Gender in Shakespeare and Early Modern Culture*. Ithaca, NY: Cornell University Press, 2004.

Novy, Marianne, 'Adopted Children and Constructions of Heredity, Nurture, and Parenthood in Shakespeare Romances', in Andrea Immel and Michael Whitmore (eds.), *Childhood and Children's Books in Early Modern Europe, 1550–1800*. London: Routledge, 2005, pp. 55–74.

The individual plays
Pericles

Cutts, John P., 'Pericles' "Downright Violence"'. *Shakespeare Studies* 4 (1968), pp. 275–93.

Dean, Paul, 'Pericles' Pilgrimage'. *Essays in Criticism* 50 (2000), pp. 125–44.

Dickey, Stephen, 'Language and Role in *Pericles'*. *English Literary Renaissance* 16 (1986), pp. 550–66.

Frye, Susan, 'Incest and Authority in *Pericles, Prince of Tyre'*, in Elizabeth Barnes (ed.), *Incest and the Literary Imagination*. Gainesville: University Press of Florida, 2002, pp. 39–58.

Gorfain, Phyllis, 'Puzzle and Artifice: The Riddle as Metapoetry in *Pericles'*. *Shakespeare Survey* 39 (1976), pp. 11–20.

Gossett, Suzanne, '"To Foster Is Not Always to Preserve": Feminist Inflections in Editing *Pericles'*, in Ann Thompson and Gordon McMullan (eds.), *In Arden: Editing Shakespeare*. London: Thomson Learning, 2003, pp. 65–80.

Jackson, MacDonald P., *Defining Shakespeare: 'Pericles' as Test Case*. Oxford: Oxford University Press, 2003.

Lewis, Antony J., '"I Feed on Mother's Flesh": Incest and Eating in *Pericles*'. *Essays in Literature* 15 (1988), pp. 147–63.

Palfrey, Simon, 'The Rape of Marina'. *Shakespearean International Yearbook* 7 (2007), pp. 140–51.

Peterson, Kaara L., 'Shakespearean Revivifications: Early Modern Undead'. *Shakespeare Studies* 32 (2004), pp. 240–66.

Relihan, Constance C., 'Liminal Geography: *Pericles* and the Politics of Place'. *Philological Quarterly* 71 (1992), pp. 281–301.

Skeele, David, *Thwarting the Wayward Seas: A Critical and Theatrical History of Shakespeare's 'Pericles' in the Nineteenth and Twentieth Centuries*. London: Associated University Presses, 1998.

(ed.), *'Pericles': Critical Essays*. New York and London: Garland, 2000.

Williams, Deanne, 'Papa Don't Preach: The Power of Prolixity in *Pericles*'. *University of Toronto Quarterly* 71 (2002), pp. 595–622.

Wilson, Richard, *Will Power: Essays on Shakespearean Authority*. New York: Harvester Wheatsheaf, 1993.

The Winter's Tale

Bartholomeusz, Dennis, *'The Winter's Tale' in Performance in England and America, 1611–1976*. Cambridge: Cambridge University Press, 1982.

Enterline, Lynn, '"You Speak a Language that I Understand Not": The Rhetoric of Animation in *The Winter's Tale*'. *Shakespeare Quarterly* 48 (1997), pp. 17–44.

Felperin, Howard, '"Tongue-tied Our Queen?": The Deconstruction of Presence in *The Winter's Tale*', in Patricia Parker and Geoffrey Hartman (eds.), *Shakespeare and the Question of Theory*. New York and London: Methuen, 1985, pp. 3–18.

Frey, Charles, *Shakespeare's Vast Romance: A Study of 'The Winter's Tale'*. Columbia: University of Missouri Press, 1980.

Hamilton, Donna B., *'The Winter's Tale* and the Language of Union, 1604–1610'. *Shakespeare Studies* 21 (1993), pp. 228–50.

Hunt, Maurice (ed.), *'The Winter's Tale': Critical Essays*. New York: Garland, 1995.

Kennedy, Dennis, *Granville Barker and the Dream of Theatre*. Cambridge: Cambridge University Press, 1985.

Marsalek, Karen Sawyer, '"Awake Your Faith": English Resurrection Drama and *The Winter's Tale*'. In David Klausner and Karen Sawyer Marsalek (eds.), *"Bring Furth the Pagants": Essays in Early English Drama Presented to Alexandra F. Johnston*. Studies in Early English Drama 9. Toronto: University of Toronto Press, pp. 272–91.

Muir, Kenneth (ed.), *Shakespeare: 'The Winter's Tale': A Casebook*. London: Macmillan, 1969.

Overton, Bill (ed.), *'The Winter's Tale'*. Basingstoke: Macmillan, 1989.

Sokol, B.J., *Art and Illusion in 'The Winter's Tale'*. Manchester: Manchester University Press, 1994.

Smith, Jonathan, 'The Language of Leontes'. *Shakespeare Quarterly* 19 (1968), pp. 317–27.

Snyder, Susan, 'Mamillius and Gender Polarization in *The Winter's Tale*'. *Shakespeare Quarterly* 50 (1999), pp. 1–8.

Tatspaugh, Patricia, '*The Winter's Tale*': *Shakespeare at Stratford*. London: Arden Shakespeare, 2002.

Tigner, Amy, '*The Winter's Tale*: Gardens and the Marvels of Transformation'. *English Literary Renaissance* 36 (2006), pp. 114–34.

Cymbeline

Brown, Richard Danson and David Johnson, *Shakespeare 1609: 'Cymbeline' and the 'Sonnets'*. Milton Keynes: Open University, 2000.

Collier, Susanne, 'Cutting to the Heart of the Matter: Stabbing the Woman in *Philaster* and *Cymbeline*', in Gillian Murray Kendall (ed.), *Shakespearean Power and Punishment*. London: Associated University Presses, 1998, pp. 39–58.

Frost, David L., '"Mouldy Tales": The Context of Shakespeare's *Cymbeline*'. *Essays and Studies* n.s. 39 (1986), pp. 19–38.

Gajowski, Evelyn, 'Sleeping Beauty, or "What's the Matter?": Female Sexual Autonomy, Voyeurism and Misogyny in *Cymbeline*', in Evelyn Gajowski (ed.), *Re-Visions of Shakespeare: Essays in Honor of Robert Ornstein*. Newark: University of Delaware Press, 2004, pp. 89–109.

Jones-Davies, Margaret, '*Cymbeline* and the Sleep of Faith', in Alison Findlay and Richard Wilson (eds.), *Theatre and Religion: Lancastrian Shakespeare*. Manchester: Manchester University Press, 2003, pp. 197–217.

Jordan, Constance, 'Contract and Conscience in *Cymbeline*'. *Renaissance Drama* 25 (1994), pp. 33–58.

King, Ros, '*Cymbeline*': *Constructions of Britain*. Aldershot: Ashgate, 2005.

Lewis, Cynthia, '"With Simular Proof Enough": Modes of Misperception in *Cymbeline*'. *Studies in English Literature, 1500–1900* 31 (1991), pp. 343–64.

Maley, Willy, '*Cymbeline*, the Font of History, and the Matter of Britain', in Diana E. Henderson (ed.), *Alternative Shakespeares 3*. Abingdon: Routledge, 2008, pp. 119–37.

Marcus, Leah, '*Cymbeline* and the Unease of Topicality', in Heather Dubrow and Richard Strier (eds.), *The Historical Renaissance: New Essays on Tudor and Stuart Literature and Culture*. Chicago: University of Chicago Press, 1988, pp. 134–68.

Mikalachki, Jodi, 'The Masculine Romance of Roman Britain and Early Modern English Nationalism'. *Shakespeare Quarterly* 46 (1995), pp. 301–22.

Simonds, Peggy Muñoz, *Myth, Emblem and Music in Shakespeare's 'Cymbeline': An Iconographic Reconstruction*. London: Associated University Presses, 1992.

Thompson, Ann, '*Cymbeline*'s Other Endings', in Jean I. Marsden (ed.), *Appropriation of Shakespeare: Post-Renaissance Reconstructions of the Works and the Myth*. New York and London: Harvester Wheatsheaf, 1991, pp. 203–20.

'Person and Office: The Case of Imogen, Princess of Britain', in Vincent Newey and Ann Thompson (eds.), *Literature and Nationalism*. Liverpool: Liverpool University Press, 1991, pp. 76–87.

Warren, Roger, '*Cymbeline*': *Shakespeare in Performance*. Manchester: Manchester University Press, 1989.

Wayne, Valerie, 'The Woman's Parts of Cymbeline', in Jonathan Gil Harris and Natasha Korda (eds.), *Staged Properties in Early Modern English Drama*. Cambridge: Cambridge University Press, 2002, pp. 288–315.

The Tempest

Brown, Paul, '"This Thing of Darkness I Acknowledge Mine": *The Tempest* and the Discourse of Colonialism', in Jonathan Dollimore and Alan Sinfield (eds.), *Political Shakespeare: New Essays in Cultural Materialism*. Manchester: Manchester University Press, 1985, pp. 48–71.

Brydon, Diana, 'Re-writing *The Tempest*'. *World Literatures Written in English* 23 (1984), pp. 75–88.

D'Haen, Theo and Nadia Lie (eds.), *Constellation Caliban: Figurations of a Character*. Amsterdam: Rodopi, 1997.

Dymkowksi, Christine (ed.), '*The Tempest*': *Shakespeare in Production*. Cambridge: Cambridge University Press, 2000.

Graff, Gerald and James Phelan (eds.), *The Tempest*. Boston: Bedford / St Martin's Press, 2000.

Hall, Kim F., *Things of Darkness: Economies of Race and Gender in Early Modern England*. Ithaca, NY: Cornell University Press, 1995.

Hirst, David L., '*The Tempest*': *Text and Performance*. Basingstoke: Macmillan, 1984.

Hulme, Peter and William Sherman (eds.), *The Tempest and Its Travels*. London: Reaktion, 2000.

Lamming, George, *Water with Berries*. New York: Holt, Rinehart and Winston, 1971.

Lindley, David, '*The Tempest*': *Shakespeare at Stratford*. London: Arden Shakespeare, 2003.

Palmer, D. J. (ed.), '*The Tempest*'. Basingstoke: Macmillan, 1991.

Peltrault, Claude (ed.), *Shakespeare: 'La Tempête': Études Critiques*. Besançon: Université de Franche-Comté, 1993.

Preiss, Richard, '*The Tempest*': *Shakespeare in Performance*. London: A & C Black, 2008.

Vaughan, Alden T. and Virginia Mason Vaughan, *Shakespeare's Caliban: A Cultural History*. Cambridge: Cambridge University Press, 1991.

White, R. S. (ed.), '*The Tempest*': *Contemporary Critical Essays*. Basingstoke: Macmillan, 1999.

Wood, Nigel (ed.), '*The Tempest*': *Theory in Practice*. Buckingham: Open University Press, 1995.

Zabus, Chantal, *Tempests After Shakespeare*. New York: Palgrave, 2002.

Henry VIII

Baillie, William M., '*Henry VIII*: A Jacobean History'. *Shakespeare Studies* 12 (1979), pp. 247–66.

Berry, Edward I., '*Henry VIII* and the Dynamics of Spectacle'. *Shakespeare Studies* 12 (1979), pp. 229–46.

Clark, Cumberland, *A Study of Shakespeare's 'Henry VIII'*. London: Golden Vista Press, n.d.

Dean, Paul, 'Dramatic Mode and Historical Vision in *Henry VIII*'. *Shakespeare Quarterly* 37 (1986), pp. 175–89.

Kermode, Frank, 'What Is Shakespeare's *Henry VIII* About?', in Eugene M. Waith (ed.), *Shakespeare: The Histories*. Englewood Cliffs, NJ: Prentice-Hall, 1965, pp. 168–79.

Magnusson, A. Lynne, 'The Rhetoric of Politeness and *Henry VIII*'. *Shakespeare Quarterly* 43 (1992), pp. 391–409.

McMullan, Gordon, 'Shakespeare and the End of History'. *Essays and Studies* 48 (1995), pp. 16–37.

'"Swimming on Bladders": The Dialogics of Reformation in Shakespeare and Fletcher's *Henry VIII*', in Ronald Knowles (ed.), *Shakespeare and Carnival: After Bahktin*. London: Macmillan, 1998, pp. 211–27.

Richmond, Hugh M., *'King Henry VIII': Shakespeare in Performance*. Manchester: Manchester University Press, 1994.

'Shakespeare's *Henry VIII*: Romance Redeemed by History'. *Shakespeare Studies* 4 (1968), pp. 334–9.

'The Feminism of Shakespeare's *Henry VIII*'. *Essays in Literature* 6 (1979), pp. 11–20.

Shaughnessy, Robert, '"Ragging the Bard": Terence Gray, Shakespeare and *Henry VIII*'. *Theatre Notebook* 51 (1997), pp. 92–111.

Shirley, Frances (ed.), *'King John' and 'Henry VIII': Critical Essays*. New York: Garland, 1988.

Wickham, Glynne, 'The Dramatic Structure of Shakespeare's *King Henry VIII*: An Essay in Rehabilitation'. *Proceedings of the British Academy* 70 (1984), pp. 149–66.

The Two Noble Kinsmen

Abrams, Richard H., 'Gender Confusion and Sexual Politics in *The Two Noble Kinsmen*'. *Themes in Drama: Drama, Sex and Politics* 7 (1985), pp. 69–77.

Berggren, P. S., '"For What We Lack, / We Laugh": Incompletion and *The Two Noble Kinsmen*'. *Modern Language Studies* 14 (1984), pp. 3–17.

Bertram, Paul, *Shakespeare and 'The Two Noble Kinsmen'*. New Brunswick: Rutgers University Press, 1965.

Bruster, D., 'The Jailer's Daughter and the Politics of Madwomen's Language'. *Shakespeare Quarterly* 46 (1995), pp. 277–300.

Donaldson, E. T., *The Swan at the Well: Shakespeare Reading Chaucer*. New Haven and London: Princeton University Press, 1985.

Finkelpearl, P. J., 'Two Distincts, Division None: Shakespeare and Fletcher's *The Two Noble Kinsmen*', in R. B. Parker and S. P. Zitner (eds.), *Elizabethan Theater: Essays in Honour of S. Schoenbaum*. Newark: University of Delaware Press, 1996, pp. 184–99.

Frey, Charles F. (ed.), *Shakespeare, Fletcher, and 'The Two Noble Kinsmen'*. Columbia: University of Missouri Press, 1989.

Iyengar, Sujata, 'Moorish Dancing in *The Two Noble Kinsmen*'. *Medieval and Renaissance Drama in England* 20 (2007), pp. 85–107.

Magnusson, A. Lynne, 'The Collapse of Shakespeare's High Style in *The Two Noble Kinsmen*'. *English Studies in Canada* 13 (1987), pp. 375–90.

McMullan, Gordon, 'A Rose for Emilia: Collaborative Relations in *The Two Noble Kinsmen*', in Gordon McMullan (ed.), *Renaissance Configurations: Voices/ Bodies/Spaces, 1580–1690*. Basingstoke: Macmillan, 1998, pp. 129–47.

Potter, Lois, 'Topicality or Politics? *The Two Noble Kinsmen*, 1613–1634', in Gordon McMullan and Jonathan Hope (eds.), *The Politics of Tragicomedy: Shakespeare and After*. London: Routledge, 1992, pp. 77–91.

'*The Two Noble Kinsmen*: Spectacle and Narrative', in François Laroque (ed.), *The Show Within*, Collection Astraea 4, vol. II. Montpellier: Publications de Université Paul Valéry, 1992, pp. 236–51.

Thompson, Ann, *Shakespeare and Chaucer*. Liverpool: Liverpool University Press, 1978.

Volceanov, George, 'Shakespeare's Bed-Tricks, Subverted Patriarchy, and the Authorship of the Subplot in the *Two Noble Kinsmen*'. *British and American Studies* 9 (2003), pp. 15–25.

Waddington, Raymond B., 'Entertaining the Offered Phallacy: Male Bed Tricks in Shakespeare', in John M. Mucciolo (ed.), *Shakespeare's Universe: Renaissance Ideas and Conventions : Essays in Honour of W. R. Elton*. Aldershot: Scolar, 1996, pp. 121–32.

Waith, Eugene M., 'Shakespeare and Fletcher on Love and Marriage'. *Shakespeare Studies* 18 (1986), pp. 235–50.

Wickham, Glynne, '*Two Noble Kinsmen* or *Midsummer Night's Dream Part II*?'. *Elizabethan Theatre* 7 (1980), pp. 167–96.

INDEX

Abrams, Richard 202
Accession Day Tilts 52, 66
Adams, Robert M. 8, 26
Adelman, Janet 16, 107, 181
Adès, Thomas, *The Tempest* 3
Adlington, William 48
Admiral's Men 62, 64
Adorno, Theodor W. 7
Aeneas 71
Agate, James 120
Ainley, Henry 121
Alexander Theatre, Liverpool 119
Alexander, Catherine 4
Alfred, Mike 140
Allen, Shirley S. 133
Alma-Tadema, Sir Lawrence 143
Amadis de Gaule 47
American Repertory Theatre 26
Amis and Amiloun 66
Amyot, Jacques 48
Anderson, Mary 120, 122
Anne of Denmark, Queen 39, 77
Apuleius, *The Golden Asse* 48
Ariosto, *Orlando Furioso* 47
Aristotle 47, 51, 52
Arne, Michael 115
Arne, Thomas 115, 146
Arnold, Matthew 157
Arundel, Earl of, see Howard, Thomas
Ashcroft, Peggy 197
Astraea 50, 61, 63, 77
Athenaeum, The 175
Atkins, Robert 176
Aubrey, John 188
Auden, W. H. 155–6
   The Sea and the Mirror 158–61, 169–71
Augustine, St 52
Austern, Linda 35, 44

Ayliff, H. K. 148
Aylmer, John, Bishop of London 50

Bacon, Sir Francis 108
Barber, C. L. 181
Barbieri, Carlo, *Perdita* 3
Barry, Spranger 145
Bartholomeusz, Dennis 118, 119,
   120, 133
Barton, Anne 110, 184
Barton, John 131, 139–40, 144
Bassett, Linda 127
Bate, Jonathan 153
BBC Shakespeare 139, 148, 176, 179
Beaumont, Francis 9, 21–3, 29, 39, 185–6,
   188–9, 190
   Cupid's Revenge 23
   The Knight of the Burning Pestle 82
   *The Masque of the Inner Temple and Gray's
      Inn* 38, 40, 65, 188
Beaumont, Francis and John Fletcher
   The Coxcomb 191
   A King and No King 31
   The Maid's Tragedy 41, 191
   1647 Folio 187
   1679 Folio 187, 189
Beethoven, Ludwig van 5
Begg, S. 142
Bellarmine, Cardinal 71, 85–6, 87
Benson, Frank R. 176
Bentley, G. E. 19, 26, 29, 190
Bergeron, David 72
Bergmann, Frederick Louis, see Pedicord
Berry, Philippa 72
Berry, Ralph 195
Bertram, Paul 202
Betterton, Thomas 189
Betts, Hannah 177

Bevington, David 68
Bevis of Hampton 47
Bible 49
  Bishops' Bible 84
  Geneva Bible 84
  Great Bible 61
  Henry VIII recension (1535) 196
  King James Bible 84
Billington, Michael 26
Birmingham Rep 148
Blackfriars District 33, 51, 187
Blackfriars Hall 62, 198
Blackfriars Theatre 8, 23, 29–43, 49, 51, 62,
  114, 178, 187, 188, 190, 191
Blake, William 138
Blenerhasset, Thomas, *A Direction for the
  Plantation in Ulster* 79, 81
Bly, Mary 27
Boaden, James 133
Boccaccio, Giovanni 65, 136
Boderie, Antoine Lefèvre de la, French
  Ambassador to London 29, 77, 83
Boethius 65, 68
Boétie, Etienne de la 66
Boleyn, Anne 62
Bond, Samantha 8, 124
Bonjour, Adrien 131–2
Bradbrook, Muriel 78
Bradley, A. C. 110, 156
Brathwaite, Edward Kamau 161–2,
  169–71
  Letter Sycorax 164
  Caliban 163–4
Briggs, Julia 202
Britland, Karen 3
Brook, Peter 121
Brooks, Peter 111
Brown, Ivor 27
Browning, Robert, *Caliban upon Setebos*
  156–7, 158, 169–71
Bruce, Susan 76
Bruch, Max, *Hermione* 3
Bruni, Emily 125
Brutus 71–2
Bullough, Geoffrey 180
Bulwer, John, *Chirologia, Or the Natural
  Language of the Hand. Chironomia, Or
  the Art of Manual Rhetoric* 68
Burbage, James 29
Burbage, Richard 29, 51
Burke, Kenneth 99
Butler, Martin 41, 45, 74–5, 76, 77,
  80, 85–6

Calvert, Charles and Adelaide 119–20
Campion, Thomas, *The Lord Hay's Masque*
  75–6
Cardboard Citizens 176
Carey, George, Lord Chamberlain 38
Carleton, Dudley 83, 84–5
Carr, Robert 76, 86
Carroll, Tim 144
Cartland, Barbara 102
Catherine of Aragon 62
Cecil, Robert, first Earl of Salisbury 86
Cervantes, Miguel de, *Don Quixote* 186
Césaire, Aimé 162–3, 169–71
  Une Tempête 162–3
Chamberlain, John 78, 83, 84–5
Chamberlain's Men, see King's Men
Chambers, E. K. 132, 201
Chapman, George 29, 39
  Byron plays 29
  *The Masque of the Middle Temple and
    Lincoln's Inn* 79
Chapman, George, Ben Jonson and John
  Marston, *Eastward Ho!* 82
Charles I, King 144
Charlton, H. B. 11–12
Chaucer, Geoffrey 49, 52–3, 64, 66, 68
  The Knight's Tale 9, 64–5, 66, 67, 69, 193
  The Legend of Good Women 65, 69
  The Merchant's Tale 69
  The Squire's Tale 69
  Troilus and Criseyde 65
Chedgzoy, Kate 160
Cheek by Jowl 151–2
Children of Paul's 29, 34, 36
Children of the Chapel, see Children of the
  Queen's Revels
Children of the Queen's Revels 21, 23, 29, 34,
  36, 190
Cibber, Susannah 145
Cicero 108
Cinthio, Giovanni Battista 48
City of London pageant (1559) 57
Clarke, Charles Cowden 135
Clopper, Laurence M. 69
Coghill, Nevill 128–9, 132
Coleridge, Samuel Taylor 110, 118, 138, 186
Colie, Rosalie 105
Collins, William 137
Colman, George (the Elder), *The Sheep-
  Shearing; or, Florizel and Perdita* 115
Comédie-Française 2
Condell, Henry 20, 139, 174, 187, 188
Cooke, Dominic 148–9

Cooper, Helen 32, 111, 192, 193
Copernicus 122
Cornwall, Barry 150
Covent Garden, Theatre Royal 3, 114–15,
116, 118, 145–6, 175
Crane, Ralph 95
Cranmer, Thomas 62
Craven, Hawes 143
Creswick, William 117
Cromwell, Thomas 62
Cumberland, Richard, *Palamon
and Arcite* 189

Daily Advertiser and Oracle, The 116
Daily Telegraph, The 120, 153
Damas, Léon 162
Daniel, Samuel 22, 42
Tethys' Festival 42, 77
Darwin, Charles 157
Davenant, Charles, *Circe* 174
Davenant, Sir William 44, 189, 192
The Rivals 189
Davenant, Sir William and John Dryden, *The
Tempest; or, the Enchanted Island*
1, 3, 155
Davies, Thomas 133
Day, John, William Rowley and George
Wilkins, *The Travails of the Three
English Brothers* 87
Dean, Paul 180–1
Dee, Dr John 61
Dekker, Thomas, *The Whore of Babylon* 84
DelVecchio, Doreen and Antony Hammond 179
Dench, Dame Judi 122, 151
Denny, Honora 75–6
Denny, Sir Edward 75
Devereux, Robert, third Earl of Essex 76, 86
Dexter, Sally 123
Digbie, Lord 71, 87
Dodd, William 137
Donaldson, E. T. 69
Doolittle, Hilda, see H. D.
Doran, Greg 124–5, 126
Dowden, Edward 2, 6–7, 8, 13, 15, 25,
67, 91
Drayton, Michael 160
Drury Lane, Theatre Royal 116, 118,
146, 189
Dryden, John 174
Dryden, John, *The Tempest; or, the Enchanted
Island*, see Davenant
Duffin, Ross 44
Duncan-Jones, Katherine 139, 202

Durfey, Thomas
*The Fool's Preferment; or, the Three Dukes
of Dunstable* 145
The Injured Princess; or, The Fatal Wager
144–5, 146, 147
Dyce, Reverend Alexander 190

Edinburgh Festival 176
Edward VI, King 22
Edwards, Philip 127
Edwards, Richard
Damon and Pithias 198
Palamon and Arcite 64, 198
Eggen, Arne, *Cymbeline* 3
Elam, Keir 94, 110
Eliot, T. S., *Marina* 181
Elizabeth I, Queen 22, 50, 57, 62, 63–4, 66,
71, 72, 77, 79, 197, 198
Elizabeth Stuart, Princess xi, 38, 57, 76, 78–9,
114, 188, 191
*Englands Wedding Garment, or a Preparation
to King James his Royall Coronation*
71–2, 74
English Shakespeare Company 144
Erasmus 66
Erickson, Peter 172
L'Étudiant Noir 162
Evans, Ifor 110
Ewbank, Inga-Stina 43, 131

Farnham, Willard 110
Faucit, Helena 118, 149
Felperin, Howard 111
Ficino, Marsilio 61
Field, Nathan 188
Fielding, Emma 151
Finkelpearl, Philip 186
Fitzpatrick, Joan 133
Fleetwood, Susan 151, 176
Fletcher, John xii, 9, 10, 17, 21–4, 26, 29,
32–3, 39, 61, 64–7, 91, 174, 185–201
Bonduca 188
The Faithful Shepherdess 23, 48
The Mad Lover 200–1
The Noble Gentleman 145
Philaster 22–3, 189
For plays co-authored with Beaumont, see
Beaumont
For plays co-authored with
Shakespeare, see Shakespeare
Fludd, Robert, *Utriusque cosmi maioris
scilicet et minoris metaphysica, physica
atque technica historia* 58

Foakes, R. A. 26
Forbidden Planet 3
Forman, Simon xi, 31, 113, 114, 136, 144, 151
Foxe, John 50
  Actes and Monuments 61
Franck, Jane P. 171
Frederick Henry, Elector Palatine 57, 78–9, 114, 188, 191
Freeman, Scott 183
Freud, Sigmund 160
Friedman, Susan 160
Frye, Northrop 111
Fuchs, Barbara 81, 82–3
Furnivall, F. J. 2, 25

Gair, Reavley 43
Garrick, David 146–7, 149
  Florizel and Perdita 115, 116, 118, 119
Gaskill, William 139, 151
Gentleman, Francis 147
Gentleman's Magazine, The 189
George II, King 189
George III, King 189
Gerschow, Frederic 34, 35
Gibson, Melissa 183
Giddens, Eugene 4
Gielgud, Sir John 121, 127
Gilbreath, Alexandra 125, 126, 130–1
Gillies, John 82
Gilman, Ernest 42
Girard, René 198
Globe Theatre (16th/17th century) xi, 8, 49, 62, 113, 114, 136, 173, 178, 187–8
Globe Theatre (20th/21st century) 140, 177
Goodman's Fields Theatre 114
Gossett, Suzanne 4, 9, 10, 17, 26, 76, 81–2, 87, 178, 179–80, 183
Gower, John 49, 52–3
  Confessio Amantis 52, 53, 180
Gowthwaite Hall, Yorkshire 180
Graphic, The 142
Granville-Barker, Harley 114, 120–1, 128–9, 131
Greenblatt, Stephen 81, 187–8
Greenblatt, Stephen and Charles L. Mee, Cardenio 26
Greene, Robert 49, 105, 108
  Greenes Vision 52
  Pandosto; or, The Triumph of Time 32, 51, 105, 113, 114, 128, 131–2
Grose, Carl 147–8

Guardian, The 26, 125
Guarini, Giambattista 22, 48, 192
  Compendio della Poesie Tragicomica 48
  Il Pastor Fido 48
Gunpowder Plot 84–5
Gurr, Andrew 21, 29, 30, 31, 32, 44, 68
Guthrie, Tyrone 195
Guy of Warwick 47

Haas, Virginia Westling, see Turner
Hall, Edward (1512) 39
Hall, Edward (2005) 125–6
Hall, Sir Peter 122–4
Halliday, F. E. 110
Hamilton, Donna B. 85, 86
Hammond, Antony, see Doreen DelVecchio
Hampton Court Conference 84
Hancock, Phyllida 124
Hands, Terry 176
Hardy, Robert 202
Harington, Sir John 47
Harker, Joseph 143
Hattaway, Michael 73
Hawkins, William 145–7
Hay, James 75–6
Hayman, Francis 3
Hazard, Mary E. 68
Hazlitt, William 102, 115, 116, 138, 175
H. D. (Hilda Doolittle), By Avon River 158–61, 164, 169–71
Healy, Margaret 74, 79, 181, 182
Heliodorus, Ethiopica 48
Hemings, John 20, 139, 174, 187, 188
Henke, Robert 25, 27
Henrietta Maria, Queen 87
Henri IV, King of France 85–6
Henry VII, King 77
Henry VIII, King 22, 39, 61–2, 86, 196
Henry Stuart, Prince of Wales 22, 42, 57, 64, 66, 73, 76–9, 82, 84, 114, 191
Henslowe, Philip 35
  Henslowe's Diary 19, 69
Heywood, Thomas, The Golden Age 41
Hiddleston, Tom 151
His Majesty's Theatre, London 120
Hoeniger, F. David 176
Hogarth, William 3
Holbein, Hans 62
Holderness, Graham 140–1
Holinshed, Raphael 18, 39
  The Chronicles of England, Scotland and Ireland 62, 141
Homes, Henry, Lord Kames 137

Hope Theatre 33
Hope, Jonathan 190
Hoskins, John, *Directions for Speech and Style* 98
Hosley, Richard 36
Houlbrooke, Ralph 26
Houston, John Porter 111
Howard family 86
Howard, Frances 76, 86
Howard, Henry, first Earl of Northampton 86
Howard, Thomas, first Earl of Suffolk 86
Howard, Thomas, fourteenth Earl of Arundel 84
Hoy, Cyrus 12, 190
Hunt, Maurice 26

Illustrated London News, The 142
Independent, The 176
Interludes 47
Irving, Henry 141–4, 150, 189, 202

Jackson, MacDonald P. 110, 180
Jackson, Russell 133
Jackson, Sir Barry 148
James VI and I, King 24, 29, 38, 40, 55, 57, 63, 71–9, 83, 84–6, 87
    An Apologie for the Oath of Allegiance 85
    Basilikon Doron 73, 76–7
    Speeches to Parliament 72, 73, 75
James, Henry 159
Jameson, Anna 149–50, 156
Jesson, Paul 124
Johnson, Dr Samuel 4, 135–7, 138–9, 140, 141, 147, 152
Johnson, Robert 38
Jones, David 139
Jones, Gemma 124
Jones, Inigo 39–40, 45, 54
    The Masque of Queens 40
Jones, John 11
Jonson, Ben 29, 32, 33–4, 39–40, 42, 61, 107, 160, 185
    Alchemist 22, 33, 44, 51
    Bartholomew Fair 33–4, 42, 201
    Eastward Ho! see Chapman
    Every Man Out Of His Humour 82
    Hymenaei 61, 199
    Masque of Augurs 82
    The New Inn 33
    Oberon 38, 49, 57, 77
    'On *The New Inn*' 173
    Volpone 82
Jordan, Constance 76, 182

Jourdan, Sylvester, *A Discovery of the Barmudas* 80
Jung, Karl 54

Kean, Charles 118–19, 128, 149
Kean, Ellen 119
Keats, John 135, 138, 150
Kemble, John Philip 116, 117, 118, 139, 149, 189
Kennedy, Dennis 121
Kermode, Frank 25, 110
Kiefer, Frederick 4
Killigrew, Thomas 114
King, Martin Luther 163
King's Company 114
King's Men 8, 9, 13, 20–4, 29–43, 49, 64, 122, 173, 178, 187–8, 190, 192
Kingston, Jeremy 176
Kneehigh Theatre 147–8
Knight, G. W. 195
Knutson, Roslyn Lander 21, 22, 27
Kohler, Estelle 125, 126, 127
Kyd, Thomas, *The Spanish Tragedy* 33

Lamb, Charles and Mary 175, 183
Lampedusa, Giuseppe Tomasi di 5
Laurence, Margaret, *The Diviners* 164–5, 166, 169–71
Leech, Clifford 134, 186, 201
Lennep, William Van 132
Lennox, Charlotte 113, 136, 139, 141, 152
Lewis, Matthew, *The Monk* 138
Lewisohn Stadium, New York 157
Lillo, George, *Marina* 175, 177
Lincoln Cathedral 122
Lincoln's Inn Fields 145
Lindley, David 2, 45, 49, 75, 76
Loeb Drama Center, Cambridge, MA 26
London Waits 34
Longus, *Daphnis and Chloe* 48
Lyceum Theatre, London 120, 141–4
Lydgate, John 49
Lyly, John 105
    Endymion 66
    Euphues 104, 105
Lynch, Susan 177
Lyne, Raphael 15
Lyric Theatre, Hammersmith 184

Machiavelli, Niccolo 63
MacKaye, Percy, *Caliban by the Yellow Sands* 157–8, 169, 171
MacLean, Sally-Beth 21

Macready, William Charles 115, 116–18, 149
Madonna 181
Malcolm X 163
Maley, Willy 79, 80, 149
Malone, Edmond 80, 83–4, 175, 179
Malory, Sir Thomas 47
Manning, John 68
Marcus, Leah 74–5
Margaret Tudor, Princess 72
Margeson, John 202
Marlowe, Christopher 105
Marsh, Charles 145, 146
Marshall, Cynthia 26
Marston, John 22, 29
    Eastward Ho! see Chapman
    Sophonisba 36
    The Malcontent 35, 36
Mary I, Queen 57, 62, 197
Mary, Queen of Scots 72, 73
Massinger, Philip 24, 188
Masten, Jeffrey 20
Matchett, William 129–30, 132
McCarthy, Lillah 121
McDonald, Russ 2, 3, 7, 10, 32, 111, 200
McLuskie, Kate 170
McMillin, Scott 21
McMullan, Gordon 2, 25, 33, 76, 78–9, 186,
    189, 192, 196, 201, 202
McNee, Jodi 152
Meadows, Kenny 150
Mee, Charles L., see Greenblatt
Merchant, W. Moelwyn 133
Mesguich, Daniel 2
Middleton, Thomas
    The Revenger's Tragedy 41
    Women Beware Women 41
Middleton, Thomas and William Rowley, The
    Changeling 76
Mikalachki, Jodi 149
Mill, Anna J. 69
Miller, Richard 162
Mincoff, Marco 12, 26
Monck, Nugent 176
Montaigne, Michel de 66
Montemayor, Jorge de 48
Morality Plays 47, 49
More, Sir Thomas 62
Morgan, Macnamara, Florizel and Perdita 115
Morley, Sheridan 139
Morley, Thomas 45
Morning Advertiser, The 116
Morning Post, The 118
Moseley, Charles 2

Moseley, Humphrey 186–7
Moshinsky, Elijah 139, 148
Mowat, Barbara 32, 110
Mucedorus 21–2, 23, 49, 53
Muir, Kenneth 10, 118
Mulryne, J. R. 79
Munro, Lucy 21, 23, 24, 43
Murphy, Arthur 147
Mystery play cycles 47, 63, 69

Nathan, Norman 130
Nation 121
National Theatre, London 26, 177, 184
National Theatre, London (Cottesloe) 122
National Theatre, London (Olivier) 122
Naylor, Gloria, Mama Day 167–71
Nebraska Shakespeare Festival 183
Neely, Carol Thomas 199
Nettles, John 124
Nevo, Ruth 16, 17, 26, 150, 180
New York Shakespeare Festival 194
New York Times, The 135, 139, 194
Ninagawa, Yukio 26, 177–8
Noble, Adrian 123–4, 140
Northampton, see Howard
Northumberland, see Percy
Norton, John 73
Nosworthy, J. M. 53, 110, 138–9
Nunn, Trevor 122, 131
Nutt, Joe 6–7, 9

Old Vic Theatre, London 176, 189
Orgel, Stephen 42, 45, 110
Ornstein, Robert 25
Other Place, Stratford 148
Ovid 19
    Metamorphoses 49, 50, 51, 56
Oxford Shakespeare Complete Works 10–11,
    12, 14–15, 18, 26, 151, 179

Pafford, J. H. P. 110
Paget, H. M. 142
Palamon and Arcite (anonymous Admiral's
    Men play, 1594) 64
Palfrey, Simon 26, 72–3, 87, 110, 182
Palmer, Sir Thomas, Essay of the Meanes how
    to make our Trauailes, into forraine
    Countries, the more profitable and
    honourable 82
Parker, Patricia 111
Parr, Antony 68
Parry, Graham 77, 78, 79
Parsons, Robert 85

Patrides, C. A. 68
Patterson, W. B. 73–4, 84, 85
Pearce, Joanne 151
Pedicord, Henry William and Frederick Louis
    Bergmann 153
Pembroke, Countess of, *Urania* 68
Pepys, Samuel 114
Percy, Henry, ninth Earl of Northumberland 85
Percy, Thomas 85
Peterson, Douglas L. 25–6
Peterson, Kaara L. 181
Petrarch, Francesco, *Trionfi* 56
Phelps, Samuel 118, 149, 175–6
Phillips, Augustine 35
Phoenix Theatre, London 121
Pigott-Smith, Tim 122–3
Plautus 47
Pope Clement VII 61
Pope Clement VIII 72
Pope Paul V 84–6, 87
Pope, Alexander 138
Potter, Lois 45, 76, 78, 188, 189, 191, 194, 202
Pound, Ezra 158
Priestley, Joseph 137
Prince and Princess of Wales (1742) 114
Prince of Wales (1759) 146
Prince's Men 22
Prince's Theatre, Manchester 119
Princess's Theatre, London 118, 119
Pritchard, Hannah 115, 119
Privy Council 29, 47
Proudfoot, Richard 78, 198
Prynne, William, *Histriomastix* 106
Punch 139, 176

Queen's Men 21

Ralegh, Sir Walter 77
Rank, Otto 88
Rare Triumphs of Love and Fortune, The 53
Red Bull Theatre 41
Redgrave, Vanessa 151
Redman, Amanda 176
Rembrandt van Rijn 148
Renan, Ernest, *Caliban: Suite de La Tempête*
    156–7, 169
Rice, Emma 147–8
Rich, John 145
Richard III, King 77
Richardson, Tony 176
Richmond, Hugh 202
Righter, Anne, see Barton, Anne
Roberts, Jeanne Addison 194

Robertson, Toby 176
Rose, Mark 60
Ross, David 146
Roundhouse Theatre 176, 184
Rowley, Samuel, *When You See Me You
    Know Me* 22, 61–2
Rowley, William
    The Changeling see Middleton
    *The Travails of the Three English
      Brothers* see Day
Royal Exchange, London 34
Royal Shakespeare Company 122, 123, 124,
    126, 127, 130, 131, 139, 140, 147–9,
    176, 177, 184

Sadler's Wells 118, 175
Said, Edward 2, 5–6, 7, 10, 12
Saint-Omer, English Jesuit mission 180
Saker, Edward 119
Salisbury, see Cecil
Sanders, Julie 167, 168–9, 172
Sandys, Edwin 73–4
Savoy Theatre, London 120
Schlegel, August 138
Schrickx, W. 184
Scotchman, The 118
Seneca 108, 191
Senghor, Léopold Sédar 162
Shakespeare in Love 13
Shakespeare Memorial Theatre, Stratford-on-
    Avon 151, 176, 195
Shakespeare Theatre, Washington, D.C. 177
Shakespeare, Hamnet 160
Shakespeare, Judith 160
Shakespeare, William
    All's Well That Ends Well 10, 14, 16, 55–6
    Antony and Cleopatra 91, 108, 136, 157
    As You Like It 14, 41, 45, 157
    The Comedy of Errors 17
    Coriolanus 1, 10, 14–16, 17, 37, 91, 104,
      108, 137
    Cymbeline xi, 4, 5, 7–18, 21, 22–3, 29, 30,
      31, 38, 41, 48, 50–2, 53–6, 67, 74–5, 76,
      77, 80, 85–6, 91, 95, 102, 126, 135–54,
      178, 191, 193
    Edward III 63
    Hamlet 11, 14, 26, 30, 78, 107–8, 157, 170,
      174, 188, 191
    Henry IV, Part 1 22
    Henry IV, Part 2 56
    Henry V 14, 62–3
    Henry VI, Parts 1–3 137
    Julius Caesar 14, 22, 157

Shakespeare, William (cont.)
King John 144
King Lear 1, 6, 10–13, 16, 17, 26, 50, 53, 55, 64, 87, 104, 107–8, 139, 141, 145, 149, 188
Love's Labour's Lost 39, 65
Macbeth 22, 60, 91, 92, 104, 108
Measure for Measure 10, 15
The Merchant of Venice 37, 50, 56, 59, 66, 93, 191
The Merry Wives of Windsor 22
A Midsummer Night's Dream 9, 17, 36–7, 48, 56, 65, 188, 191, 195
Much Ado About Nothing 14, 22
Othello 11, 15, 22, 50, 53, 55, 56, 107–8, 136, 149
Rape of Lucrece 53, 65
Richard II 137, 144
Romeo and Juliet 136, 137, 157, 174
Sir Thomas More 14–15
The Sonnets 105, 170
The Tempest xi, 1, 2, 3, 5, 7–18, 22, 30–1, 36, 37–8, 41–3, 47, 48, 49–52, 55, 56, 59–61, 62, 67, 80–1, 82–3, 91, 92, 95, 107, 109, 136, 155–72, 178, 185, 191, 193
Timon of Athens 6, 104, 107–8
Titus Andronicus 37, 53, 137
Troilus and Cressida 10, 14, 45, 65, 137, 157
Twelfth Night 14
The Two Gentlemen of Verona 17, 191, 198
The Winter's Tale xi, 4, 5, 7–18, 21, 22, 30, 31, 32, 38, 48, 49–52, 53, 56–9, 60, 61, 63, 65, 67, 68, 82, 91, 93–4, 95, 96–7, 98–9, 101, 103, 104, 105, 108–9, 113–34, 123, 149, 178, 192, 193
First Folio xi, 8, 9, 10–13, 14, 17, 19, 36–7, 61, 93, 95, 132, 139, 151, 161, 174, 187, 188, 201
Second Folio 174
Third Folio xi, 174–5, 201
Fourth Folio 175
Oxford Shakespeare Complete Works, see Oxford
Shakespeare, William and John Fletcher
Cardenio xi, 9–18, 22, 26, 91, 185–7, 188
Henry VIII; or, All is True xi, 3, 4, 9–19, 22, 31, 39, 50, 51, 55, 56, 61–4, 76, 78–9, 86, 91, 95, 157, 174, 185–98, 200
The Two Noble Kinsmen xii, 4, 9–18, 31, 38, 64–7, 76, 78–9, 91, 145, 174, 185–201

Shakespeare, William and George Wilkins
Pericles xi, 4, 7–18, 23, 26, 32, 33, 41, 48, 49–53, 55, 60, 62, 64, 67, 68, 74, 76, 81, 82, 83–4, 87, 91, 94–5, 97–8, 99–100, 101, 102, 103, 107, 109, 140, 173–84, 185, 188, 193, 201
Shapiro, Michael 43
Sharpe, Robert 6
Shaw, George Bernard 140, 142–3
Shepherd, Mike 148
Sheppard, Samuel, The Times Displayed in Six Sestiads 173
Sher, Sir Antony 125, 126, 130–1
Shirley, James 24
Arcadia 173
Siddons, Sarah 116, 118, 189, 197
Sidnell, Michael J. 68
Sidney, Sir Philip 102, 105, 107, 108
Arcadia 47, 49, 66, 68, 105
Apologie for Poesie 47, 48
Simonds, Peggy Muñoz 56
Sisson, C. J. 13, 184
Smallwood, Robert 133, 178
Smuts, R. Malcolm 77
Snyder, Susan 160
Somerset, Edward, fourth Earl of Worcester 86
Sophocles, Oedipus at Colonus 5
Spanish Infanta 57, 72, 77
Speaight, Robert 12, 133
Spedding, James 189–90
Speght, Thomas 68
Spencer, Charles 153
Spencer, Sir Stanley 124
Spencer, Theodore 194
Spenser, Edmund 19, 52, 84, 105, 108
The Faerie Queene 71, 77, 105
St Clair, William 153
St John, William M. 135
Start Here Productions 144
Stationers' Register xi, 186
Stern, Tiffany 30
Stettin-Pomerania, Duke of 34
Stimpson, Marguerite 177
Strachey, Lytton 2, 91
Strauss, Richard 5
Strong, Roy 45, 69
Suffolk, see Howard
Sullivan, Sir Arthur 3
Sutherland, James 110
Swinburne, Charles Algernon 150

Tasso, Torquato 48
Aminta 48

Tatspaugh, Patricia 3, 133
Taubman, Howard 139
Taylor, Gary 11–13, 26, 37
　Cardenio 26
Taylor, Paul 176
Taylor, Robert, *The Hog Hath Lost His Pearl* 173
Tennenhouse, Leonard 154
Tennyson, Alfred Lord 135, 150, 190
Terence 47
Terry, Ellen 142, 150, 197
Theatre for a New Audience 148
Theatre Royal, Covent Garden, see Covent
　Garden
Theatre Royal, Drury Lane, see Drury Lane
Theatres Royal, London (1815) 139
Theobald, Lewis 186
　Double Falsehood; or, The Distrest Lovers
　9, 26
Thompson, Ann 69, 140
Thorndike, Ashley 22, 110
Tillyard, E. M. W. 25, 177, 178–9
Times Literary Supplement 139, 196
Times, The 116, 117, 120, 143, 175, 177
Tippett, Sir Michael, *The Knot Garden* 3
Tompkins, J. M. S. 179
Townshend, Aurelian, *Tempe Restored* 54
Traversi, Derek 25
Tree, Herbert Beerbohm 113, 120, 189, 192, 196
Tresnjak, Darko 194–5
Trewin, J. C. 133, 148
*True Declaration of the State of the Colonie
　in Virginia, The* 80
Turner, Robert Kean and Virginia Westling
　Haas 132
Twine, Laurence, *The Pattern of Painful
　Adventures* 180

Ulrici, Hermann 25
Underdowne, Thomas 48
Universal Museum 115
Urfé, Honoré d' 48

Valdes, Diego Flores de 84
Valdes, Don Pedro de 83–4
Vaughan, Virginia Mason 3
Venezky, Alice 133
Vickers, Sir Brian 180, 190
Vincent, Isabella 146
Virgil 19, 49, 97
　Aeneid 49, 60, 64
　Eclogue Four 63–4
　Georgics 50
Virginia Company 80

Waith, Eugene M. 69, 202
Waldron, Francis Godolphin, *Love and
　Madness; or, the Two Noble
　Kinsmen* 189
Walker, Mike, *Marina Blue* 3
Walkley, Thomas 189
Wallace, Jennifer 152
Warburton, William 136–7, 139
Warner, Marina 166–7
　Indigo 166–7, 168, 169–71
Warren, Roger 123, 133, 179
Watermill Theatre, Newbury 125
Weber, Bruce 202
Webster, John
　Induction to *The Malcontent* 35
　The Duchess of Malfi 38
Wells, Robin Headlam 45
Wells, Stanley 110, 123, 133, 201
Westminster Gazette, The 121
Whitehall Palace 49, 114
Whitney, G. 68
Wiggins, Martin 31
Wilkins, George 8, 9, 91, 174, 179–80, 182,
　185, 201
　The Miseries of Enforced Marriage 179
　*The Painful Adventures of Pericles
　Prince of Tyre* (prose romance)
　18, 174, 179–80
　Pericles, Prince of Tyre see Shakespeare
　*The Travails of the Three English
　Brothers* see Day
Williams, Deanne 181
Williams, Tam 125–6
Wilson, Daniel, *Caliban: The Missing Link*
　156–7
Wilson, M. Glen 133
Wilson, Richard 181
Wittreich, Joseph A. 68
Wolsey, Thomas 62
Woodfill, Walter L. 44
Woodward, Peter 123
Worcester, see Somerset
Worden, Blair 195, 202
Wright, George T. 111
Wrigley, E. A. 26–7
Wynyard, Diana 121

Yates, Frances A. 68, 69
Young, Alan R. 69

Zabus, Chantal 165, 171
Zimmerman, Mary 177
Zurcher, Amelia 180–81

Cambridge Companions To...

AUTHORS

Edward Albee edited by Stephen J. Bottoms

Margaret Atwood edited by Coral Ann Howells

W. H. Auden edited by Stan Smith

Jane Austen edited by Edward Copeland and Juliet McMaster

Beckett edited by John Pilling

Aphra Behn edited by Derek Hughes and Janet Todd

Walter Benjamin edited by David S. Ferris

William Blake edited by Morris Eaves

Brecht edited by Peter Thomson and Glendyr Sacks (second edition)

The Brontës edited by Heather Glen

Frances Burney edited by Peter Sabor

Byron edited by Drummond Bone

Albert Camus edited by Edward J. Hughes

Willa Cather edited by Marilee Lindemann

Cervantes edited by Anthony J. Cascardi

Chaucer edited by Piero Boitani and Jill Mann (second edition)

Chekhov edited by Vera Gottlieb and Paul Allain

Kate Chopin edited by Janet Beer

Caryl Churchill edited by Elaine Aston and Elin Diamond

Coleridge edited by Lucy Newlyn

Wilkie Collins edited by Jenny Bourne Taylor

Joseph Conrad edited by J. H. Stape

Dante edited by Rachel Jacoff (second edition)

Daniel Defoe edited by John Richetti

Don DeLillo edited by John N. Duvall

Charles Dickens edited by John O. Jordan

Emily Dickinson edited by Wendy Martin

John Donne edited by Achsah Guibbory

Dostoevskii edited by W. J. Leatherbarrow

Theodore Dreiser edited by Leonard Cassuto and Claire Virginia Eby

John Dryden edited by Steven N. Zwicker

W. E. B. Du Bois edited by Shamoon Zamir

George Eliot edited by George Levine

T. S. Eliot edited by A. David Moody

Ralph Ellison edited by Ross Posnock

Ralph Waldo Emerson edited by Joel Porte and Saundra Morris

William Faulkner edited by Philip M. Weinstein

Henry Fielding edited by Claude Rawson

F. Scott Fitzgerald edited by Ruth Prigozy

Flaubert edited by Timothy Unwin

E. M. Forster edited by David Bradshaw

Benjamin Franklin edited by Carla Mulford

Brian Friel edited by Anthony Roche

Robert Frost edited by Robert Faggen

Elizabeth Gaskell edited by Jill L. Matus

Goethe edited by Lesley Sharpe

Günter Grass edited by Stuart Taberner

Thomas Hardy edited by Dale Kramer

David Hare edited by Richard Boon

Nathaniel Hawthorne edited by Richard Millington

Seamus Heaney edited by Bernard O'Donoghue

Ernest Hemingway edited by Scott Donaldson

Homer edited by Robert Fowler

Horace edited by Stephen Harrison

Ibsen edited by James McFarlane

Henry James edited by Jonathan Freedman

Samuel Johnson edited by Greg Clingham

Ben Jonson edited by Richard Harp and Stanley Stewart

James Joyce edited by Derek Attridge (second edition)

Kafka edited by Julian Preece

Keats edited by Susan J. Wolfson

Lacan edited by Jean-Michel Rabaté

D. H. Lawrence edited by Anne Fernihough

Primo Levi edited by Robert Gordon

Lucretius edited by Stuart Gillespie and Philip Hardie

David Mamet edited by Christopher Bigsby

Thomas Mann edited by Ritchie Robertson

Christopher Marlowe edited by Patrick Cheney

Herman Melville edited by Robert S. Levine

Arthur Miller edited by Christopher Bigsby (second edition)

Milton edited by Dennis Danielson (second edition)

Molière edited by David Bradby and Andrew Calder

Toni Morrison edited by Justine Tally
Nabokov edited by Julian W. Connolly
Eugene O'Neill edited by Michael Manheim
George Orwell edited by John Rodden
Ovid edited by Philip Hardie
Harold Pinter edited by Peter Raby (second edition)
Sylvia Plath edited by Jo Gill
Edgar Allan Poe edited by Kevin J. Hayes
Alexander Pope edited by Pat Rogers
Ezra Pound edited by Ira B. Nadel
Proust edited by Richard Bales
Pushkin edited by Andrew Kahn
Rilke edited by Karen Leeder and Robert Vilain
Philip Roth edited by Timothy Parrish
Salman Rushdie edited by Abdulrazak Gurnah
Shakespeare edited by Margareta de Grazia and Stanley Wells
Shakespearean Comedy edited by Alexander Leggatt
Shakespeare on Film edited by Russell Jackson (second edition)
Shakespeare's History Plays edited by Michael Hattaway
Shakespeare's Last Plays edited by Catherine M. S. Alexander
Shakespeare's Poetry edited by Patrick Cheney
Shakespeare and Popular Culture edited by Robert Shaughnessy
Shakespeare on Stage edited by Stanley Wells and Sarah Stanton
Shakespearean Tragedy edited by Claire McEachern

George Bernard Shaw edited by Christopher Innes
Shelley edited by Timothy Morton
Mary Shelley edited by Esther Schor
Sam Shepard edited by Matthew C. Roudané
Spenser edited by Andrew Hadfield
Laurence Sterne edited by Thomas Keymer
Wallace Stevens edited by John N. Serio
Tom Stoppard edited by Katherine E. Kelly
Harriet Beecher Stowe edited by Cindy Weinstein
August Strindberg edited by Michael Robinson
Jonathan Swift edited by Christopher Fox
J. M. Synge edited by P. J. Mathews
Tacitus edited by A. J. Woodman
Henry David Thoreau edited by Joel Myerson
Tolstoy edited by Donna Tussing Orwin
Mark Twain edited by Forrest G. Robinson
Virgil edited by Charles Martindale
Voltaire edited by Nicholas Cronk
Edith Wharton edited by Millicent Bell
Walt Whitman edited by Ezra Greenspan
Oscar Wilde edited by Peter Raby
Tennessee Williams edited by Matthew C. Roudané
August Wilson edited by Christopher Bigsby
Mary Wollstonecraft edited by Claudia L. Johnson
Virginia Woolf edited by Susan Sellers (second edition)
Wordsworth edited by Stephen Gill
W. B. Yeats edited by Marjorie Howes and John Kelly
Zola edited by Brian Nelson

TOPICS

The Actress edited by Maggie B. Gale and John Stokes
The African American Novel edited by Maryemma Graham
The African American Slave Narrative edited by Audrey A. Fisch
Allegory edited by Rita Copeland and Peter Struck
American Modernism edited by Walter Kalaidjian
American Realism and Naturalism edited by Donald Pizer

American Travel Writing edited by Alfred Bendixen and Judith Hamera
American Women Playwrights edited by Brenda Murphy
Ancient Rhetoric edited by Erik Gunderson
Arthurian Legend edited by Elizabeth Archibald and Ad Putter
Australian Literature edited by Elizabeth Webby
British Romanticism edited by Stuart Curran
British Romantic Poetry edited by James Chandler and Maureen N. McLane

British Theatre, 1730–1830, edited by
Jane Moody and Daniel O'Quinn

Canadian Literature edited by Eva-Marie Kröller

Children's Literature edited by M. O. Grenby
and Andrea Immel

The Classic Russian Novel edited by Malcolm
V. Jones and Robin Feuer Miller

Contemporary Irish Poetry edited
by Matthew Campbell

Crime Fiction edited by Martin Priestman

Early Modern Women's Writing edited by Laura
Lunger Knoppers

The Eighteenth-Century Novel edited
by John Richetti

Eighteenth-Century Poetry edited by John Sitter

English Literature, 1500–1600 edited by Arthur
F. Kinney

English Literature, 1650–1740 edited by Steven
N. Zwicker

English Literature, 1740–1830 edited
by Thomas Keymer and Jon Mee

English Literature, 1830–1914 edited by
Joanne Shattock

English Novelists edited by Adrian Poole

English Poetry, Donne to Marvell edited
by Thomas N. Corns

English Poets edited by Claude Rawson

English Renaissance Drama edited by
A. R. Braunmuller and Michael Hattaway
(second edition)

English Restoration Theatre edited by Deborah
C. Payne Fisk

Feminist Literary Theory edited by
Ellen Rooney

Fiction in the Romantic Period edited by
Richard Maxwell and Katie Trumpener

The Fin de Siècle edited by Gail Marshall

The French Novel: from 1800 to the Present
edited by Timothy Unwin

German Romanticism edited by Nicholas Saul

Gothic Fiction edited by Jerrold E. Hogle

The Greek and Roman Novel edited
by Tim Whitmarsh

Greek and Roman Theatre edited by
Marianne McDonald and J. Michael Walton

Greek Lyric edited by Felix Budelmann

Greek Mythology edited by Roger D. Woodard

Greek Tragedy edited by P. E. Easterling

The Harlem Renaissance edited by
George Hutchinson

The Irish Novel edited by John Wilson Foster

The Italian Novel edited by Peter Bondanella
and Andrea Ciccarelli

Jewish American Literature edited by
Hana Wirth-Nesher and Michael P. Kramer

The Latin American Novel edited by
Efraín Kristal

The Literature of Los Angeles edited by
Kevin R. McNamara

The Literature of New York edited by
Cyrus Patell and Bryan Waterman

The Literature of the First World War edited by
Vincent Sherry

The Literature of World War II edited by
Marina MacKay

Literature on Screen edited by Deborah Cartmell
and Imelda Whelehan

Medieval English Literature edited by
Larry Scanlon

Medieval English Theatre edited by
Richard Beadle and Alan J. Fletcher
(second edition)

Medieval French Literature edited by
Simon Gaunt and Sarah Kay

Medieval Romance edited by Roberta L. Krueger

Medieval Women's Writing edited by
Carolyn Dinshaw and David Wallace

Modern American Culture edited by
Christopher Bigsby

Modern British Women Playwrights edited by
Elaine Aston and Janelle Reinelt

Modern French Culture edited by
Nicholas Hewitt

Modern German Culture edited by Eva Kolinsky
and Wilfried van der Will

The Modern German Novel edited by
Graham Bartram

Modern Irish Culture edited by Joe Cleary and
Claire Connolly

Modernism edited by Michael Levenson

The Modernist Novel edited by Morag Shiach

Modernist Poetry edited by Alex Davis and Lee
M. Jenkins

Modern Italian Culture edited by Zygmunt
G. Baranski and Rebecca J. West

Modern Latin American Culture edited by
John King

Modern Russian Culture edited by
Nicholas Rzhevsky

Modern Spanish Culture edited by David T. Gies

Narrative edited by David Herman

Native American Literature edited by Joy Porter
and Kenneth M. Roemer

Nineteenth-Century American Women's Writing edited by Dale M. Bauer and Philip Gould

Old English Literature edited by Malcolm Godden and Michael Lapidge

Performance Studies edited by Tracy C. Davis

Postcolonial Literary Studies edited by Neil Lazarus

Postmodernism edited by Steven Connor

Renaissance Humanism edited by Jill Kraye

Roman Satire edited by Kirk Freudenburg

The Roman Historians edited by Andrew Feldherr

The Spanish Novel: from 1600 to the Present edited by Harriet Turner and Adelaida López de Martínez

Travel Writing edited by Peter Hulme and Tim Youngs

The Twentieth-Century English Novel edited by Robert L. Caserio

Twentieth-Century English Poetry edited by Neil Corcoran

Twentieth-Century Irish Drama edited by Shaun Richards

Victorian and Edwardian Theatre edited by Kerry Powell

The Victorian Novel edited by Deirdre David

Victorian Poetry edited by Joseph Bristow

War Writing edited by Kate McLoughlin

Writing of the English Revolution edited by N. H. Keeble